WORLD RELIGIONS IN AMERICA: AN INTRODUCTION

WORLD RELIGIONS
IN AMERICA

An Introduction

JACOB NEUSNER
Editor

WESTMINSTER/JOHN KNOX PRESS
Louisville, Kentucky

Literary Editor: Naomi Pasachoff

Book design by Publishers' WorkGroup

Cover design by Aavidar Design Inc.

First edition

This book is printed on acid-free paper that meets the American National Standards Institute Z39.48 standard. ⊗

Published by Westminster/John Knox Press
Louisville, Kentucky

PRINTED IN THE UNITED STATES OF AMERICA

2 4 6 8 9 7 5 3 1

Library of Congress Cataloging-in-Publication Data

World religions in America : an introduction / Jacob Neusner, editor. — 1st ed.
　　p.　　cm.
Includes bibliographical references.
ISBN 0-664-22053-3 (alk. paper)
ISBN 0-664-25300-8 (alk. paper ; pbk.)

　　1. United States—Religion.　　2. United States—Religion—1960–
I. Neusner, Jacob, date–
BL2525.W67　1994
200'.973—dc20　　　　　　　　　　　　　　　　　93-32886

CONTENTS

ACKNOWLEDGMENTS

As organizer and editor of this project, I acknowledge with real thanks the contributions of many people. It is right and proper to name each one.

The literary editor of this book is Naomi Pasachoff. She read each chapter as it came in and corresponded with the various authors, making numerous important suggestions for the improvement of the early drafts. An accomplished textbook writer in her own career, she brought to the study of religion those skills of presentation to students that have made her one of the country's leading writers of science textbooks, and text-books for the synagogues' schools of Judaism. We were fortunate indeed for her participation in this volume, and all of the authors join me in expressing our thanks to her.

The study-guide material is the work of Dr. Mark Ledbetter of Huntingdon College, Montgomery, Alabama. The weight of his contribution may be simply stated: Without it, the book would be much less effective as an instrument of teaching. All parties to the book concur that he has given us just what we needed, and it is his skill as a teacher that has shaped the study-guide material.

My thinking about the need for a project of just this kind—combining the study of world religions with a close reading of religions in America—was shaped in conversations with Professor William Scott Green of the University of Rochester. No detail of the planning of this book, the definition of its purpose, the outline of its chapters, and its execution throughout, was finally defined without discussion with him. He has served not only as a consultant, but as an active partner in the conception and completion of the book.

A word of thanks and admiration goes, also, to the authors of the various chapters. I learned about religion, as well as about the study and teaching of religion, from each chapter in succession as it reached me. First, all authors kept to our timetable, and none caused a day of delay, so we were able to produce the book within that precise schedule projected at the outset. Readers who have organized academic projects will know how high praise that simple sentence accords to every author in this book. Second, each one of them gave thought to the program and problems of the book, responding to my questions and taking up my intellectual challenge for them: Can we talk to young Americans about the things they see and know from day to day, so that out of the known they may learn about what the here and now represents? Can we discover the character of religion throughout the world through the facts of religions in America? Those who use this book will concur that every author answered these questions, and that all of them did so in an imaginative and passionate way.

I wanted the authors to write out of emotion and commitment, as well as objective learning—to tell young people what they cared about and why, not only what they know and how they know it. Every chapter in this book has met that aspiration. If the book engages its intended audience, it is because each of these authors has responded to the challenge, and I am proud of having worked with all of them.

Beyond what I owe to all of them equally, I am personally obligated to three of the authors. First, Professor Andrew M. Greeley of the University of Chicago was my other conversation partner in the formation of the book; most of what I know about religion in America, how it should be studied, and why it is important, I learned from his writings and from conversation and letters exchanged with him. It is from his imaginative and original thought that I got the idea for the book to begin with. Second, Professor Martin Marty made a contribution to my chapter that he cannot have realized he was offering. When I conceived of this book, I did not know whether or not anyone could carry it off. I wanted major scholars to write for young Americans. I wanted every American student to find himself or herself in the pages of this book. I wanted the book to express passion and commitment to learning about religion as a critical component of intellectual life. I also did not know whether I personally could write a chapter that would serve. I had no model in my own mind for what I needed to do; I knew only that we, and I, faced a mighty worthwhile challenge in writing. The first of the chapters to come back to me came—predictably—from Professor Marty, who is justly famed in the study of religion both for the quantity and the quality of his writing, and also for the vitality and excellence of his thinking. His chapter assured me that the project was feasible, because he provided precisely the kind of writing that I had hoped to elicit for the book. Once I read his chapter, I knew the work could be done, and I also had a model for my own chapter. I do not claim to write nearly so powerfully as he does, but he at least gave me a standard by which to measure my own work. Third, I had invited the late Professor John Meyendorff to write the chapter on Orthodox Christianity. Shortly after he signed the contract, he died suddenly and unexpectedly. Left with a deadline I wanted to preserve and an unassigned chapter I deemed essential to the book—Orthodox Christianity sometimes being slighted in the study of Christianity in the world today—I turned to Professor Jaroslav Pelikan. Overburdened with a vast range of important scholarly projects, he accepted the assignment and produced a chapter that admirably met the needs of the book. Professor Pelikan's willingness to take up the burden at the last minute represents a gift beyond the measure of the law, and I am thankful to him for his understanding and cooperation.

It remains to express my thanks, finally, to my own university, the University of South Florida, and to its Department of Religious Studies. This book was born out of what I learned about teaching when I came to Florida. In a university shaped by a commitment to public service—we call ourselves "the full service university on the urban frontier"—and committed to excellence in teaching and scholarship for that massive public that we uniquely address, I undertook a different and, I think, a more *adult* kind of teaching: students of all ages, conventional and unconventional, bringing to me all sorts of commitments and motivations, capacities and concerns. In this university, which is more profoundly American than any that I knew before, and is more deeply committed to the future of this country than some places framed around considerations of preferment and status, a book such as this became possible. Indeed, it became necessary. Not only so, but in doing my work as organizer and editor of numerous projects in academic learning and teaching, I have found generous support. In times of fiscal crisis, the University of South Florida has provided a large research expense fund, as well as other media of practical assistance for my work. I express my thanks to the administration and faculty of the University of South Florida for giving to me and my work a warm welcome and for securing a long-term future in a most comfortable and generous setting in which to pursue it. Nothing that I have done since coming here in 1990 would have been possible in any prior setting in my career.

JACOB NEUSNER

CONTRIBUTORS

Malcolm David Eckel, *Boston University*
Robert S. Ellwood, *University of Southern California*
John L. Esposito, *Georgetown University*
Elizabeth Fox-Genovese, *Emory University*
Sam Gill, *University of Colorado at Boulder*
Justo L. González, *Columbia Theological Seminary*
Andrew M. Greeley, *University of Arizona and University of Chicago*
William Scott Green, *University of Rochester*
Gerald James Larson, *University of California at Santa Barbara*
Martin E. Marty, *University of Chicago*
Jacob Neusner, *University of South Florida*
Peter J. Paris, *Princeton Theological Seminary*
Jaroslav Pelikan, *Yale University*

JACOB NEUSNER

Introduction

This book introduces you to the world's religions in the United States today. Such an introduction is important because to understand America,* you have to know about religion. Most, though not all, Americans say they are religious, and the world's religions flourish in today's America. Most Americans would agree that "in God we trust." But each does so in his or her quite special way, and that is what makes religion in America interesting. This book does not advocate religion, or any particular religion. Its purpose is only to describe and explain religion as an important factor in American society.

AMERICANS ARE
A RELIGIOUS PEOPLE

Most Americans are religious. They believe in God. They pray. They practice a religion. They explain what happens in their lives by appeal to God's will and word and work, and they form their ideal for the American nation by reference to the teachings of religion: "one nation, under God." This statement, from the Pledge of Allegiance, describes how most Americans view our country. Americans act on their religious beliefs. Nearly all Americans (92.5 percent) profess belief in God. A majority prays from day to day and week to week. Most Christians go to church every week; nearly all Jews observe the Passover festival and most keep

---

*Although Canadians, Mexicans, and Latin Americans of South America also are Americans, this work concentrates on the United States in particular, and in these pages we use "Americans" to mean citizens of the United States.

1

the Days of Awe (New Year, Day of Atonement) and other religious celebrations. Religiosity is a fundamental trait of the American people and has been from the very beginning.

THE RELIGIONS OF THE WORLD FLOURISH IN TODAY'S AMERICA

Americans are not only a religious people. We also are a people of many religions. Most of the religions of the world are practiced in America. About 60 percent of the American people are Protestants (among them, 19 percent are Baptists, 8 percent Methodists, 5 percent Lutherans, and the other 28 percent divided among many groups). Another 26 percent are Roman Catholics. About 2.5 percent are Jews, most of whom practice Judaism. Somewhat less than 1 percent practice Hinduism, and about the same number practice Buddhism. Only 7.5 percent of the American people profess no religion at all.

One cannot understand America without making some sense of its diverse religious life. The marvel of America is its capacity to give a home to nearly every religion in the world, and the will of the American people to get along with one another, with the rich mixture of religions that flourish here. This book presents not only the better-known religions of America, Christianity and Judaism, but also the religious world of Native Americans, African Americans, and Hispanic or Latin Americans, as well as the old religions newly arrived in this country, such as Islam (0.5% percent of the American people), Hinduism, and Buddhism.

America Began Because of Religion: Religion played a fundamental role in America's development by Europeans. The eastern part of this country was settled by people from Great Britain as an act of religion. The Southwest was founded by people from Spain and Latin America as an act of religion.

New England was settled by British Puritans from East Anglia; Virginia and the Chesapeake area, by British Anglicans (Episcopalians); Pennsylvania and New Jersey, by British Quakers; and the Appalachian South, from West Virginia and western Pennsylvania south through Piedmont North and South Carolina, by British Presbyterians from the area around the Irish Sea, the border regions of Scotland and Northern England, and the Irish counties of Ulster, in particular.

The first European settlements in Texas, New Mexico, Arizona, and

California were established by Roman Catholic missionaries and soldiers coming north from Mexico, who wanted to bring Christianity to the native peoples. Many of the place-names in the American Southwest were given by Hispanic pioneers, who acted in the name of Jesus Christ and the Roman Catholic faith. The earliest European explorers and settlers in the Midwest, from Detroit to New Orleans, were Roman Catholic missionaries and traders from Quebec, in French Canada.

From colonial times onward, many groups that joined in the adventure of building the American nation brought with them their religious hopes and founded in this country a particularly American expression of religions from all parts of the world: Africa, Asia, Europe, and Latin America. Entire American states and regions took shape because of religiously motivated groups—for example, Utah and the intermontane West through the Latter-day Saints ("Mormons"). So our country is a fundamentally religious nation, and in our country today, nearly every living religion is now represented in a significant way.

IS AMERICA
A CHRISTIAN COUNTRY?

Some people think America is basically a Christian country because different forms of Christianity have predominated through its history and have defined much of its culture and society. The vast majority of Americans who are religious—and that means most of us—are Christians. But to be a true American, one can hold another religion or no religion at all. The first religions of America were those of the Native Americans. And although Protestant and Roman Catholic Christianity laid the foundations of American society, America had a Jewish community from nearly the beginning; the first synagogues date back to the mid-seventeenth century. Today this country has become the meeting place for nearly all of the living religions of the world, with the Zoroastrian, Shinto, Muslim, Buddhist, and Hindu religions well represented. Various religious groups from the Caribbean and from Africa and Latin America likewise flourish. What you learn in this book is that nearly every religion in the world is practiced by some Americans.

AMERICA IS DIFFERENT

Other countries have difficulty dealing with more than a single skin color, or with more than a single religion or ethnic group, and nations today break apart because of ethnic and religious difference. But America holds together because of the American ideal that anyone, of any race, creed, color, language, religion, gender, sexual preference, or country of origin, can become a good American under this nation's Constitution and Bill of Rights, its political institutions and social ideals. And while religions separate people from one another, shared religious attitudes, such as a belief in God, unite people as well.

America is different because, except for Native Americans, it has always been a land of immigrants. From the very beginning, but especially since World War II, people have come to this country from all parts of the world. Today the great religious traditions of the world are practiced in America, where many of them have become distinctively American. This book presents the world's religions both as they flourish universally and also in their distinctively American forms.

WHY STUDY THE WORLD'S RELIGIONS
IN THE AMERICAN SETTING?

America is the right place in which to study the religions of the world because nearly all of them can be found here (and in nearby Canada). But America is religiously more interesting than most countries in another way. Not only do we have Judaism and the various kinds of European Christianity, we also have Christian traditions deriving from places besides Europe, for instance, from Africa, China, Korea, Japan, Southeast Asia and the Pacific islands. To give one example, the Unification Church, which began in Korea, flourishes in America today. Distinctive forms of Christianity from Latin America, both Pentecostal and Roman Catholic, have also become part of the tapestry woven by world religions into the fabric of American society. All of these important components of religion in America are described in this book.

WHAT YOU WILL LEARN IN THIS BOOK
ABOUT RELIGIONS IN PARTICULAR

This book first examines religions one by one, and then religion in America in general. We start with the first set of religions to exist in America, the diverse faiths of Native Americans. We turn next to Protestant Christianity, because the founders of the earliest American settlements, in Virginia and Massachusetts, were Protestants. Because Protestants form the most complex and also the largest single component of religious life in America,

Protestant Christianity is treated in a chapter twice as long as those devoted to the other American representatives of the religions of the world. African Americans have formulated a distinctive religious expression within Protestant Christianity, and they were among the earliest settlers, so we turn next to African American religious life.

Next we discuss Catholic Christianity, represented in the eastern part of the United States nearly from the beginning, and also the foundation religion of the great Southwest. Because Hispanic Americans today comprise nearly half of all Roman Catholic Christians in the United States, we take up Hispanic religious life in America, both Roman Catholic and Protestant.

We then turn to Judaism, a most ancient religion that has produced a strikingly contemporary and distinctively American statement of its own. We learn much about America from how Judaism has evolved within this country's open society.

We then turn to the American religions that have achieved importance on the national scene in our own day—newer religions of this country, but older religions of humanity—Islam, Buddhism, and Hinduism. We pay attention, also, to the religious traditions brought to the United States by Japanese, Korean, and Chinese immigrants, many of whom are Christian but some of whom practice other religious traditions of the eastern shores of Asia.

Each chapter treats its subject in accord with a single plan: How do we encounter this religion today? What is its definition and history? In what ways does the American expression of this religion teach us about religion in America and what being religious in America means? In answering these questions, the authors tell you about world religions in general and also about world religions in America in particular. Having mastered the contents of these chapters, you should be able to make sense out of the great religions of the world as America knows them, and also the diverse meanings of religious life in America.

WHAT YOU WILL LEARN IN THIS BOOK
ABOUT RELIGION IN GENERAL

To make sense of our country's complex life—its politics, culture, society—we need generalizations. An understanding of religion in general, and not just particular faiths, sheds light on these aspects of American life. We therefore consider three questions that pertain to all religions. The first concerns the relationship between religion and society:

How does religion shape American life? The second concerns how religion is shaped in this country by women: What do we learn about religion from the ways in which women are religious? Finally, we turn to the immediate question of politics: How does religion affect the political life of this country? Our political system carefully distinguishes state from church, so that no governing body may favor or discriminate against a particular religion or religion in general. But religious people—that is, nearly all Americans—bring to politics important religious beliefs and commitments. How religion comes to expression in American political life teaches us much about religion.

WHY THIS BOOK DIFFERS
FROM OTHER BOOKS ABOUT THE
WORLD'S RELIGIONS IN AMERICAN LIFE

In general, up to the end of World War II people defined the three religions of the United States as Catholicism, Protestantism, and Judaism. The other great world religions, such as Islam, Buddhism, and Hinduism, were not broadly represented here. In addition, it was not widely recognized that African Americans had formed a powerful and distinctive statement of Protestant Christianity, and that Latin Americans had formed in this country an equally important and distinctive expression of Catholic Christianity; and the importance of Pentecostal Christianity in Latin America was just then emerging. So chapters on how other world religions, besides Christianity and Judaism, or on how other non-European formulations of great religions flourished in America would not likely have been written just a few decades ago.

And, if the truth be told, half a century ago chapters on Catholic Christianity and on Judaism might also have been left out, since not a few people saw America as not only Christian, but also—and exclusively— Protestant. According to this school of thought, "others"—not white, not Protestant, not Christian, not European, not English-speaking, or not from the northwestern part of Europe (Britain, excluding Ireland, Germany, or Scandinavia)—really were not authentic Americans at all. That is what made them different and somehow abnormal, just as in that time people thought it was "normal" to be a man and not "normal" to be a woman. But that narrow conception of what it means to be an American—and normal—is no longer taken seriously. We now accept that Americans come in all colors, shapes, and sizes, in both genders, and from every corner of the world. We now know that anyone can become a real

American. And America has the power to make its own all the religions of the world. In America, there is no "other." Everyone is one of us. That is the message of this book: we all belong. Therefore, all of us bear the same tasks and responsibilities to make this a better country.

HOW TO STUDY ABOUT OTHER RELIGIONS

The future of America depends on the answer to the question, How are religions going to relate to one another in this country? Shall we refight in our own country the world's religious wars, Protestant against Catholic, Christian against Jew, Muslim against Hindu, and so on?

Religions think about outsiders, that is, other religions, in four ways.

1. *Exclusivist:* "My religion is not only true, but it is the only truth." This view of religious truth is natural to many believers, whether or not their religion officially takes such a position. If I believe something about God, how can I imagine any other belief is valid?
2. *Inclusivist:* "My religion is true for me; your religion is true for you." This position is common in a tolerant society, such as, in general, America is. It is sometimes called "relativism," meaning that truth is relative to the person who holds it; if you think up and I think down, for you it's up and for me it's down. Religious beliefs can be true only for those who hold them.
3. *Pluralist:* "Every religion has something true to tell us." God works in ways we do not always understand. We had best try to make sense of each of those ways. One way of doing so is to realize that different religions ask different questions, so you really cannot compare the statements of one religion with those of another.
4. *Empathetic Interest in Other People:* The way taken in the pages of this book concerns not whether religions are true (which in the end is for God to decide) but how all religions are interesting and important. We maintain here that every religion has something to teach us about what it means to be a human being. Here we take a different path from the one that leads us to questions about religious truth. It is a path that carries us to a position of empathy for our fellow Americans, in all their rich difference.

We are trying to understand others and to explain ourselves in terms others can understand. That is the American way: to learn to live happily with difference, and not only to respect but to value the other. We teach the lesson that religion is a powerful force in shaping society, making history, and defining the life and purpose of individuals and entire groups. That is why we want to understand religion—and, among the many true and valuable things about religion that there are to comprehend, that is what we in particular want to teach in these pages.

HOW WILL YOU KNOW WHETHER THIS BOOK HAS SUCCEEDED?

If, when you meet someone of another religion, you find yourself able to understand what is important to that person about the religion he or she believes, then the course in which this book has been used is a success for you. The goal of this course is to help you better understand the world you live in, which means understanding the people you meet. America is a huge and diverse country, and the secret of its national unity lies in its power to teach people to respect one another, not despite difference but in full regard for difference. We like one another as we are, or, at least, we try to. And when we do not succeed, we know we have failed our country. A good American is a person who cares for the other with all due regard for the way in which the other is different.

STUDY QUESTIONS

1. Do you believe that most Americans are religious persons? If yes, explain why you think so, and give specific examples of persons "being religious" or "acting out" their religion to support your answer. If no, explain why you think so, and give specific examples.
2. Why do you think that America has such religious diversity? Is this a positive and/or negative feature of American society?
3. Why would Christians tend to describe America as a Christian nation? Why should persons be careful in defining America in this way? Should we/Can we talk about "being religious" in America and include everyone, Christian and non-Christian?

1

SAM GILL

Native Americans and
Their Religions

When Americans are asked to say what distinguishes our country from all other nations in the world, it isn't long before we begin to talk about Native Americans. When talking about Native Americans it isn't long before we say something about dances, rituals, ceremonies, spirituality, and stories. Today people the world over, but especially Americans, look to Native Americans to find inspiration, a spiritual centeredness, a religious connectedness to the land and to nature. Native American religions frequently play a role in film, television, and literature. Native American religions are important to the way we think about America. Significantly, Native American dancers represented the United States in the festivals that opened the 1984 Summer Olympic Games in Los Angeles.

There are four predominant categories of Native American religions in today's America. Each category is distinguished not only by its form but also by its history. First, today many Native American religions are identified with specific cultures. We will call them *tribal traditions*. These religious cultures have been developing for hundreds, often thousands, of years. Each tribal tradition has its distinguishing character and history, but we find some common traits and attributes among them. For example, all of these traditions have a strong attachment to the specific landscape where they originated and continue to flourish.

Second, missionaries were often successful in introducing Christianity to Native Americans. Today Christianity is their most widely practiced religion. Native American Christianity has taken on characteristics distinctive to specific Native American communities. There are fascinating surprises here.

Third, Native Americans have developed new religious forms that extend beyond specific tribes, yet are distinct from European American religions. The most widely practiced of these is *peyote religion,* institutionalized as the Native American Church.

Finally, when Native Americans of different cultures talk to one another they often emphasize how they and their cultures differ. But when Native Americans of different cultures talk about their histories, or find themselves joined together to deal with the U.S. government or with Christian missionaries, they talk about an identity they hold in common, whatever their tribal identities. This "Indian" identity is often expressed as an alternative to the modern, technologically based, capitalistic and materialistic character of much of America. Though this identity is political, it is also religious in that it strives to recover ancient sensitivities, particularly those that connect people religiously to the land, to nature, and to all living things. This Native American religiousness, called *Indian spirituality,* is at once old and new. It is the form of Native American religion publicly most observable in today's America.

The following presentation of Native American religions in today's America will explore each of these four categories more fully.

TRIBAL TRADITIONS

Since a time thousands of years before Columbus, hundreds of relatively small groups of people have lived on the lands we now know as the Americas. Many of these groups continue to exist today. It is difficult to know in much detail the religions of these peoples before Europeans began to write descriptions of them, and even these records are rather sketchy until this century. There are some clear defining traits, however, that are present today as in the past.

The peoples of these cultures self-consciously distinguish themselves from their neighbors. They speak different languages than other tribes around them. They have distinctive houses and styles of clothes. Every tribe has rules defining marriages. Some tribes are patrilineal—that is, they transmit lineage through the father as we do when we receive our father's family name. Many other tribes are matrilineal—that is, a woman and her daughters and granddaughters are the lineage of the family. All of these many cultures tell their own stories, perform their own rituals, and have ritual leaders or medicine societies. All of these cultural factors, and many other things, make each of these cultures distinctive. So we must always think of Native American tribal traditions as many and varied.

Today in North America there are still more than one hundred Native American tribal traditions. Most Native Americans now speak English, but many also speak their native languages. Many Native American communities understand that keeping alive their own native language is important to the survival of their culture.

Oral Traditions

While there are many Native American languages, none of them are written. You may have heard about a Cherokee man named Sequoya who developed a way to write the Cherokee language, but this is an exception and is not even much used by Cherokees. Native American tribal religious traditions are shaped by the fact that these languages are not written. Just think about how important scriptures, written histories, and interpretive writings are to Christianity, Judaism, Islam, and other religions in America. Native American tribal traditions are composed of stories told orally by one person to others and of rituals passed from one generation to the next.

Though the lack of a written tradition may involve some shortcomings, it also ensures that the religious lives of Native Americans have a sense of immediacy, urgency, and relevance. Native American traditions are always on the edge of extinction because what is not remembered, kept vital, or seen as important enough to pass on to the next generation, is irrecoverably lost. The wisdom, experience, knowledge, and achievement of a people gained throughout their history must be borne in the memories of the living members of the culture. Every person bears a responsibility for the whole history and wisdom of her or his culture.

America is obsessed with the development of literacy, the very emblem of civilization and the measure of superiority in the world. The verbal SAT score is a primary measure of our secondary educational system. Native Americans are not unaware of literacy. Some have even suggested reasons for resisting it. A member of the Carrier tribe in British Columbia told anthropologist Diamond Jenness, "The white man writes everything down in a book so that it might not be forgotten; but our ancestors married the animals, learned their ways, and passed on the knowledge from one generation to another."[1] An old Inuit (Eskimo) woman told the Danish ethnologist Knud Rasmussen, "Our forefathers talked much of the making of the world. . . . They did not understand how to hide words in strokes, like you do; they only told things by word of mouth, . . . they told many things . . . which we have heard repeated time after time, ever since we were children. Old women do not fling their words about without meaning, and we believe them. There are no lies with age."[2]

The Zuni in New Mexico tell stories of their origins. In the earliest era the ancestors of the Zuni people lived in dark, crowded caves deep within the earth. The Sun Father sent his two warrior sons to lead the people out. When they emerged as "sunlight people" the Sun Father told them to travel in search of their home, "the middle place of the world." During their travels the people found a rain priest. Their own rain priest prayed with him, and together they made it rain. A water strider, an insect that skates on the surface of the water, came along and stretched its legs out to the edges of the earth. Where its heart touched the earth marked the middle. The Zuni had finally found *itiwana*, the middle place of the world.

The Zuni see the world as divided into sections corresponding mainly with the four cardinal directions, but they also consider the regions above and below as important. The Zuni are matrilineal. Each person is born into her or his mother's family and receives her clan, a named social designation. Each clan is associated with one of these directions. For example, if your mother's clan is Evergreen-oak, this is your clan. Evergreen-oak, green even in winter, is associated with the north and with winter. Yellow, the color of morning and evening light in winter, is associated with northern clans. One's clan determines the range of occupations and religious activities one has. Because the north correlates with war and destruction, a person in the Evergreen-oak clan would be encouraged to engage in war-related occupations and religious activities. One must always marry outside of one's own clan.

The Zuni priesthoods stand at the pivot and meeting place of all these divisions. For the Zuni the center represents totality and summation. The Zuni annual calendar is divided at the solstices into two halves, each containing six lunar months. Around the time of the solstices are twenty-day periods of intense religious activities, known as *itiwana*, marking the center or turning places within the yearly cycle.

The Zuni village, known also as *itiwana*, bears the prestige and power of a center place, of being at the conjunction of all places in the universe.

The Seneca, who live in upper New York State, tell stories about a woman who fell from the sky into this world. A flock of birds caught this woman. The world was then covered by water, so the only support they could find for her was on the back of a turtle swimming in the water. One by one many animals tried to dive to the bottom of the water to get a bit of earth from which to make the world. After many failed, one finally succeeded, and the Earth Maker, a creator, expanded this bit of soil into the present earth, which is supported on the back of the turtle.

The woman who fell from the sky gave birth to a daughter. The daughter was the mother of corn as well as of twin boys who represent the negative and positive forces constantly at struggle in life.

We may think that no one could really believe such a fanciful story, and we might even be a little suspicious of anyone who claimed they believed it. These stories are, however, quite interesting, and they are among the ways Native American people express such important things as what they understand to be good and bad, how the world came to be, what makes life meaningful, and how to relate to one another. These stories tell how a particular Native American culture understands the world.

This kind of story, which we call a myth, can be used in very serious ways. For example, for decades the Navajo and Hopi peoples have been in conflict over lands declared for their joint use by a U.S. government treaty. Though there have been many court battles and efforts made by the federal government to resolve the situation, the peoples themselves remain unsatisfied. Several years ago the Hopi and Navajo tribal chairpersons met in public to discuss this conflict. Both appeared dressed in business suits. Both were well versed in the law and government policy. Each, when it was his time to speak, told the story of the creation of the world. Each showed how the particular landscape in question is essential to the identity of the people in his tribe.

The Hopi tribal chairperson described how the Hopi people were led out of the lower worlds onto this surface of the earth through an emergence hole (*sipapuni*) in the canyon of the Little Colorado River. From there they migrated in clan groupings to their present homes atop the mesas in northeastern Arizona.

The Navajo tribal chairperson told the story of how, before the Navajo world was created, the Navajo ancestors traveled through worlds below this one. Eventually they emerged at a location somewhere in the four corners region, where present-day Arizona, Utah, Colorado, and New Mexico meet. The Navajo world was then created, bound by four mountains, one in each of the four cardinal directions, each identified with a mountain that Navajos can see in their land today.

For both these modern tribal leaders the religious authority of their people's stories of creation is more important than any legal or governmental authority. Both cultures depend for their very lives upon the land they occupy. Each culture's identity depends on its creation story and on living in the landscape created for it. Besides being charming and interesting, these stories are the basis for a meaningful life for individuals and cultures.

Art and Architecture

Let's now consider Native American art and architecture. Native Americans' homes are commonly models of the universe. This makes homes religiously important. Every architectural feature, every way a house is used, reflects something meaningful. The way Native Americans build, divide up, and use parts of their houses correlates with their way of life. Many Native Americans perform ceremonials in the home. Yet there is also specialized religious architecture. *Sweat lodges,* found in many styles throughout North America, are small houses in which people go to purify themselves, to learn religious information, and to talk about serious things. Pueblo people use *kivas,* partly underground rooms, for performing rituals. Large Eskimo ceremonial houses called *qasgiq* are entered through a tunnel and a hole in the floor. These houses contain marionettes; for use in dramatic performances there are screens, behind which the performer can dress or otherwise prepare; even the entry tunnel and the skylight window are used to dramatic effect. Enormous clan houses of the Pacific Northwest have elaborately painted fronts and doorways that represent an orifice of the body of a mythic ancestor. Just imagine that every time you enter your house you step through the mouth or vagina of a mythic ancestor!

The designs on clothing, pottery, baskets, and tools frequently correspond with images from stories, features of the landscape, and clan symbols. By wearing clothing and using pottery and baskets, Native Americans are reminded of their stories; they are surrounded by the patterns that they associate with what makes their life and culture meaningful. For example, Navajos believe that closed circles constrict movement and thereby life. To bring harm to another, one need only draw a closed circle around her or his house. Navajos insist on openings in all encircling designs. The characteristic design woven into Navajo wedding baskets is always open, and the opening corresponds with the beginning and ending coil at the center and perimeter of the basket. The border designs in Navajo weavings always have a thread carried from the interior to the outside signifying the opening for the movement of life. A personified rainbow surrounds sandpaintings (discussed below) on three sides, being open on the east.

It is more appropriate to think of Native American art as a verb, as "arting," to focus attention on the creation process and the use of the objects produced. In Eskimo carving, the carver picks up the raw material, a piece of ivory or stone. Turning it about, the carver tries to see the shape contained within. To assert one's will upon the material is not the goal of carving. Rather the carver serves as an agent to reveal or release a shape already in the material—a seal, a bear, a whale.

Navajo sandpainting, so commonly known in the craft or fine art form, is always a part of a ritual process in traditional Navajo culture. Sandpainting is a ritual act of curing performed as a part of healing ceremonials that last many days. These pictures are associated with stories about heroes or heroines who are cured of some illness they suffer. Sandpaintings are made on smooth, clean sand bases on the floors of Navajo *hogans* (houses). They are often ten feet or larger in diameter. The elaborate designs must be produced accurately, but none of the hundreds of paintings that can be prepared exists anywhere in permanent form. Their every detail must be remembered by the medicine people who know these ceremonials. When the painting is finished, the person to be treated walks upon and sits in the middle of the painting. The medicine person or a masked spirit being known as *ye'ii* begins to treat the person. The medicine person's or the ye'ii's hands are moistened with an herbal medicine lotion and placed on the story figures in the picture. Particles of sand are transferred from the body parts of each figure in the sandpainting to the corresponding body parts of the suffering person. This identifies the person with story. The painting is smeared in this process. After the ritual is performed upon the sandpainting, the medicine person destroys and removes it from the hogan. For Navajos, a sandpainting functions less as a work of art than as a tool to make a healthy human being and world. What a sandpainting helps create is beauty of the highest order.

For Native Americans art and arting have a religious aspect. By making and using art Native Americans continue the creation process begun so long ago by gods and ancestors.

Rituals

The rituals of Native American tribal traditions are rarely performed simply to celebrate or commemorate some event or time. Native American rituals are performed to bring something about—a stage of life, a successful hunt, a change in season. In other words, rituals do more than celebrate something already done.

Girls' puberty rites are performed throughout the region west of the Rocky Mountains. The Apache people call their girls' puberty rite the Sunrise Dance. After an Apache girl begins menstruation her family may sponsor a Sunrise Dance involving not only the extended family but the whole community. After days of preparation accompanied by social dances in the evenings, the formal ceremonial begins. In an elaborate buckskin dress the initiate dances to songs that tell the stories of creation. The girl is identified with White Shell Woman, and through her dance she reenacts the events that created the world, when White Shell Woman had sexual union with the Sun. During this rite the pubescent girl is identified with the powers that created the whole world. Contact with her, even being present at the ceremony, promotes health and life. Near the end of the ceremonial, baskets of fruit and candies are poured over the girl's head. Everyone present scrambles for the goodies, made powerful by their contact with the girl.

The Apache, and similarly the Navajo, are exceptional in their approach to female coming-of-age. Many cultures, in contrast, consider menstrual blood a pollutant, and menstruating females are isolated from the community.

Among tribes throughout the northern Plains and Northwest, males come of age by fasting for a vision. A Lakota (Sioux) male wishing to complete his passage to manhood seeks a vision through a period of ritual and fasting. Isolated on a hilltop he fasts and offers prayers using a pipe and pointing its stem in each of the four directions—north, south, east, and west. He humbles himself before the powers of the world; he cries for a vision. Visions are described by visionaries as sequences of images strong in their potential for meaning. After a vision, the visionary consults with medicine men who help him discover the possible meanings of the vision. These images serve as a guide to be consulted throughout life. When a man must make decisions at the crossroads of life, he will look to his vision for help. The vision thus serves as a guardian spirit or a spiritual helper available in times of need.

A fascinating example of the transformative powers of ritual is the Hopi initiation of eight- to ten-year-old children, who thus begin their formal religious lives. Much of Hopi religion involves the frequent appearance of masked dancers, known as *kachinas*, representing spiritual messengers. For more than half of every year dancing and performing kachinas are common in Hopi villages. Before their initiation, children do not see either unmasked kachinas or unoccupied masks. When they undergo their initiation rites, the children hear stories about the kachinas, especially about their origins. They go to a nighttime kiva dance from which they have always been excluded. The kachinas enter the kiva where the children await. What is important is that these kachinas do not wear masks. When the children see that what they thought were spirits are actually their uncles and fathers, they are shocked, angered, and disenchanted. They wonder if they will ever be able to trust adults again.

This seems harsh treatment for children and it is. But the children learn something very important through this experience. They have up till now seen the world naively, believing that the world is exactly as it appears to be. This disenchantment gives them the experience that there is more to the world than meets the eye. As they begin to participate in their religious lives, they listen to the stories with greater care. This initiation by disenchantment opens the children to the world of mystery, beauty, and power that can only be known through devoted participation and can only be experienced with a sensitivity attuned to the reality that surpasses the merely physical.

The Sun Dance was prohibited in the late nineteenth century by U.S. government regulation. It has returned in recent years, especially among tribes in the northern Plains. The Sun Dance is an annual ritual involving everyone in the community. The world is re-created and renewed in this new year's rite. All the people are released from grievances and social strife. Everyone is rededicated to his or her role as woman, man, leader, hunter, warrior, or child. The Sun Dance provides an opportunity to perform vows made in return for favors asked of spirit beings. These vows often take the form of physical suffering. After the ritual construction of a Sun Dance lodge, dances are performed by individuals attached to the center pole of the lodge by leather thongs and skewers, which are inserted through the dancer's pectoral muscles. These dances are central to the Sun Dance ceremonial. The dancer's suffering fulfills a vow made in promise for some spiritual favor and serves to humble the dancer before the spiritual powers.

The Sun Dance innovatively combines features from old fertility rites of corn-growing peoples who lived along the rivers in the central and eastern Plains with the hunting rituals of cultures that hunted buffalo and other game on the Plains. For thousands of years physical survival of Native American peoples depended upon some combination of successful hunting, gathering, agriculture, and fishing. It is little surprise that animals and plants are central to the religions of tribal traditions. Not only are such animals and plants used as powerful ritual objects, they express central religious concepts. The buffalo, whose head adorns the center pole in the Sun Dance lodge, designates the source and power of life itself.

Corn, corn pollen, and cornmeal are used ritually by all agricultural Native American tribes. Corn, in a personified form, plays a major role in ritual and myth. The Cherokee tell a story of Selu, a woman who is corn, who provides food for her family by rubbing epidermal waste from her skin or by defecating. When her children discover how she produces food, they consider it witchcraft and decide to kill her. Knowing of their plans, Selu instructs them to plow an area of ground and to drag her bleeding body over the upturned soil after they kill her. They do as she asks, and where her blood touches the soil corn plants grow. Many Native American cultures tell stories of a corn woman who magically provides corn to feed her people. When mistreated she leaves, and her departure marks the beginning of the human cultivation of corn. In some southwestern tribes, at initiation a child is given an ear of corn, known as a corn mother, as a guide and protector. Pollen or cornmeal strewn or sprinkled is a blessing and an act of prayer.

Even though the horse was introduced to North America only with the coming of the Spanish in the sixteenth century, it has become central to many tribal traditions. The most respected of Navajo songs are the horse songs, which depict its cosmic dimensions:

Its feet are made of mirage
Its gait is a rainbow
Its bridle of sun strings
Its heart is made of red stone
Its intestines are made of water of all kinds
Its tail of black rain
Its mane is a cloud with a little rain.[3]

From the circumpolar region southward throughout much of North America, bears have played a religious role for thousands of years. Along the Pacific Northwest Coast, Raven is a creator and major culture hero who brings light to the world and shapes culture. Tobacco is widely used in the rituals of Native American tribal traditions as a potent spiritual "medicine." The list of plants and animals with religious significance could go on and on.

Here is what must be remembered to this point: Native American tribal traditions, though different one from another, are nonetheless similar in some respects. These traditions are directed toward the creation of a meaningful life for the people within a specific landscape that has been sanctioned by a tradition based on primordial events recorded in mythology. Native American tribal traditions foster a closeness to and respectful interdependence with the natural world.

Shamanism

Health and healing are common concerns of tribal traditions. Some of these traditions, such as the Navajo, use health and healing to address almost all concerns. Some traditions, especially those in the Arctic and down the Pacific Northwest Coast into California, practice shamanism. Caution is needed when using the term *shaman*. Many have used it to name any religious or spiritual specialist. The term comes from tribal cultures in Siberia and refers to individuals who use ecstatic techniques— that is, it designates those who know how to enter into a trance. Through trances shamans enter the spiritual world to seek help in resolving human problems, most often illness.

Today in America the Pomo, a California tribe, continue to use shamans. These individuals, often women for the Pomo, sing and shake long rattle staffs in preparation for entering a trance. Kneeling beside the sick person, the shaman then breathes rapidly while blowing incessantly on a bird-bone whistle. Eventually the shaman's body begins to quiver and convulse, showing that she or he has entered into trance.

After entering a trance the shaman examines the body of the sufferer by passing a quivering hand over it. This locates the illness, believed to be a malevolent object—a bone, a worm, an arrow, an insect—that has intruded into the body. These objects are often thought to be "shot" by witches. The shaman sucks out this evil object. As it enters the shaman's body, there is a noticeable convulsion. The shaman spits the object in the fire or in a bowl of water to destroy it. Some cultures actually display for all to see the object that has been removed.

Another form of illness treated by shamans is conceived as the loss of the life form, sometimes called the soul. The Salish people of the Pacific Northwest engage troupes of shamans who ritually paddle canoes in search of the lost life form; that is, they dramatize this journey by sitting in a canoe in the healing lodge. They recover the life form in dramatized ritual battles and then paddle back to return it to the sufferer.

Ecstatic techniques are used in North America to find lost objects or relatives, to learn of the future, to ensure success in hunting, and to conduct the deceased to the land of the dead. Shamanism always involves the use of ecstatic techniques by an individual to call upon forces in the spiritual world to intervene in human affairs.

An individual is often called by a powerful vision or dream to enter a shamanic career. A persistent theme in these dreams, as well as in the initiatory rituals, is the aspiring shaman being stripped to a skeleton and reconstituted as a shaman. This theme suggests that a shaman gains power through a death and rebirth experience. Still, shamans require extensive training beyond these initiatory experiences.

Perhaps because Native American tribal traditions are shaped by an essential connection with a specific landscape and by an authority structure based on myths telling of primordial events, it may appear that these traditions do not change, that they do not have histories. But extensive changes have often taken place within these tribal traditions. Native Americans are not helpless recipients of changes brought on by others. Because many of their traditions bear the responsibility for the ongoing creation of the world, Native Americans often creatively manage their own histories. There is no greater evidence of this than the fact that so many tribal traditions not only have survived but continue to thrive in the face of half a millennium of almost constant onslaught by powerful visitors from other lands.

NATIVE AMERICAN CHRISTIANITY

When Columbus met Native Americans, all their religions were tribal traditions. One of his first observations of these new peoples was that he believed they could be easily Christianized. Missionaries soon began their work in this new land. In today's America not a single tribal tradition has escaped the influence of Christianity. Many Native American communities today are primarily Christian. Many other communities have extensively incorporated Christian elements into tribal traditions. Others, particularly those forced to become Christian, compartmentalized their religious lives by publicly practicing Christianity while secretly continuing their own tribal traditions. The discussion of several cultures will exemplify these several types of Native American Christianity.

The Pueblo Peoples of the Southwest

Though it is often thought that American history moved across the continent from east to west and that American religious history began with the founding of Jamestown in 1607, the first meeting between Native Americans and Europeans was at Zuni in present-day New Mexico. The conquest of Mexico led to explorations north into the American Southwest. The first Franciscan missionaries attempted to establish themselves among the pueblo peoples by 1580. Santa Fe was a provincial capital city in 1610, a decade before the *Mayflower* sailed. Franciscan missionaries accompanied Spanish explorers, and by the early seventeenth century mission churches had been built in pueblos throughout the Southwest. These churches are the largest buildings in most pueblo villages. The church in the village of Acoma, which sits high atop a mesa, required the forced labor of hundreds of pueblo people to hand-carry the building materials to the mesa top, including many enormous roof support beams from trees cut as far away as a hundred miles. Pueblo peoples were forced, sometimes on punishment of beatings or even death, to be baptized and to practice Christianity publicly. Missionaries discouraged the practice of the tribal traditions and even destroyed pueblo ceremonial paraphernalia such as altars, costumes, and masks. Little wonder this treatment did not endear Christians and Christianity to pueblo peoples.

Although the people were forced to practice Christianity, the tribal traditions of these pueblos survived and persisted by going underground. These practices became so secret that almost nothing is known about the religions of several pueblos still apparently quite vital today. This public practice of Christianity complemented by the secret and private practice of tribal traditions is sometimes called "compartmentalization."

As the centuries have passed, missionaries have become far less oppressive of Native American tribal traditions. Although the compartments remain, with less pressure the pueblo antagonism toward Christianity has diminished. Christianity has earned a meaningful place in the lives of many pueblo people today, complementing their tribal traditions.

The Yaqui

Among the most creative interactions between tribal traditions and Christianity are those of the Yaqui, who currently live in several Arizona communities. The Yaqui lived in present-day Sonora at the time of the conquest of Mexico. For a long time they effectively resisted Spanish influence. Finally, in 1617, they invited Christian missionaries (who were Spanish) to live among them. Almost overnight the Yaqui willingly transformed their culture and religion, taking on many Christian forms. In 1767, after more than a century, under pressure from the Mexican government, which was demanding economic and social change and rejecting everything Spanish, the Yaqui asked the missionaries to leave. In the century that followed, however, even without the presence of missionaries, they continued to practice and develop traditions that had distinctive Christian forms.

The Mexican government finally conquered the Yaqui in fierce military engagements and dispersed the culture. Some formed communities in southern Arizona. By the beginning of this century they began once again to practice their traditions. Central among these is the elaborate ritual process that unfolds during the forty days of Lent. The elements of the Christian Passion can be recognized in this ritual, but they are interpreted as representing the universal struggle between good and evil. The evil forces are portrayed by soldiers dressed in black known as *Pilates* and by groups of masked figures known as *Chapayekas*. Holy Week, the climax of this ritual season, includes the capture of the church by the evil forces, the crucifixion of Jesus (represented as an icon), and the return to the church of the good. The final struggle between good and evil occurs on Easter Saturday. An effigy figure of Judas is placed in the center of the plaza that extends in front of the Yaqui church. Midmorning the Pilates and Chapayekas march into the plaza in two long lines, prepared to assault the church and return to power. At the signal of the ringing church bell, the evil forces rush the church, which is defended by children and old women armed with flower petals and green leaves representing the transformed blood of Christ. These prove to be stronger weapons, and evil is repelled. The masked figures leave their swords, daggers, and masks at the foot of the Judas effigy and rush to the church to rededicate themselves to Christ and the good. Judas is torched, and as he, along with all the masks and swords, explodes into fire, the whole Yaqui village erupts into fiesta.

Native American Christian Communities

Throughout America today we find Native American communities that are primarily Christian, peoples who have little or no practice of what we have called tribal traditions. These Christian communities often have distinctive tribal designations. Others are identified generically as Indian, without tribal designation, especially in the large Native American communities in many cities. Although Americans of European ancestry introduced Christianity to Native Americans, Native American clergy and leaders have increasingly taken over the leadership of churches in these communities. Many young Native Americans have trained for Indian ministry in institutions such as Cook Christian Training School in Phoenix. Native American Christian communities are most commonly fundamentalist in their theology, conservative in their practice, and often revivalistic and evangelical.

As Native Americans became Christian, they gained a certain freedom from being the objects not only of missionization, but also of academic scrutiny. As Christians they no longer seemed unknown or exotic. As a result very little is known about most of these communities. What are these religions? How are they related to tribal traditions? A scholar named Thomas McElwain recently did a study that gives us some hints. He studied Christian hymns that had been translated from English into Seneca for the 1834 publication of a Seneca Christian hymnal. He simply translated the Seneca back to English, examining especially the words in Seneca used for God. He found that the hymns express the religious ideas of Seneca tribal traditions much more than those of Christian theology.[4]

Many Native American Christian communities have responded innovatively to the pressures of Christianization, being able at once to continue older tribal traditions or ideas in new forms (and forms that have little compatibility with their own), to incorporate some aspects of the invading traditions, and coincidentally to diffuse the pressures of conquest and the intrusion of academic studies.

NEW RELIGIOUS MOVEMENTS

For Native Americans, religion is essential to life and cultural identity. In performing rituals and telling stories, Native Americans discover and create the meaning of life in the world. Religion provides some of the tools needed to go through the cycle of life, to hunt and grow food, and to deal with life's crises.

Throughout American history Native Americans have suffered wars, epidemic diseases, and forced displacements. They changed their way of life when horses, sheep, and new weapons were available from Americans. A never-ending progression of technologies, from electric appliances to pickup trucks, has introduced irreversible change to Native American cultures. The way Native Americans govern themselves has changed too. When they were forced as nations to negotiate with U.S. federal and state governments, Native Americans were compelled to develop new political and legal organizations, tribal councils, and governments that have little resemblance to former tribally distinct methods of governance. Literacy, schooled education, missionization, and the ceaseless treatment of Native Americans as objects of academic study, often motivated by the belief that these cultures were soon to become extinct, have forced many changes. Often outsiders invented images of Native Americans that served as standards by which the lives of actual individuals have been measured. These images, whether negative (the bloody savage) or positive (the noble savage) were always inventions.

Crisis Cult Movements

Sometimes the cumulative pressure of these intruding forces reached crisis proportions, and the Native American response often took the religious form of crisis cult movements. These movements, led by a visionary or prophet, helped renew and strengthen threatened cultures.

They required Native clothing, language, hunting, and cultivation, while consciously rejecting American clothing, English language, schooled education, Christianity and missionaries, the use of alcohol, metal tools, and firearms. Finding themselves living in strange territories, with no way to continue practicing the ways of life that distinguish them, Native Americans have followed visions of those who saw the cataclysmic end of this world and the return of a former world, a world before European influences.

By the beginning of the nineteenth century, Seneca culture was facing a major crisis. Seneca people had been drawn away from Seneca ways through Christianization, education in schools, employment for wages, and the use of alcohol. A Seneca man named Handsome Lake typified the people at the time. He was an alcoholic and no longer knew how to be Seneca. He fell ill, and many thought he had died. As he lay motionless in his bed he had a vision in which he received good news about the future. He learned how to revitalize the Seneca through the introduction of a new religion. Though there were difficult times ahead for Handsome Lake and for the Seneca, this religious movement, born of crisis, eventually became established and continues to serve the Seneca people.

During the nineteenth century many Native American cultures were pushed to the limits of their abilities to survive. The transcontinental railroad was completed. The great herds of buffalo were destroyed. Native Americans were confined to reservation lands on which they could not hunt or farm. Many Native American cultures began to face the possibility of extinction.

Throughout the northwestern United States during the last half of the nineteenth century many crisis cult movements arose. The most widespread was the Ghost Dance movement of 1890. A Paiute man named Wovoka had a vision that foretold the cataclysmic end of the world as it had become, followed by a return of the world that existed before the Europeans came. Those Native Americans who practiced the rituals of the movement and lived according to its tenets believed they would survive the cataclysm, that the dead humans and animals would return, and that the land would be renewed. The Ghost Dance ritual was a circular dance in which dancers fell into trances and often saw visions of the dead journeying back to the world of the living.

The Ghost Dance movement ended in the tragic massacre by U.S. troops of hundreds, including many women and children, at Wounded Knee at the end of December 1890.

The Native American Church

Peyote, a small hallucinogenic cactus, has long been used in ritual in Native American cultures in Mexico, especially in the area where the cactus grows. Late in the nineteenth century, a new religion with distinct ritual forms involving the ingestion of the cactus began to spread northward into Texas and through the Plains. Early in this century, in an effort to use this hallucinogen legally, the religion was formally constituted as the Native American Church. Comparing the use of peyote to the Christian sacrament of the Eucharist, Native Americans, though not at the time considered U.S. citizens, mounted a legal defense based on protection under the law of the free practice of religion. Though the legal battles continue, the Native American Church has thrived and by mid-century was widely practiced not only by Plains tribes, but also by many others.

Native American Church meetings are all-night singing and prayer meetings. They may be held in any form of lodge, although the plains *tipi* is the most popular. Built on the floor of the lodge is a crescent-shaped altar carved from tip to tip with a design of the peyote road. This road represents the life lived according to the direction of the peyote spirit. A large peyote button, representing Chief Peyote or the peyote spirit, rests on the center of the altar. A water drum provides the rhythmic accompaniment for the singing. A beaded staff, feather fans with beaded handles and gourd rattles are other ritual implements used in the meetings.

The meetings begin at sundown and end at dawn. Meetings are called for specific purposes: the illness of a member of the community, the celebration of a special event, even the preparation of a student for school examinations. A leader, known as the road chief, begins by stating the purpose of the meeting and inviting everyone to direct prayers to this need. Throughout the night peyote songs are sung—often in a Plains language, regardless of what tribe is singing the songs—to the accompaniment of rattle and drum. The beaded staff is passed around the meeting, and the person holding it becomes the singer. The drum, fan, and rattle are also passed. Periodically peyote is passed and eaten by the members. While members may experience visions, particularly increased intensity of colors and other sensations, the primary purpose is to increase concentration and the sense of community. It should be noted that peyote is not eaten to induce intense individual hallucinogenic experiences. Native American Church communities are often very conservative. The Native American Church is effective in the treatment of drug and alcohol abuse.

The Native American Church is distinct from tribal traditions in that it is practiced by Native Americans from many tribes. It can incorporate elements of Christianity; for example, the peyote spirit may be identified as Jesus. Passages from the Christian Bible may be incorporated in the ritual. Unlike Native American Christianity, however, peyote religion was not introduced by Europeans. Like tribal traditions, the Native American Church is distinctly Native American. The Native American Church need not threaten individual cultural identities. Indeed, there are often tribal variations in the ritual practice. The Native American Church links Native Americans together, forging a common identity out of their shared history of oppression.

NATIVE AMERICAN SPIRITUALITY

Early in the nineteenth century, faced with the displacement from ancestral lands by the American westward expansion, a Shawnee man named Tecumseh and his brother Tenskwatawa fought for Native American survival. They believed that cooperation among the various native cultures would provide more effective resistance than the separate efforts of many tribes. Military and political strength was the foremost concern, but there was also a vision of a common Indian religion. This perspective marks a shift from trying to accommodate the European American presence to the acknowledgment that Native Americans, despite significant cultural differences, held more in common among themselves than they did with those who were threatening their existence.

Especially since the middle of this century leaders have described what distinguishes all Native American peoples. These distinctive traits are religious in character, but the term *spirituality* will be used here to emphasize that the view is self-consciously anti-Western. The term *religion* denotes Christianity to many Native Americans; the term *spirituality* avoids this connection while suggesting an attitude of respect and reverence toward every aspect of life.

Notably, the rise of Native American spirituality has been associated with the print medium. Those who have shaped it are those who have written, or at least whose words have been written and published. There is perhaps some irony in this, but it has also made Native American spirituality the most known and accessible of all forms of Native American religions. The movement has served to mediate between mainstream American culture (whose primary access to other cultures is through print) and tribal cultures (which remain exclusively oral). No single book has been more important to the rise of Native American spirituality than

Black Elk Speaks, recorded and developed by the non-Indian author John Neihardt. The extent of Neihardt's contribution has given rise to considerable controversy, yet many Native Americans see this book as equivalent to a holy book. *Black Elk Speaks* is complemented by *The Sacred Pipe,* in which Black Elk tells Joseph Epes Brown about the seven rites of the Oglala Sioux. Many other Native Americans have participated in the development of Native American spirituality. Vine Deloria, Jr., schooled in Christian theology and the law, has written books widely read by Native Americans and other Americans alike. The fiction of Leslie Silko and N. Scott Momaday has shown that one of the spiritual centers of Native American traditions is storytelling.

Those Native Americans most influential in developing Native American spirituality have retained close contact with their specific tribal traditions. In describing their own tribally based spirituality, they have seen themes, images, and concerns common among all Native American peoples.

Native American spirituality encourages the continuity of tribal traditions, but more so the embracing of a common Indian identity. Native American spirituality exists in an arena of intense awareness of the crises and difficulties Native Americans face. Native Americans share a history of oppression and a pride and confidence in their heritage that has given them the strength to survive.

Understandably, the tenets of Native American spirituality are expressed largely in opposition to majority American culture. Native American spirituality condemns the very things its proponents identify as distinctive of most Americans: capitalism and the accompanying materialism, rational thought and literacy, political and economic policies that encourage the exploitation of the land and peoples, and Christianity. Native American spirituality builds upon its ancient roots in the American soil and a spiritual way of life that reveres the land as a mother, often formalized as Mother Earth, and respects as kin all plants and animals, indeed, all of nature. This perspective strongly holds that Native American spirituality not only is superior to the religion and culture of most Americans, but that it also holds the promise for saving the whole of America from a course of destruction.

Native American spirituality encourages the continuity and revitalization of the myths and rituals of tribal traditions. It has virtually no distinctive mythology apart from tribal traditions, though in its place is an extensive body of anecdotes, stories, and literature about Native American oppression and mistreatment by European Americans, and about the apparently foolish and destructive ways of these oppressors. Native American spirituality has embraced pipe ceremonies and sweat lodge rites. The dancing, singing, drumming, and ceremony of powwows have become the principal form of expression for many Native Americans.

Native American spirituality is widely popular among non–Native American peoples. This popularity is at once a backlash against what are considered negative aspects of our American heritage and a sign of respect for the Native American religions.

Though it may seem that Native Americans are largely gone, a people of movies and books, it must be remembered that today millions of people identify themselves as Native Americans. Further, as we have learned in this chapter, Native Americans have rich and diverse cultures including many forms of religious practice.

NOTES

1. Diamond Jenness, "The Carrier Indians of Bulkley River," *Bureau of American Ethnology Bulletin,* no. 133 (Washington, D.C., 1943): 540.

2. Knud Rasmussen, *The People of the Polar North: A Record* (London: Kegan Paul, Trench, Trubner & Co., 1908), 99–100.

3. Adapted from Pliney E. Goddard, *Navajo Texts,* Anthropology Papers, vol. 34 (New York: American Museum of Natural History, 1933), 164.

4. Thomas McElwain, " 'The Rainbow Will Carry Me': The Language of Seneca Christianity as Reflected in Hymns," in *Religion in Native North America,* ed. Christopher Vecsey (Moscow: University of Idaho Press, 1990), 83–103.

STUDY QUESTIONS

1. Discuss the stereotypes often associated with Native American religious traditions. How has reading this chapter changed your understanding of Native American religious traditions?
2. What are the four predominant categories of Native American religions in today's America? How do they function? What do you see as the important characteristics distinguishing these categories? How are they similar?
3. Native American languages are not written languages, at least not in their original forms. What do you see as the implications, positive and negative, of an oral tradition versus a written tradition? What would you gain from your religious tradition if your language were only oral? What would you lose from your religious tradition?
4. What is a story? Why is "story" important for any religious tradition? The Native American tradition? Describe or create a religious story from your religious tradition that functions like a story in the Native American religious tradition.
5. Explain how Native American art can be described as having a religious function. Give examples of Native American art and describe its role in the religious lives of its people.
6. Religious ritual plays a significant role in the lives of Native Americans. Define ritual. How would you distinguish ritual from habit? Describe at least two rituals from Native American religious traditions and discuss their functions.
7. Explore the relationship of Native American religious traditions with Christianity. How did the two traditions become so intimately connected to one another? Give several examples of how each tradition has influenced the other. What do you think has been lost and/or gained by this relationship?

ESSAY TOPICS

The Role and Function of the Shaman in Native American Religious Traditions

Native American Art: Exploring a Religious Tradition Through Images

Native American Religious Traditions and Christianity: Conflict and Compromise

31

WORD EXPLORATION

The following words play significant roles in any discussion of Native American religious traditions and are worth careful reflection and discussion.

Tribe	Native American	Oral Tradition
Medicine Person	Shaman	Sacred
Rite of Passage	Ritual	

FOR FURTHER READING

Beck, Peggy V., and Anna L. Walters. *The Sacred: Ways of Knowledge, Sources of Life*. Tsaile, Ariz.: Navajo Community College Press, 1977.

Capps, Walter H., ed. *Seeing with a Native Eye*. San Francisco: Harper & Row, 1976.

Gill, Sam. *Native American Religions: An Introduction*. Belmont, Calif.: Wadsworth Publishing Co., 1982.

Silko, Leslie. *Ceremony* [a novel]. New York: Viking, 1977.

Talayesva, Dan C. *Sun Chief: The Autobiography of a Hopi Indian*. New Haven, Conn.: Yale University Press, 1942.

2

MARTIN E. MARTY

Protestant Christianity in the World and in America

TAKING ROLL CALL OF PROTESTANTS

Suppose you rang a bell and exactly one hundred students responded to form an assembly. Suppose they represented a precise sample of adult America. If you were to ask them (as you probably would not in public), "What is your religion?" you would find that sixty of the hundred would say that they are Protestant. If people in the United States engaged in holy wars the way people did in other times and still do in some other places, you would be very worried if you were one of the two or three Jews in the assembly. You would be concerned if you were one of the much larger but still outnumbered group of twenty-six Catholics. Things could be especially bad for you if you were one of the eight who said that you had "no religion."

Not to worry—as they say nowadays when they want us to be at ease—because those sixty Protestants would never be able to form a single team to gang up on you. First of all, they have no reason to be angry with you; most of them have many friends who are not Protestant, and they would not want to hurt their friends. Even more of them would not consider religion the main reason to take sides on anything; race or income would more likely define who is "in" and who is "out."

There are two even better protections for the 40 percent of Americans who do not say that Protestantism is their religion. First, American law and custom make holy war difficult to carry out, and also irrelevant. Two hundred years ago in the Bill of Rights the founders distinguished between citizenship and religious belief. Some say they thus "separated church and state." This means, among other things, that religious majorities cannot use the law to take action against minorities and that minorities are protected. Along the way, Americans have also developed some habits of tolerance. These are not perfectly consistent habits, but very seldom does someone suffer or die in America because of a religious issue.

The other reason for protection, one that will help you understand your or your neighbor's Protestantism, is this: Protestants differ very much from each other. It would be hard to get them to agree on everything. Who would give marching orders? For what purpose would they attack? Only ten out of a hundred adults would call themselves simply Protestant when asked. Instead, nineteen of them would say their religion was Baptist. Baptists form the largest group of white Protestants, and more than half of the African Americans in your assembly would also say they are Baptist. Further down the line, eight of these one hundred Americans would be Methodist, five Lutheran, three Presbyterian, and so on.

A GLANCE AT THE MAP AND
THE LANDSCAPE

These numbers give you some idea of what your neighborhood would look like religiously if it were a perfect miniature of the whole United States. Few neighborhoods, however, are good miniatures. You might be living and attending school in Rhode Island, for instance, where sixty out of a hundred people are Roman Catholic and few Protestants are in sight. Or you might get an opposite and wrong picture of American Protestantism if you live in South Carolina, where only six out of a hundred people are Catholic and almost all the people say their religion is Protestant.

Most people do not look different from others because of their religion. Your neighborhood more probably looks like it does because of the buildings on its landscape. If we think of Protestants as a species, we will want to track them to their habitats. If they are active in practicing their faith, they are likely to be found, at least occasionally, in a church. Although some Protestants worship in homes or rented spaces, most go to specific buildings for which they or people who came before them have paid. These take all kinds of forms. On the heights in Harlem, for example, we find the Episcopal Cathedral of Saint John the Divine, which was begun over a century ago and will probably never be finished; the funds for a project of this scale are simply not available. Even unfinished, it is the largest Gothic cathedral in the world. You would feel very small under its great vaults and arches. If you have traveled to Europe or know your architecture, you would think while in this cathedral that you were in a Catholic building of the Middle Ages. You would imagine the same thing on the heights of Washington, where another huge Gothic beauty often called "Washington National Cathedral" towers.

Just a few blocks from the cathedral in Harlem, you might find a Protestant church located in a storefront. The congregation would be largely made up of black or Hispanic citizens—many Mexican or Puerto Rican people whose grandparents were Catholic have now turned Protestant. You would see folding chairs, perhaps a stand for a Bible, a piano, a cross—and a crowd, since these humbler places often attract large congregations.

A few blocks from the cathedral in Washington you will find Protestant church buildings that look like those on calendars or greeting cards that make America look like a New England village: simple but stately, white or brick meetinghouses with plain windows. If you want to portray a rural midwestern or southern landscape, you will probably show, somewhere in the distance, a typical steeple with some bells in it.

From this variety of habitats, you will see that the style of the architecture does not set Protestants apart or help you to group them. The abundance of buildings suggests, however, that they do gather to worship God and to meet each other for an hour or two most weeks. After meeting, they disperse. We have to find other ways to help account for the remaining 166 or 167 hours of the week.

PROTESTANTISM ALPHABETIZED
IN DENOMINATIONS

Try the Yellow Pages of the phone book in the section called "Churches." Although the list includes, for example, synagogues and mosques, most of these listings will be of Protestant denominations. ("Denomination," by the way, is a word invented to help us keep track of all the groups without saying anything good or bad about them. If you want to keep Protestant friends, don't say they belong to this or that Protestant "sect." Denomination is a neutral term.)

Protestant denominations run alphabetically from A, not to Z, but assuredly to U, V, and W. The number of listings may dazzle you; it also makes a point about Protestant varieties. We mentioned those nineteen Baptist citizens. In a large city like Chicago it takes four pages, twenty-four columns of small print, just to provide names, addresses, and phone numbers of the Baptist congregations. Most remarkably, they come in fourteen varieties, including "Independent-Fundamental," "Mission-ary," "Free Will," and "Southern" (even though this is a northern city!). These individual churches often have colorful names—not just "First Baptist," but also "Cristo En La Ciudad," "Acme," "Aimwell," "Eureka," "Jordan River," "Original Rising Star," and "Traveler Rest." Protestants usually get to name their own churches, and they like these names to suggest what they cherish, which helps them feel at home.

So far all you would know from this quick tour is that many of your classmates and neighbors (and perhaps you yourself) call themselves Protestant, and that they come in a wide variety of denominations and do things—we mentioned only worship, so far—at an equally wide variety of places called churches. If this were all that Protestantism meant, we would have done no more to help explain America to most Americans than if we said there were many kinds of locusts or automobiles, without saying why they exist, what they do, who fears them, or who has good hopes for them. The rest of this chapter will discuss the meanings of Protestantism.

LOOKING BACKWARD TO EXPLAIN THE PRESENT

When you set out to explain what life in a group of people means, you have to look backward to determine why they exist as a group, where they came from, and how they got here. Thus if you see people in military uniform you need to know their country and why that country stations troops where it does. If they are in very old uniforms, you might find that this is a civil holiday and they are going to reenact an old battle. If you see a woman in a long white dress with a man in a tuxedo and they are heading from a Protestant church to a limousine, you will have to understand the customs, handed down from the past, that lead people to dress that way and to go to such places in order to get married.

Many Americans at the end of the twentieth century are Protestant and go to Protestant places to do Protestant things, whatever they are. They have been doing this since the beginning of the seventeenth century, and what they do now is partly explained by why and when they came here. It is important to learn this, because the white Protestant ancestors of so many people today had most of the thirteen original American colonies pretty much to themselves, both in numbers and especially in having the power to set the terms for life around them.

Protestants do not have that kind of power in the nation today, but the nation is what it is today because they once had that kind of power. They may not know their own background; they probably take it for granted and would be surprised to learn the details. Whether you are Protestant or not, you will soon know something of that background and history, and you will begin to have an advantage over those who cannot explain why so many things today are as they are. Most of us Americans are not used to looking at our past to explain our present, and few of us have learned to look for the deposits, traces, and legacies left by religious forces. These pages are an exception that we like to think of as an opportunity.

SETTING THE STAGE:
THE EUROPEAN BACKDROP

Let's call what follows "The Protestant Drama." Thinking of it that way—and its story *is* dramatic—allows us to get behind the American scene for a prelude, a plot before the scene unfolds. This is necessary because Americans did not invent Protestantism; they imported it from Europe and tried to spread it to Native Americans just as, eventually, they found themselves sharing it with people of African descent.

Europe was the original scene of operations. The opening event was a movement that today goes by the name of the Protestant Reformation. (There were also Catholic Reformations going on at the same time.) The word *reform* as we use it today usually has a moral ring. Not long ago, "Correctional Institutions" were called "Reform Schools." A young person whose life took the wrong form would be sent to such a place to be "reformed." This language may be familiar: "Young man, I want you to reform and be home by eleven o'clock every night; and keep your room straightened out!" The term has other uses as well. A company that has a bad sales record might be called upon by its board to reform, which might mean to bring in new management or to design better ways to go about its business.

REFORMATION AND THE BIRTH
OF PROTESTANTISM

Almost five centuries ago in Europe, especially in northern Europe and the British Isles, leaders began to claim that the Christian church of their day, what we call the Roman Catholic Church, needed moral reform. It had to straighten out, bring in new management, and go about its business in better ways. In those days, Catholicism was not something you would find in a long listing of choices, the way you do in the Yellow Pages today. For a thousand years it had been a monopoly. Catholic Christians fought to keep their rivals, the Muslims, from taking over Europe, a battle that did not end until 1492—the year Columbus sailed—when Muslim armies were defeated in their European stronghold in Spain. (Had the Muslims prevailed, you would probably see mosques, not churches, across the American landscape.)

For hundreds of years Catholic Christians had also kept Jews from expanding their communities, moving about freely, or having religious influence. Often they persecuted and killed Jews; at best they segregated them in close communities, which in Italy began to be called *ghettos*. By the way, in the same year of Columbus, 1492, Spain expelled Jews and sent them into hiding and refuge. Europe was not to be Muslim or Jewish; it was to be Christian.

For some time after 1492 it was equally clear that Europe was also not supposed to be Protestant. The word was not even invented until 1529, when some "re-formers" of Catholicism presented a document that used the word "protest." (Protestants by and large do not like their name, since it sounds defensive and negative. That is partly why they more often say they are Baptist or Lutheran or Methodist than Protestant. But in the history books and to the polltakers, they are also Protestant.)

Catholic Christianity took mainly two forms. In Eastern Europe, from Greece through Russia, it was called Orthodox. You will find various Orthodox churches in the Yellow Pages, but fewer Orthodox peoples came to America than did Roman Catholic and Protestant peoples. The Eastern churches by and large ignored the Protestant Reformation and the Catholic reactions to it. What we call Western or Roman Catholicism—Roman because it was governed by and obedient to the bishop of Rome, the pope—was the subject of attack by reformers.

Today it is hard to picture how strong the Catholic hold was on Europe. For a thousand years its popes, bishops, and priests had a monopoly on formal religion. They even shared political power with kings, princes, and magistrates. Popes crowned emperors and emperors influenced popes. They might compete; they might argue; they might even go to war against each other. But they did not disagree on the basic idea that Christianity and the Church were necessary for running the state, for determining its laws, for blessing its battles. The Church was an owner of vast lands and wealth. It was represented in every village and in every corner of life.

Priests did the marrying and burying and recorded the marriages and burials for the state.

The priests and their Church were corrupt, said restless parties in Bohemia, England, Germany, Switzerland, France, and the Netherlands. The leaders in these northern places could take advantage of local pride, of national goals, and of resentment against Rome, which was then often drawing wealth and power across the Alps to Italy. But even Catholics then and especially now admit that the Church needed reform. Priests often were corrupt. Monopolies become casual about the rights of people, and Catholicism was no exception. Often the common people were held in virtual bondage. They feared that if they displeased the Church they would be condemned to an eternity in hell. To get into heaven they believed they had to do what the church wanted, often at great expense to themselves.

The Protestant reformers, including John Hus (1372–1415) in Bohemia, John Calvin (1509–1564) in Switzerland, John Knox (1513–1572) in Scotland, and most of all Martin Luther in Germany, did not make bad morals their main point of attack. When they said "straighten out!" they concentrated on the *teachings* of the Church. They all agreed that not the pope, but the ancient sacred scriptures that they called the Bible should be the authority in religion. Catholicism made demands on people who wanted to be right with God. The reformers in turn said that people would be free only when they realized that Christian faith meant God was generous, gracious, and gift-giving, the assurer that they could be "saved" without earning their way to heaven in the life to come. Eventually the protests led the reformers to walk away from the Roman Catholic Church or to be expelled from it.

A VARIETY OF ESTABLISHED OFFICIAL PROTESTANT CHURCHES

Soon there were churches called Reformed, Lutheran, Anglican (after "England") or Episcopal, or Presbyterian (because they were ruled not by a pope but by presbyters, elders who were not official ministers). The Protestant Reformation was not complete, however, at least not by the standards of most later Protestants. The leadership did not do what American's founders did. They did not "separate church and state"; they basically changed management! When a king or a prince converted from Catholic to Protestant, as kings and princes did in England, Scandinavia, and elsewhere, all the people were expected to follow. Protestants, like

Catholics, persecuted Jews and tried to punish dissenters. These dissenters were usually Protestants who rebelled against Protestantism, reformers who wanted to go further with reform. Still, reform did go far enough that the Bible and not the pope became the authority in these places. Preachers did preach that God's grace mattered and that human good works only followed because people loved God and not because they had to please him.

THE RISE
OF PROTESTANT ENGLAND

After Columbus, it looked as if the Americas would be Catholic. From 1492 until 1607 almost all the settlers in what Europeans called the New World were from Spain and Portugal. Catholic France was also beginning to move toward settlement, and it later colonized parts of what is now Canada. Protestant princes and kings were still busy gaining power, purging Catholics, and developing nationalism. These processes were slow on the European continent. But during that American Catholic period, Protestant England was growing powerful and ambitious. The British began exploring, and their entrepreneurs were looking for a place in which to invest. America beckoned.

Some English Christians, hoping to convert Native Americans and lead them to heaven, which they did not think Catholic missionaries were doing, said they wanted to turn North America into a vast mission field. Some critics said that the English were never serious about converting or serving the people they called the Indians or natives or savages; they only talked about saving them in order to keep a good conscience about plundering their lands. Motives of nations are usually quite mixed, and plenty of motives went into the English mix.

EPISCOPAL VIRGINIA AND
THE SOUTH

The English were sure, however, that they were destined to settle in America and that where they did, they and their official religion, no longer Roman Catholic but Anglican Catholic or Episcopalian, would go with them. They settled first in Virginia. Most of the Virginians and then the Carolinians went to America for reasons of investment and economy. They soon forgot about educating and saving Indians, especially after these Native Americans rose up in a bloody rebellion one spring day in

1622. As investors and not as exiles fleeing from repression, many of them did not think much about religion at all—but when they did, they thought Protestant. They brought along chaplains and ministers or priests, and from the first they held worship services. Before long they made the Episcopal church the legal monopoly in Virginia and elsewhere. They passed laws forcing people to go to church and to follow Episcopal teachings and practices. Fortunately, many would say, they were not good enforcers of these laws, so there was not much persecution. But the law still gave Episcopalians great privilege.

In those early years of settlement a prophet would have predicted that in the future every American would be Episcopalian and that the laws would be dominated by the Episcopal leadership and its will. Yet fewer than two out of a hundred Americans today call themselves Episcopalian, and even in Virginia only three out of a hundred citizens do (as opposed to thirty-one who call themselves Baptists!). Many things happened to prevent an Episcopal takeover. The first and most important of these, however, resulted from the rise of another party in English Protestantism, a party that settled New England and had more influence on the later United States.

That rival did not extinguish Episcopal influence. Remember the cathedrals towering over Manhattan and Washington? They are Episcopal, but both of them, especially the one in Washington, are used by the nation at large for non-Episcopal events (such as burials of admirals and presidents, or celebrations of military victories and the return of peace). Episcopalians do not dominate anywhere, but they tend to be represented everywhere, North and South. Most of the southern colonial founders of the nation, people named Washington and Jefferson, Mason and Madison, were Episcopalians. Many of America's wealthy and educated people have been Episcopalian, so they make up a disproportionate share of the *Who's Who in America* list. They were soon outnumbered and outinfluenced, however, by their rivals to the north.

NEW ENGLAND AND THE
PURITAN NORTH

These rivals were called the Puritans. It seems to be a habit for Protestants to breed generations who feel that others have not gone far enough. Puritans were British Protestants who after around 1559 argued that Episcopalianism was too much like the Roman Catholicism it had left: it looked too formal and ceremonious, too heartless and routine. Puritans wanted a religion that moved the people's hearts as much as it reached their heads or controlled their conduct. They also expected more strict observance of the faith, and promoted the notion that Christians had a covenant with God that God and they had to keep. God would be their God and they would be God's people. God would be gracious and they had to be disciplined. Many of these Puritans felt uncomfortable or were even persecuted in England. They tended to be educated people, middle class, ambitious, and restless about their own future security and their children's faith. They had to act upon their need to establish a pure community and their desires to worship freely. One of their leaders, Francis Higginson (1588–1630), made it clear that they were not saying farewell to the Church of England but in the New World they wanted to advance the work of reformation, which they were not able to do in the English context.

Before they could take action, however, they saw the rise of a more radical party. Remember the word about Protestant logic: there is always someone who will go further. You know the people who went further, because we call them the Pilgrims. In their black suits and dresses, with their silver buckles and trusted guns, they now appear on cardboard table decorations on Thanksgiving Day. Schoolchildren sing about the "land where our fathers died, land of the Pilgrims' pride." High school students know about them through Nathaniel Hawthorne's *Scarlet Letter*, or through attacks on them for being too strict and stuffy, or even because of later persecution of witches at Salem. Students are also taught to admire them as people of conviction who worked to express their liberty.

These "Pilgrims," which is what they called themselves, were Puritans who became "Congregationalists," which meant they allowed for no authority—no popes, no bishops, no presbyters—beyond the local congregation. The familiar New England "town meeting" was their ideal for the way to address concerns of church and state. They did not even need ministers, though in time some were welcomed. These independent English people first took refuge in the Netherlands, but found their children adopting the worst practices of their neighbors. They needed a place apart and sailed, as you know, on the *Mayflower* and some successor ships. They settled in a place they called Plymouth in 1620. Ten years later the more moderate Puritans settled Massachusetts Bay at Boston, and some of their party later branched off to found New Haven and Connecticut.

These lovers of liberty essentially loved their *own* liberty. They were sure that they were God's elect people, chosen as the people of Israel had been of old. They read the Hebrew Scriptures, which they called the Old Testament, and saw themselves in the plot. They passed laws they thought were influenced by the laws of Moses. (Jews have a right to say that their scriptures had a great influence on early America, not because there were many Jews here but because the Puritans found it easier to make their laws match the Ten Commandments of their Old Testament than Jesus' Sermon on the Mount from their New Testament.) Puritans like to talk about living by a covenant with God. They did not welcome Jews, Catholics, Episcopalians, or anyone but their own kind. The liberty they wanted was the liberty to be themselves, to have things their own way, to set up a new Israel, a new Zion in the wilderness.

Eventually they were to lose out, too. The stricter Pilgrims of Plymouth were outnumbered and did not prosper as did the Puritans of Massachusetts Bay, who kept attracting English Puritans and who did prosper and propagate. But that did not mean that strictness disappeared from Protestantism. Soon a new group of dissenters came along to complain that even Puritanism was turning formal and routine. Where was the heart? they asked. People could no longer assume that their children would automatically inherit the religion of their parents.

Each individual had to make a choice, a decision for God, a response to Christ. People had to "own" the covenant. In language more familiar now than then, they had to be "born again," starting over, as it were, as new beings no matter how evil they had been from birth. They had to form vital congregations of their own. One group thought that baptizing children, pouring water over the heads of infants who did not know what was happening to them, was a kind of magic, a mere routine. These people would baptize only adults who converted and spoke up for themselves. They called themselves Baptists.

THE BAPTISTS AND METHODISTS
MOVE SOUTH AND WEST

Baptists from England had already settled in Rhode Island when the new Baptists in Massachusetts and Connecticut started splitting the Puritan Congregational churches. Others moved south, spreading quickly through the backcountry of Virginia and the Carolinas. Here was a kind of democratic faith, one that appealed to emotions and the desire for community. When America west of the Appalachians opened up for settlement, at least in the South, these Baptists surged across the mountains and won converts. Today, Baptists predominate in nearly every county in the South (except in the southernmost portions of Florida, Louisiana, Texas, and in the Southwest).

Back in England another Protestant party set out to reform the Episcopal church. Guided by a reformer who wanted to be holy and perfect, John Wesley (1703–1791), they eventually went their separate way as Methodists. Many Methodists came to America, and after the American Revolution they spread across the South and West. Not as democratic as the Baptists, they used superior organization—they had bishops, superintendents, and ministers who "rode the circuit" to gain converts—to become rivals to the Baptists. From the middle colonies they won what we might call the north of the South and the south of the North; their greatest contributions on the map of American religion run from Baltimore and environs, where they were organized in 1784, to Kansas and the Great Plains in general, though they are well represented in most parts of America. The nineteenth century also saw the rise of at least two large black churches, the African Methodist and the African Methodist Episcopal Zion. The Methodists were the largest Protestant body for more than a century.

That these Baptists and Methodists influenced America is obvious to anyone who knows the history of slavery and abolition. In the South they were generally for slavery; in the North they often opposed it. Both churches split before the Civil War, and the Baptists never came back together. The same two denominations had a big role in reform movements, most notably Prohibition (1919–1933), which forbade the sale of alcohol in America. (Many of them still oppose drinking of alcohol, but they have given up trying to pass laws prohibiting others from doing so.)

Baptists believe very much in liberty and human rights. They helped produce the separation of church and state in America and continue to work for human freedom. President Jimmy Carter was a Southern Baptist who said his faith moved him to work for human rights in other nations, even where such intervention caused complications in his foreign policy. Methodists, especially Methodist women, helped gain suffrage for women and were active in political and social causes. They long represented one of the great success stories in American Protestantism because of their rapid growth and influence in the society. In the 1960s, however, they began to decline in membership and influence.

VARIED INFLUENCES FROM THE MIDDLE COLONIES

Between the Episcopal South and the Puritan Congregational North were several "middle colonies," whose Protestantism still influences America.

These colonies, unlike the other nine, never did set up ("establish") by law an official church for which everyone had to pay taxes. In Pennsylvania, a radical Protestant group led by William Penn, the quiet and pacifist (peace-loving) people called Quakers, wanted a "holy commonwealth" in which Native Americans, Quakers, and anyone else would be free to follow the Spirit. The Quakers were soon outnumbered. But they acquired such a reputation for their witness for peace and a passion for ethical living that they have had an influence beyond their small numbers. To the back country of Pennsylvania came non-English-speaking Protestants, not all of them welcome. These included small Baptist-type groups from Europe such as Mennonites and Brethren, people of peace who were disturbing to their neighbors because they were so different, set apart and apparently unworldly. Today a small group of these, the Amish, is best known. A much larger group were the Lutherans from Germany, whose descendants now make up the third largest Protestant group, thanks also to later immigrations to the Midwest in the nineteenth century.

Dutch of Reformed background settled New Netherland, especially New Amsterdam, today's New York and New York City. They wanted an established church, but for purposes of trade and commerce they found themselves having to tolerate others. By 1654 they saw the settlement of Jews (fugitives from Spain in 1492, who came now fleeing Brazil and looking for new opportunity) and many other peoples and religious groups. Perhaps because they found that they could not enforce a religion and had to make room for everyone, these New Yorkers were the "winners" in determining the future shape of America. Today we call American society "pluralist," which means, as the expression goes, "any number (of religions, in this case) can play"; many groups coexist, and all are free to worship as they please.

From Scotland and the Scotch-Irish lands came the Presbyterians, a hardy breed of people who were ruled by elders; who hated Episcopalians in the British Isles; whose leaders loved true doctrine; and whose poor people spread from Philadelphia to the unsettled lands just east of the Appalachians. From there they poured forth into the West with the Baptists and Methodists if in lesser numbers. Like the other groups they split between North and South, but recently they have come together. Not officially established, they nonetheless became part of "the establishment." If many U.S. Presidents were Episcopal, many others were Presbyterian, as were people of wealth and influence. As Presbyterians moved west, they built colleges, spread literacy, promoted reform legislation that had to do with temperance, education, and the like, and in general also exerted influence beyond their numbers.

AWAKENED AMERICA, ENLIGHTENED AMERICA

You can see that beginnings have much to do with outcomes in the American Protestant drama. With that in mind, we now examine two more events in colonial times that gave shape to America and continue to influence us today. The first event was later called the "Great Awakening." For several decades before the American Revolution, from New England to Georgia, local pastors stirred their people with vigorous prayer and preaching and saw many conversions. Traveling revivalists also upset establishments and fired up hearts and minds. These revivalists got the public talking about religion, and many converted to their churches. It is hard to measure such an event precisely, but the Awakening seemed to spread ideas of freedom of choice, the need for personal decision, and the premium upon individual liberty. Some historians think that these "awakened" people, being democratic in their anti-establishment outlook, provided much of the energy and many of the soldiers for the Revolution, the call for independence and the birth of the United States.

How does the Awakening affect us today? It helped spread the notion that religion is not something one inherits (as a Jew does by being a child of a Jewish mother) or acquires with the territory (as Catholics and earlier Protestants did, before church and state were "separated"). Religion is rather a matter of choice. Today some Jews try to convert people of Jewish inheritance to be "practicing Jews." Many Catholics know they have to stir people who were baptized Catholic if their faith is to make a difference in their lives. The evangelizing Protestant groups, who call for a "born again" experience, grow faster than those who do not. If Americans consider religion a matter of heart more than head, of choice more than inheritance, they do so in part because of habits acquired in the Great Awakening.

At the time of the Revolution, a new kind of Protestantism was being born in England and among the educated and elite people in the colonies. Scholars call this movement the Enlightenment. Those who welcomed its light were anti-Catholic—as were most of America's founders, George Washington being a rare partial exception—but they also feared the power of those Protestant ministers who insisted that to be a good citizen one had to be a converted church member who made and obeyed laws based on God's revealed will as recorded in the Bible. These Protestant churchgoing people—among them Thomas Jefferson, James Madison, George Washington, and John Adams—respected the Bible and the central Christian figure, Jesus, but they believed that God was revealed in (note the capital letters) Nature and Reason and Law. These were available to all thoughtful people of goodwill. No religion should be established or forced on people. These Enlightened statesmen linked up with Baptists and other "outsider" Protestants to attack insiders. Through the First Amendment they ensured that the United States Congress would "make no law respecting an establishment of religion, or prohibiting the free exercise thereof." It was this act that Jefferson somewhat too dramatically called the erection of a "wall of separation between church and state." There was no wall, or, if there was, it was always porous. But this distinction, however incomplete, was something Catholics in the Middle Ages and official Protestantism in the colonies had not known.

From the time of the First Amendment, Protestants, and eventually, Catholics, Jews, and others, were free to compete for the soul of America. This did not mean that they always engaged in fair and friendly competition: rivalries and hostilities at times were fierce. Some Protestants feared that this free market in religion would mean the end of churchgoing and the moral influence of faith. To their surprise the opposite happened. People *liked* to be persuaded rather than coerced; they chose freely, but they chose. Protestants in the United States are far more active in their churches than are their counterparts in Europe. These voluntary churches set up voluntary organizations to educate, spread their moral vision, and reform America. Much of the tradition of voluntarism in America, evidenced today by the energy put into United Way or the Red Cross, can be traced to these Protestant voluntary groups. To this day, most of the hours and dollars Americans donate, they donate through religious groups, many of them Protestant.

THE IMPORTANCE OF BELIEFS
IN PROTESTANTISM

Americans not content to hear that a group performed services long ago, like to ask, in effect, What have you done for me lately? Informally, non-Protestants ask this of Protestants. That Protestants dominated and largely shaped colonial America and then kept control, power, or influence as America turned more secular (which means less dependent upon religion for public choice) and more pluralist, tells us much but not everything about today's Protestantism. To understand those sixty out of a hundred people who call themselves Protestant or members of Protestant churches, we have to look at what is going on now. We already said that most Americans are not highly history-minded, and many Protestants know less about their own history than you just read in these few pages. So, What have they done lately? What are they doing now?

They are believing.

To understand a faith, a set of religious organizations, you have to ask why it exists. What do its adherents think about reality? A faith would not exist or would never survive if it did not successfully convince its followers to look at the world in a different way than if they did not believe and belong. In most respects, Protestants and Christians as a whole are just like everybody else. When they are sick they go to a physician and want high-tech medicine. When they want to know the weather, they do not go to a magician; they consult a meteorologist, who may have a slightly better record than did ancient readers of signs in the sky. When they vote, they usually do not like it if religious voices are too noisy telling them how to vote or whom to elect. They use the same technological logic that their neighbors do to run computers, fill prescriptions, or invest in the stock market, and with about the same record of success and frustration. Sometimes, especially if they call themselves liberals or modernists—a distinct minority—they are so much like everyone else that the faith cannot hold the interest of its members, especially the young. That is partly why those who stress the differences, people called evangelical or Pentecostal or fundamentalist, seem to have stronger groups and grow more successfully.

To understand faiths we have to talk about beliefs and worldviews. Do not expect anything neat here. There are so many scores of Protestant denominations because their leaders and members differ on beliefs. Within these denominations there are endless varieties. Lacking a pope who has final authority to decide about doctrines, and depending upon a Bible they can interpret so many ways, Protestants will not agree on the details—or perhaps even many of the essentials—of teachings. They may even differ on how important beliefs themselves are.

THE ROLE OF CREEDS

If you want to understand Jews, you do not ask which doctrines or dogmas or tenets they believe. Jews deal more with a story than a doctrine. Muslims will respond by reciting laws rather than by listing dogmas. Catholics can provide precise lists of what the official church sets forth as beliefs, but to the average Catholic it is a faith made up of scores of practices. Some Protestants, such as Quakers, resist the idea of doctrine. Most Baptists, Disciples of Christ or members of the Churches of Christ— movements from the nineteenth century that claim to be dependent on the New Testament alone—will say that to determine faith, the Bible, not creeds (formal statements of faith), is all one needs, can have, or should have.

Lutherans, Episcopalians, Presbyterians, and many others will tell you, however, that they believe the Bible, but that they also interpret it using creeds. These belong to the whole catholic church (but not *Roman* Catholic, mind you!) of which they are a part. They also supplement these creeds with documents from the Reformation era. For Lutherans this means the Augsburg Confession, for Episcopalians the Thirty-Nine Articles, for Presbyterians the Westminster Confession, and so on.

If you go into a Lutheran or Episcopal or Presbyterian church, don't expect the members to be able to tell you all about these confessions and articles. Just because the guidebooks say that these are official or charter documents that help define the church, this does not mean that they are best-sellers or even that they are read at all by most congregants. Scholars in the seminaries debate them, and sometimes during a quarrel between factions in a church both sides will claim these creeds. But they exert their influence in subtler, more diffuse, and often half-forgotten ways.

In this introduction to Protestantism, we cannot hope to detail all the particular teachings. We can only offer some illustrations. For instance, two of the original parties, the Lutheran (third largest in American Protestantism) and Calvinist-Reformed-Puritan (in combination the most influential), both believe that God is gracious and all-powerful. But Lutherans start by asserting that God is gracious; whatever else they say, including anything about God's power, they will say in such a way that grace remains central, that God's loving initiative is primary and talk about God's power is secondary. Ask them whether God, being all-powerful and all-knowing, "knew" or "destined" in advance who would be the elect people, and they will say that because God is gracious, those who respond in faith and care about the answer can deduce that God somehow elected them. Ask the Calvinist the same question and he or she may very well say that God did elect or foreknow outcomes. Should that not terrify someone who may not have been selected? Not really. Remember, says the Calvinist, God is also a God of grace, so you should feel confident in God's love. Neither of these teachings is "neat"; neither seems fully logical to the outsider. But to those who share these faiths, they match the reality the believers find in the Bible, their hymns, their prayers, their hearts, and their lives.

THE ROLE OF THE BIBLE IN
PROTESTANT BELIEF

What can be said about Protestant doctrine? Here we have to paint with a very broad brush, leaving details to others or to your further inquiry. The two things to be said right off are that (1) Protestantism is a branch of Western Christianity, as opposed to the offspring of Eastern Orthodoxy, and (2) it is that part of Western Christianity that rejects the authority of the pope at Rome and all that goes with his office. For the rest, things remain wide open. Let's look at the broad outline.

Protestants make much of their Bible, which includes the Hebrew Scriptures, which speak to Jews but which Christians reinterpret until Jews hardly recognize them—think what calling *your* book the "*Old* Testament" (or "Covenant") would do to a faith! Protestants also rely on the New Testament, the four Gospels telling the stories of Jesus and the earlier letters of Paul the apostle and others who spread the word of Jesus and told Asians, Europeans, and North Africans what Jesus meant. Most Protestants believe that these Testaments are *somehow* inspired by God, which means they are set apart from merely human documents. A large conservative minority even says that they are "inerrant"—free from error or infallible—that a loving God would have taken care to preserve the original manuscripts from any mistakes, even in trivial details of geography. Most Protestants say that the Bible speaks with God's authority, which God risks in a world where there are many changes and accidents, arguments and interpretations. The more liberal among them acknowledge that they use their own reason and experience to connect the witness of the Bible to their lives.

GRACE, FAITH, AND GOOD WORKS
IN PROTESTANTISM

Most Protestants stress that God, being gracious, chooses to show love and favor by wanting to include all people in the divine reach, to "save" them all from whatever limits or ails them—their shortcomings or sins, their death, or "the devil," by which they mean everything from a literal figure to the forces of evil.

God shows this grace through Jesus Christ. His disciples called him "rabbi," which means "teacher." This rabbi taught, did wonders, attracted a following, and was put to death. Christian anti-Semitism arose from the fact that in the Gospels, the people responsible—alongside the Romans, who carried out the execution—were, like Jesus, Jews. Today the historic accusations that Jews were "Christ-killers" tend to be remote memories for most Protestants. Official Protestantism seems to do what it can to revise interpretations so that the Gospels will not be used against Jews. Most Protestants today are taught that not Romans, not Jews, but they themselves, through their own faults, in effect "put Jesus Christ on the cross."

Most Protestants believe that death was not the end of the Jesus story. Somehow—don't expect agreement on detail—the story continues with the announcement that Jesus was "raised from the dead," resurrected; God did a new thing through this Jesus, who comes to be called "the Son of God." Protestants believe that their death will not be the end of their story, either; with Jesus, they will be part of a new creation, a new life. This does not mean that they do not fear dying. They just have a sense—which may range from vague to precise—that their dying does not end the reach of God's love to them.

Along with their biblical grounding and the story of grace and faith in Jesus Christ, the teacher, victim, and risen one, Protestants have any number of other doctrines that flow out of the logic of these basic ones. To take one major illustration: whoever observes Jews, and Catholics, and Muslims in action knows that to them the conduct of life, both as a people and as individuals, is extremely important. Protestants often like to say that those three and some other faiths are "legalistic," motivated by fear of a judging God whom the followers have to please. But don't accept that statement categorically. Some good advice: when you want to know what someone believes, ask him or her. Don't depend upon even the most sincere attempts to represent others, and certainly do not be content with caricatures. God—the same God, many Protestants will say, for all the faiths just mentioned, faiths that are their kin—is seen as loving and gracious in all of them.

In many arguments, however, Reformation-era Protestants and their heirs found that wherever law and legalism ruled, they defined themselves best, not as people who did not care about "good works" or morality, but as those who simply wanted to relocate where efforts to follow God's ways came in. They insisted that doing good did no good, so far as being right with God was concerned, *before* one experienced grace.

Doing good was always good for its own sake, of course. It helped one's neighbor and made for healthy citizenship. But in Protestant faith, the doing of good was to flow from the experience of grace. Because God has shown love, the believer, after receiving divine gifts, puts those gifts to work, empowered to love and serve others.

THE PRESENCE OF GUILT
AND MORALISM

However much Protestants say that theirs is a religion of grace, of gifts, of the receipt of love, they do not always act accordingly. Many of them have heard and believe the message of grace, but they still feel and act guilty. As Protestants continue the Reformation, they have to keep reminding themselves that when they push guilt on their own faithful believers, they are contradicting themselves. Some Protestant youth react and rebel because they have felt the hand of repression or guilt. Others may become moralistic and legalistic; that is, they act as if Protestant church life is essentially a matter of being handed a list of do's and don'ts, which make impossible demands and leave them unhappy. Again, their teachers will ordinarily tell you that such an approach is based on a misunderstanding of the grace of God, but they are aware that the impulse to turn faith into a matter of responding to commands is very strong, and that makes it difficult to keep grace central in Protestantism.

From all this it is clear that Protestants do not believe that all is well for humans if and as they live their lives apart from faith in God. That is part of their worldview. This does not mean that most of them believe you must be a believer or a Christian or a Protestant or their kind of Protestant to be a good citizen. They will usually vote for their party or the candidate with their political viewpoint over a fellow church member. Nor do they think that only Protestants are moral or virtuous or capable of doing good. Most of them link up freely with non-Protestants for good causes, and admire people of any faith or no faith who feed the hungry, bring peace, provide housing, take care of the ill, and so forth. They argue instead that, as fortunate as these expressions of good may be, they do not bring peace to the restless heart, answers to the deepest questions of life, a sense of authority or identity, or an experience of being "saved," the way faith in the God of the Bible and grace through Jesus Christ bring these. The human, in old-fashioned but still vivid terms, is a sinner and needs God's help.

ALL BELIEVERS ARE PRIESTS:
A HIGH VIEW OF
LAYPEOPLE

Another Protestant teaching that somehow persists is that all believers are equal before God. When Protestant founders set out to reform the Roman Catholic Church—and even today, after much Catholic reformation—they saw that the clergy had a special status, a special set of rights, a special closeness to God that made laypeople into second-class citizens of God's kingdom. (Remembering our rule to let faiths speak for themselves, we have to say that Catholics will not all and always regard that view as being accurate or up to date.) Protestants assert that all believers are "priests," that all people have equal access to God. The parents washing diapers, the homemakers taking out the garbage, the people behind the plow or at the computer, the laypersons reading the prayer book, are as deeply involved in holy callings or "vocations" as are monks and priests and nuns.

HOW PROTESTANTS GOVERN
THEMSELVES

Not all Protestants have put this democratic belief into practice in their organizations. Democratic forms of church life can produce great pressure for conformity. Some denominations vote on the truth or falsehood of doctrines, and thus look much like Catholics with their councils. Because almost all denominations have professional, ordained ministers or clergy, and because so many of them function well in their roles, there tends to be general respect for the offices of the clergy. Protestants call these "minister," sometimes "preacher," often "the Reverend," or, to symbolize a warm leadership role, "pastor." But when showing such respect, the laity are not to become second-class citizens.

Protestants govern themselves in many different ways. For instance, Episcopalians (and some Scandinavian Lutherans), like Orthodox and Roman Catholics, believe that their leaders, their bishops (which means "overseers"), get their authority when other bishops engage in a rite of "the laying on of hands." They believe that this rite has continued in unbroken succession ever since Jesus laid hands on his first disciples or apostles and gave them authority. Methodists, as in today's large United Methodist Church, or Lutherans in the also large Evangelical Lutheran Church in America, have bishops as well. But they see the bishop's office

53

not as essential but as being *beneficial* to the life of the church. Presbyterians have presbyters, or lay elders; and Congregationalists of the Puritan tradition (now usually part of the United Church of Christ), along with Baptists, insist that congregations are the main seat of authority. They may link up for common practices, however, in "synods" or conferences or even through bureaucracies that have no official doctrinal support.

Speaking of the point where faith, practice, and government meet leads us to the ecumenical movement. This movement, begun around 1910, tried to address the issue of too many Protestantisms, too much competition and divisiveness, too little interaction between Protestants and other Christians. From it issued in 1908 a Federal Council of Churches; in 1951, a National Council of Churches; and in 1948, a World Council of Churches. These ecumenical or unitive organizations do not attract as much attention in the churches or the public press as they used to, but the ecumenical spirit lives on. Protestants are unimaginably closer to each other than they were before they began to federate or form cooperative councils.

If there has been an ecumenical movement to bring Protestants together, there also have been movements away from traditional Protestantism. The Mormons' Church of Jesus Christ of Latter-day Saints has added *The Book of Mormon* to the Bible as a basis for their faith. The Mormons share many aspects of Protestant life; but they believe that God is a physical being who once was a human and that humans can become gods and goddesses in the life to come, and those beliefs keep them at a distance from conventional Protestants. Later in the nineteenth century came Christian Science, a movement stressing spiritual healing. Jehovah's Witnesses appeared at about the same time. This was and is a group that stands entirely apart from all others, whom they consider to be opposing the purposes of Jehovah God. The Witnesses' particular views of the return of Christ and their zealous mission work set them apart. Much of what we are saying about Protestant life and worship does not apply to them. Yet their founders were all Protestant, and many almanacs and encyclopedias list them with Protestantism.

RITES OF WORSHIP

If beliefs or doctrines in endless detail are not vivid to most Protestant church members, one must look elsewhere to find them doing characteristic or distinctive things. A natural place to look is where we started, in the buildings to which the Yellow Pages served as a guide. Their collective habitats more often than not are churches, where a chief activity is worship.

Protestants believe that one of their duties and delights is to come together to praise God. They believe in the doctrine of creation, or, better, they believe that a divine creator made and makes the billions of stars in the billions of galaxies, and has a hand in the ongoing creation of the present world and of all life in it.

Most Protestants square their belief in continuing creation with modern science, with evolution. Fundamentalists and some other conservative parties believe that the two are opposed. Because they are quite vocal about what is taught in respect to origins of the universe, the world, and humans, they draw more attention than does the majority. But both wings believe that they are to show wonder in the face of the created order and the Creator. God, whom Jesus addressed as "Father," is the Creator. As Jesus prayed to the Father, they will sing or say praises to the Creator. That openness to a personal God who hears prayer, who welcomes praise, who wants people to gather, is a mark of most Protestants.

(Here we should say that some offsprings of the Protestant impulse, notably in the Unitarian Universalist Association, are uneasy about being called Christian. One wing of that body, whose ancestry is largely New England Congregational, defines itself as humanist. It gathers for meetings, messages, and worship, too, but does not focus on a personal God, and makes a point of expecting great freedom of expression, whether directed to God or not.)

So Protestants gather for worship and praise. Roughly one-third of the people who call themselves Protestant and one-half of those who are on the church rolls worshiped last weekend. Almost all did so on Sunday, but some Seventh-Day Adventists and Seventh-Day Baptists hold Sabbath or Saturday worship. Protestants have some disadvantage in calling for people to gather for worship. Orthodox and Catholic Christians believe that something goes on in church that cannot go on elsewhere. Their view of the presence of Christ in the bread and wine of the Eucharist or Mass or Last Supper—a rite they believe Christ instituted the night before he died—means that you have to be there to get the full benefit of what is offered. Some Protestants, notably many Episcopalians, believe the same. Many others have a view that Christ is thus present, but they cannot as clearly make the point that something is missing if one is not present for this "presence."

This means that Protestants are always being urged or are urging each other to go to church. Many of them see church as a kind of voluntary association, a gathering of like-minded people who choose to come together for common purposes. When the polltaker comes by to ask whether one can be considered a good Christian if he or she does not worship regularly, the vast majority of the clergy will say "no" but the vast majority of the people—except in very conservative bodies—will say "yes," though regular churchgoing certainly is important. You might say that the clergy have a vested interest in having good crowds. It gives them power and assures the support of their institutions. But the belief goes deeper than that. Most Protestant leaders agree with Orthodox and Catholic teachings that the church of Jesus Christ is a body, a communion, a reality, a people, before an individual finds it advantageous to join.

Protestantism has just enough of the classic Jewish sense of a "people," as well as the classic Catholic sense that there is a community called the Body of Christ, to make churchgoing vital. It also has a heavy dose of individualism that seems to make churchgoing part of a buyer's market, a bargain, a free choice. Despite some confusion over these conflicting claims, the presence of tens of millions of Protestants in worship each week astonishes visitors from Protestant Europe, where attendance is low. It may also astonish visitors from Protestant sub-Saharan Africa or Oceania, where the percentage of believers who worship regularly may be much higher!

On whatever grounds, the invitation to gather for worship pulls congregations together, and there one best sees Protestantism in action. The rest of the time religion seems to be a private affair, rarely visible and not always spoken up for. But behind stained-glass or storefront windows, inside sanctuaries, in front of a cross in a picnic grove, or wherever Protestants gather, they may take for granted that what they do there is obvious. To a visitor, whether another kind of Christian, an unbelieving inquirer, a Jew, a Muslim, a Hindu, or a Buddhist, the rites and practices may seem very mysterious.

READING OF SCRIPTURES
AND PREACHING

Surprisingly, a Jew might find it easiest to understand Protestant worship because it derives from the synagogue. The reverent reading of the Scriptures is a major element in worship. Someone then applies what is read to life today, in the act called *preaching*. This person, specially trained and usually an ordained minister, rises to face the group and give voice to a shared faith. The preacher—formerly always a man but now, except in a couple of large conservative groups, quite possibly a woman—takes the Bible reading and applies it to life. The speaker may display good voice or bad, exact grammar or imprecise syntax, some excellent points and some meanderings, but somehow the people conceive of this elaboration of Scripture as "the preaching of the Word of God." They like to have it applied to their daily living. In some churches the sermon will be more of a lecture, something like comment on current affairs or a book review. But that is still the exception.

To get a sense of what is intended in preaching, one should attend a black church, a Baptist, Methodist, or other congregation in the African American tradition. There will be little talk about a doctrine of biblical inerrancy or authority, but it will be clear that the Bible is the authority. The Bible provides a kind of scenario or script for the life of the people. The congregation, one might say, seems to be part of the plot, and everything is made contemporary. One expects to find Pharaoh in City Hall, or false prophets promising peace when there is no peace down the street. Martin Luther King, Jr., and others in the succession of black leaders have played the role of a Moses, pointing to a Promised Land. God is on the move, they say, and the people will do well to take part in that movement. Here is liberation from oppression. Here is dignity for those who are usually trampled. Here is hope for the hopeless. Such preaching took rise in times of slavery and provided meaning in the worst of segregation times. Even among upper-middle-class blacks, where the forms of worship might be a bit more staid and discreet, preaching first addresses the people *as* a people, and then as individuals who need to experience grace and make new resolves.

PRAYER, PRAISE, AND SONG:
THE GIVING OF GIFTS

Along with the preaching there is prayer, which seems to be common to most religions wherein a personal God is addressed. The prayers may be very formal, inherited from books of grand style and refined by centuries of usage. They can also erupt from the heart and be brought forward by people who are present. Nothing is too trivial, because nothing in the life of faith is trivial: the congregation is asked to pray for a young woman in military service and in harm's way; for a couple who had a child; for those fighting addiction and trying to free themselves from substance abuse. The prayers then reach out to the overlooked, the homeless, hungry, and despised. Protestants also take from Jesus the signal to love their enemies, and are taught to pray for them. Prayers and praises often take the form of songs, by choirs, soloists, or the whole congregation. With a few passive exceptions, Protestants say theirs is a singing church. Spirituals and gospel music in black denominations; plainsong and chorales and Victorian anthems and folk music—all mix in various Protestant groups.

Most Protestant worship will include an offering, the bringing forward of money gifts. To grudging members or suspicious visitors this may look like money-grubbing by solid and greedy institutions. To people who have caught on to what is going on, this is more than an act of survival, of self-support, of a means to keep the building heated and lit and the ministers paid, the organ in tune and the hymnals in shape, the roof from leaking and the windowsills painted. It is even more than a means to provide seminaries to train ministers and publishing houses to spread the word; more than an instrument to support works of charity and mercy, to buy blankets and food for refugees, or to support development where there is threat of famine.

The giving is conceived as an act of worship, usually called *stewardship*. Protestants who grasp this concept say that in their stewardship they are acknowledging that God is the source of whatever they have; they have it on loan, as it were. By turning back part of it, they show that their possessions do not rule them, that they are free, that they can part with what dominates many lives and becomes an idol. This is the ideal, of course, and the reality may often differ from it.

RITES AND SACRAMENTS

Although Sunday is the big day of the week for most Protestants, they tend to celebrate other special days. Only a few groups, who see the festivals as inventions of Catholicism, avoid churchly observance of Christmas, the birth of Christ, and Easter, his resurrection. Many take note of certain seasons, such as the four weeks of Advent for the preparation for Christmas, or the six weeks of Lent, a serious time in which people ready themselves to follow the story of Jesus' death and resurrection. Many also recognize certain heroes, heroines, and saints, though they do not pray to these saints.

Two special rites or sacraments stand out. We have already referred to both. Although a few groups, such as Quakers, avoid sacraments, almost everyone else baptizes. Protestants disagree over whether or not to baptize infants, and whether baptism must be by immersion in water. They also differ over its meaning. It is somehow the initiation rite that begins or deepens the Christian life. Those who baptize infants see it as a pure act of God's grace that initiates a lifelong growth in grace. Adult baptism depends upon a conscious profession of choice, a decision of faith.

The night before Jesus died, according to the Gospels, he had a supper with his disciples. This lives on in the Lord's Supper, Holy Communion, or the Eucharist, which means thanksgiving. Protestants see this variously as a memorial, an observance, a deepening of faith, a spiritual union with Christ, or an actual if special form of presence of the same Jesus Christ who is also present in the preached Word of God. Some Protestants, such as the Disciples of Christ and many Episcopalians and Lutherans, commune every week; others enjoy this sacrament less frequently.

WOMEN, CHILDREN, AND YOUTH

The congregation is likely to have more women than men, though there are many elements in Protestantism that have appealed equally to men. Some women have accused this faith of being so interested in production, achievement, aspiration, and dominance that it has a "macho" cast. They argue—and many men agree—that its male adherents must recover the freedom to be vulnerable, to heal because one understands suffering, to stay close to the processes of life that women as mothers know so well, and to keep the poetry of faith. The women's movement has affected Protestantism considerably. Some women have disdained it for being patriarchal. Most believing Protestant women who want to change things have stayed around to help reform the churches, and their reinterpretations of the Bible and of Christian themes bring not only controversy but vitality to Protestantism.

As for the young, before, during, or after worship they may be in Sunday school or church school. There the simpler biblical stories become a part of their lives. They may have handiwork and craft projects that help make the landscape of Israel, the scene of Bible stories, vivid for them. Elsewhere in the same building, high-school-aged members may be pursuing more advanced studies, often discussing how to apply biblical teachings to their own lives as they take on more responsibility. What does the church have to say about sexuality and marriage, about drugs and lifestyles, about the choice of careers and professions, about morals and ethics? These Protestant young people are also likely to have banded together in various organizations, some of them extremely successful and dynamic and some of them, to say the least, less so. There they gather for recreation, retreat, performing service, studying, and eating mountains of pizza. (Pizza is a borrowing from the Italian Catholic world that is now universal among younger Protestants, as casserole dishes at church suppers seem to be among older ones.)

EXTENSIONS OF PROTESTANT LIFE

In that parenthesis we tucked the clue that Protestant church life is not all supposed to be grim. Those who leave it behind tend to dismiss it as dull, dour, and boring. Those who stay with it find many of their best friends and most profound attachments there. In the loneliness of the modern city an alert Protestant congregation will have a young adults' social group where people meet, sometimes to find their marital partner but more often to find their friends. They laugh and work together. Then tragedy strikes; one in their number is abused or deserted or stricken with illness. Where the laughs had been, there come tears, or gentle gestures of support. Protestantism is by no means unique in offering this benefit as part of its package. But where it does not find a way for people to enjoy each other's company and to find means of bonding, it does not stand much chance of being vital or even surviving. Protestantism intends to be a faith that moves from weekend and sanctuary to weekday and workday and play time.

PROTESTANT INDIVIDUALISM IN POLITICS AND ECONOMICS

Protestantism is usually defined as a faith that appeals to individualists. When Martin Luther (1483–1546), in a moment that lives in Protestant mythology, thundered to the emperor that he would not abandon his stand unless convinced by Scripture and sound reason, he was standing for the idea that no pope, no authority, no collection of people, can take responsibility for each person's faith. This means that each person has to be equipped to make decisions. For that reason, Protestantism tended to promote literacy, having been born at about the same time as movable type and the printing press. Now it was possible to put the Bible into the hands of the people and to expect them to read it. Protestantism became a kind of religion of the printed page, and some parts of it have trouble making sense of the electronic age. Other parts—one thinks of those that are represented by televangelists—have become masters of electronic media. But the printed page has been the base of the spread of Protestant ideas.

Those ideas permeate the culture. A moment ago we mentioned individualism. The belief in what one scholar calls "the exalted individual" carries far beyond the encounters between a reformer and an emperor or a pope. It reaches far outside the sanctuary of a church. In colonial America, when the evangelists told backcountry people that they should decide about the truth of faith no matter what the official established preacher said, they started spreading the contagion of freedom. Some of these converts resented the Congregational or Episcopal church, for which they had to pay taxes even if they opposed it. When the time came to decide on independence from England, many of them carried this resentment into the political realm, along with the intoxicating idea that they had a responsibility to be free.

One should not make *too* much of that kind of connecting between religion and political and economic life. Human motives are too tangled and church memberships too varied to let us trace all such connections. But where they exist, they do suggest how many aspects of life the faith is to touch and direct. When Protestants of the Enlightenment and Protestant dissenters linked to promote freedom through the Bill of Rights, they bought into a logic that made Protestant support of slavery—and Protestantism was long the main support system for the idea of slavery—into a travesty. In England, evangelical Protestants were major players in the abolition of slavery; in America, the record was mixed. But blacks in slavery and as free persons found ideas of individualism ready at hand in their biblically based Protestant faith and their local Protestant congregations.

This individualist idea carried over into economic life as well. One great scholar, Max Weber (1864–1920), looking at Switzerland, Germany, and England, decided that modern economics, with its support of capitalism, had roots in Protestantism, especially in Calvinism. He spoke of "the Protestant Ethic," an idea that remains controversial; rivers of ink have been spent on books supporting or demolishing it. After all, there were capitalists in Venice before there were Protestants. There are capitalists in Japan, which is largely unmoved by Protestant Christianity.

Weber was not all wrong, however. In Protestantism, for better and for worse, religion came to be a matter of choice. One read the Bible and chose not to stay Catholic. One made up one's mind and decided to follow the preaching of this revivalist and not that one. One worked through the Yellow Pages and found a congenial denomination and then chose which form the expression of faith took. At the same time, one chose independence and freedom in politics. Along came Adam Smith (1723–1790), whose *Wealth of Nations* appeared in 1776, the very year of American independence. He did not make his case for capitalism on Protestant grounds, and Protestant social thinkers have always found fault with his ideas. But some of what he observed matched many Protestant ways of doing things. One assessed situations, made calculations, used one's judgment, decided to be a steward, and then invested. The investment might be the long day's work or the money one needs to become an entrepreneur.

THE SOCIAL SIDE OF
PROTESTANTISM

The majority of Protestants in America—and elsewhere, as exuberant forms of Protestantism spread throughout Catholic Chile and Guatemala, for example—are supportive of individualism, enterprise, competition, and capitalism. But there are other points of view within Protestantism. The Puritans were not simply economic individualists; their New England towns lived with a sort of planned economy. For a hundred years Protestants in movements such as the Social Gospel or Christian Socialism, while rarely endorsing the violence and class warfare that went into Marxism-Leninism, did advocate workers' cooperatives, some nationalization of industry, some limits on private property, and considerable support for the welfare state. This social preaching was probably always a minority voice, belonging to theologians, elected or appointed leaders, journalists, and the like. But it too had some biblical basis and some effects in the political world.

PROTESTANTISM IN THE
PUBLIC WORLD

Our foray into economics shows how controversial Protestantism can be when it leaves the sanctuary. Some Protestant denominations, notably Quakers, Mennonites, and Brethren, are "peace churches" that promote pacifism in the face of war. Other Protestants, in the old establishment style and often through nationalistic instincts, have been quite militaristic, ready to go whenever conflict attracts American energies.

Why pay attention to Protestantism, then, if it is so divided on such an issue? On every issue? It cannot be because Protestantism as a whole has an answer or The Answer. Although some of its task forces, boards, and bureaus sometimes give the impression that they speak for the church (and are on occasion even authorized to do so), most members pay no attention or resist if they think that such speaking is unrepresentative or even wrong. Many members do, however, show that they welcome the act of designating people who are supposed to have special competence to take on special tasks. These people make studies and try to set the terms for teaching, for speaking *to* the churches. When truly crucial issues appear, Protestants may put their energies to work in the public arena. Thus much of the historically white Protestant movement eventually linked up with black Protestant civil rights leadership—many of whom were clergy—to promote legal changes. But such moments of agreement are rather rare.

Take an issue which tears America apart today: abortion. The polltaker finds that 10 or 20 percent of the people believe it is always wrong. About the same percentage believes that only choices, not lives, are at stake: "A woman's body is her own to do with what she wants." Some fundamentalist churches are entirely in the former camp and some liberal ones are almost entirely in the latter. But the vast majority of Protestant churches and believers are in the company of the perhaps 70 to 80 percent of Americans who have problems of conscience with and moral distaste for abortion but who can envision numerous circumstances in which women must be free to choose it. Therefore it is hard for any commission to speak *for* the church body in helpful ways. And the speaking *to* each such body has to be so full of qualifiers that it may not settle much. Still, the exercise of discussing abortion, euthanasia, addiction, and health care practices is something most Protestants feel is urgent and, overall, beneficial, even if it does not leave their churches at peace.

THE PROTESTANT PARTIES
AND SCHISMS

Several times we have referred to "liberal" or "modernist" Protestantism, on the one hand, and "conservative," "evangelical," or "fundamentalist," on the other. It is impossible to complete a picture of Protestantism without noticing these informal names and parties that divide clusters of denominations or run right through them. Once again, we should start by getting a sense of the numbers. Ask a hundred Americans what they prefer in religion, and twenty-four of them are likely to list membership in denominations characterized as "moderate," or they will describe themselves as "moderate Protestants." Eight or nine will say "liberal" depicts them or their church—such as the Episcopalians, the Presbyterians, or the

United Church of Christ. Nine will list "black Protestant" denominations or preferences. Some spinoffs from Protestantism, which other Protestants do not regard as in their camp, such as Mormons (1.5 percent), are in a class by themselves.

That leaves about sixteen out of a hundred who belong to denominations of or accept the designation "conservative Protestant." This includes Southern Baptists, Churches of Christ, Adventists, and especially the groups called evangelical, fundamentalist, and Pentecostal. Members of these last three groups will insist that they are the oldest, that they represent the two-thousand-year-old essentials or "fundamentals" of doctrine and practice, which they received from the inerrant Bible and have preserved from the time of Jesus.

The historian will say that, although these groups have roots in earlier conservative Protestantism, they took their present shape in this century as a reaction to modernity. They saw liberal and modernist Protestants saying that evolution was "God's way of doing things," and that the Bible did not have to be inerrant to carry authority. They thought some liberals were getting too worldly, too much like everyone else. So they reacted. They reached for what they considered to be "the fundamentals"—the inerrant Bible, and literal beliefs in Jesus' being born of a virgin, or that he would physically come to rule for a thousand years and end world history as we know it.

If modernists started finding too much to like in other religions and thought that God would save more or less everyone, so they could stay at home or engage in humanitarian missions, these reactive parties insisted that God would condemn those who condemned themselves by being unbelievers. For this reason they evangelize, meaning they spread God's good news and try to make converts. Pentecostals especially believe that God the Holy Spirit is immediately available to us. They stress divine healing, and they speak or sing in languages that are unintelligible but which they interpret. At the very least, they want to provide an alternative to most Protestantism, which they think lacks fervor and commitment.

The fundamentalist-evangelical-Pentecostal movements and the liberal-moderate-modernist flanks came to a kind of schism earlier in this century and now engage in a less-than-peaceful coexistence. Now that they are no longer united in anti-Catholicism, that not being a part of any large Protestant movement today, they have nothing around which to coalesce. They might struggle for control of the same church body, as fundamentalist Southern Baptists did when they took power from traditionally conservative Southern Baptists. Some fundamentalist, evangelical, and Pentecostal Christians choose to work chiefly outside denominational patterns. They have their own moderate spokespersons, such as Billy Graham, and their own celebrities, such as the televangelists. They used to appear to be nonpolitical but have turned quite political in recent years.

Because mass media often misrepresented them, evangelicals, fundamentalists, and Pentecostals fought back with television stations of their own or by boycotting programs they did not like. Because they disagreed with *Roe v. Wade*, the U.S. Supreme Court decision permitting some abortions, they worked for a constitutional amendment to counter it. Because they disagreed with court decisions ruling out Bible reading and school prayer, they carried on battles for "Creationism" in the science class and for amendments that would allow for prayer. Some built Christian schools of their own.

THE EXPRESSIONS OF
PROTESTANTISM CLOSE TO HOME

It would be misleading, however, to suggest that either the elites of liberal Protestantism who make statements on public affairs which so many of their own fellow members ignore or the vocal leaders of New Christian Right Protestantism who gain the limelight represent the main agenda of most Protestants.

For most Protestants in your school, as elsewhere, church life extends first and foremost to home and personal life. When they cannot make sense of chaos, they try to find the hand of the God of Moses and Abraham and Jesus active in the confusing plot of history. When they feel guilty or oppressed or lonely, they believe that by supporting each other, by praying and speaking up, they can make Jesus Christ somehow vivid and can recognize his presence. When they fear disease, suffer illness, or face death, they expect the Bible stories they learned, the sermons they heard, the songs they sang, the prayers they prayed, and the company they kept at church to comfort and be with them. They expect to be challenged to do good works even as they expect to complain about the institutional church or organized religion.

THE PROTESTANT REFORMATION CONTINUES

If Protestants protest against the Protestant churches, including their own; if they think the reformers did not complete the task and that the church needs more reform—they are simply acting as Protestants are supposed to. This chapter would not be complete if somewhere we did not use a scholarly sounding term that makes one stop to stumble and, perhaps, to think. The early Protestants insisted, in Latin, that *ecclesia semper reformanda*, the church was always in need of being reformed.

Today's Protestants and their leaders still believe that, though they may find this belief uncomfortable when applied to themselves. They know that they are never supposed to sit back and think they have come to the fulfillment of the kingdom of God. But they do not like to have their own members point out how far short they have fallen, how much they need to do to see more unfolding of what they believe God's purposes to be. They find it easier to criticize Catholics and Jews, Muslims and Hindus, Buddhists and "secular humanists" or unbelievers, than to apply the Word of God critically to their own enterprises.

If Protestants are to be true to themselves, however, they must be ready for further protest and reform. They have had such ideas since their very beginnings, and they never know when, in the midst of routine organized church life, when everyone looks comfortable and smug, someone will come along and say "Thus saith the Lord!" and convince them to follow. That is why no chapter on Protestantism can present the final word. There is change every day. There is supposed to be.

STUDY QUESTIONS

1. How do you explain the "variety" that is called Protestantism? Give specific examples of the characteristics that have contributed to such variety. In light of such difference, does tolerance exist among different denominations? If so, how do you explain this tolerance? Be specific.
2. Explore what is meant by "The Protestant Drama." Who are its characters? What is its plot? Historically, how does the drama begin and develop?
3. What is Protestantism's relationship to Catholicism? What were the theological issues that led to the formation of the Protestant church? Develop, in particular, the role of the priest, the Bible, and how one is "saved" in discussing the Protestant Reformation.
4. Discuss the development of the earliest Protestant church in the United States. What were the motives behind the Protestant church's early development in this country?
5. Describe the historical and theological development of Puritanism in the United States. What are the major contributions of Puritan thought to contemporary Protestantism? To American government?
6. What is the Great Awakening? Why is the element of religious choice so crucial to understanding it? Do you see any connection between the Great Awakening in early American religious history and the development of the New Religious Right in the United States today?
7. What significant, if not unique, role do the Bible, the church, the "priest," grace, good works, faith, and guilt play in a Protestant's theology? What is "uniquely" Protestant about each of these theological issues? Give specific examples of these issues at work in contemporary Protestantism.
8. Define Protestant individualism. Is there a "social" side to Protestantism? If so, describe its function in society. If not, defend your position. What influence has Protestant individualism, as well as its social dimension, had on American politics?

ESSAY TOPICS

Jonathan Edwards: Puritan Spokesperson
The Protestant Sacraments: Baptism and Communion
The Bible Belt: Protestantism in the South
Going West: The Protestant Missionary Movement
The Great Awakening, Its Leaders and Its Theology
Protestantism and American Politics: Strange Friends?

WORD EXPLORATION

The following words play significant roles in any discussion of American
Protestantism and are worth careful reflection and discussion.

Denominationalism	Ministers	Good Works and Faith
The Protestant	Protestant	The Great Awakening
Work Ethic	Individualism	Politics
Free Will	The Bible	Puritanism
Creeds	Guilt	

3

PETER J. PARIS

The Religious World of African Americans

The African American churches are the oldest and most important institutions in their communities. Some scholars claim that they predate the African American family because the latter had no independent existence during the period of slavery. Since African American religion has always been predominantly Christian in character, this essay will center largely on its gradual development from the time of slavery up to the present day.

Unlike the vast majority of white Americans, African Americans did not come to this country voluntarily. Rather, they arrived on these shores in chains. Their descendants are the survivors of the Atlantic crossing historians refer to as the "middle passage." Packed like sardines in the humid bellies of slave galleys, these African peoples experienced indescribable suffering. Continuously exposed to the nauseous stench of feces, vomit, and vermin and the putrid smell of death, countless thousands perished en route. Those who survived the middle passage were delivered to the auction block in the slave marketplace, where they were sold like commodities to the highest bidder. Unlike the European settlers who came voluntarily to this country in search of freedom and wealth, Africans came in bondage, condemned to a life of misery and suffering.

In 1619, one year before the arrival of the *Mayflower*, twenty African slaves aboard a Dutch man-of-war were put ashore in Jamestown, Virginia. The American slave trade is said to have begun when the captain of that galley decided to trade his slaves for food. Yet this was not the first time Africans had arrived on these shores. Many of the earliest explorers and settlers brought domestic slaves with them. In fact, evidence shows that Christopher Columbus's cargo included African slaves.

Ruthlessly uprooted from their families and tribes, these African newcomers to this country suffered the unspeakable nightmare of slavery for two and one-half centuries. Ironically, slave traders and owners were often devout Christians who saw no contradiction between their religion and the practice of owning slaves. Their deep conviction that African peoples were not fully a part of the human race meant that they felt no moral obligations toward them whatsoever. In fact, they viewed the slaves as part of their livestock; hence, they had a legal right to do with slaves whatever they wished.

As a result, the slaves were forced to labor from sunrise to sunset with minimum food and lodging. They inherited at birth a social status that excluded them from liberty and freedom. Any infractions of the rules could result in such arbitrary punishments as whipping, torture, disfigurement, or death. Slave women suffered the additional violence of constant rape and wanton abuse. Further, their children could be wrenched from them at any time and sold so far away that no possible trace of them could ever again be found.

Ironically, the colonial states institutionalized this cruel and treacherous system at the beginning of their history. Although the quest for freedom had inspired both the American Revolution and the new Constitution of the Republic, the system of slavery was left intact for nearly another century. This tragic historical fact has plagued the destiny of all Americans, both white and black, ever since. A lingering legacy of white racism remains deeply rooted in the American psyche and culturally ingrained in all of its institutions. As a result, white and black Americans alike have been shaped both morally and religiously by the experience of slavery and the enduring presence of white racism.

AFRICAN AMERICAN SPIRITUALITY

Throughout the seventeenth and much of the eighteenth century African slaves had no other choice than to continue their own cultural traditions in this alien land. No rapid assimilation to the American cultural ethos was possible for them. Yet their white owners repudiated and disallowed all African cultural practices. Whenever the slaves were discovered engaging in such activities they were severely punished. Consequently, in underground locations African traditions were preserved and the substance of African American religion was born.

Not surprisingly, very few Africans became Christians during the first century of American slavery due in large part to two principal reasons.

First, the Euro-American view that Africans were subhuman implied that the latter did not possess souls; hence, no effort was made to convert them to Christianity. Second, these Euro-Americans who believed differently about the nature of African humanity feared that if slaves participated with whites in a common religion, they might soon want to extend the notion of religious equality to the sphere of civil equality and thereby threaten the security of the slave system.

As a result, throughout much of the seventeenth and eighteenth centuries, African slaves were repulsed by Christianity because they viewed it as the religion of slave owners and, hence, not as a resource for the well-being of slaves. Their early rejection of Christianity reflected the African understanding that a people's religion is synonymous with their lifestyle. In other words, they believed that a people's lifestyle mirrored their religion and vice versa.

The African understanding that religion is synonymous with life implies that all life is sacred. Thus, unlike Western peoples, Africans (then and now) had no appreciation for the Western idea of secularization. The rejection of Christianity by the African slaves did not mean that they had no religion. On the contrary, African peoples have always believed that religion permeates every dimension of human life. Similarly, they have believed that religion serves the good of its devotees and is strongly opposed to its enemies. Thus, the slaves had no difficulty in viewing slave-owning Christianity as inimical to the well-being of slaves. Accordingly, slave narratives are replete with descriptions of the disrespect that slaves expressed toward their masters' religion, which they experienced as an evil force intending their moral and spiritual demise.

Due to the circumstances of their departure from Africa, the American slaves had no choice but to leave their cultural artifacts behind. Yet they brought with them to these shores the spiritual substance of their culture, deeply embedded in their collective self-understanding. Gradually, these people shaped a new world of spiritual and moral meaning by appropriating and interpreting various elements in their new environment in accordance with their African understandings. Thus, the condition of slavery did not cut them off from their ultimate source of meaning, God, whom they knew by many names and who was for them the source and ground of all their religious and moral values.

Thus, despite the massive suffering endured for three and one-half centuries of slavery, the acculturation of the Africans to their new environment did not result in a total loss of their former religious and moral understandings. On the contrary, African slaves were able to preserve many of the formal features of their most fundamental spiritual beliefs and moral values. This astounding accomplishment was due to their ability to make many of the Euro-American cultural expressions, including Christianity, serve as vehicles of cross-cultural transmission—a feat that involved no small amount of creative ingenuity.

Gradually, the slaves designed creative ways of expressing African meanings and values through the cultural forms of Western songs and stories. By amalgamating various African and Western elements, the African slaves adapted many of their traditional religious beliefs and practices to Christianity. Eventually, this process led to the birth of a peculiar hybrid religion that we call African American Christianity—which, incidentally, cannot be understood apart from the history of slave-owning Christianity and the response of the slaves to it.

THE CONCEALED CHURCH

Sometime around the middle of the eighteenth century a growing number of slave owners had been persuaded by Christian missionaries to believe that slaves who converted to Christianity adapted more agreeably to the conditions of bondage than those who did not. Most slaveholders at the time opposed such a prospect because they assumed that if slaves experienced ecclesial equality in church membership they would aspire to civil equality as well. After they became convinced, however, that both civil law and local custom had long established the fact that the conversion of slaves to Christianity implied no change in their civil status, many gradually relaxed their opposition to slave conversions for at least two reasons: (1) their own personal conversion to Christianity sometimes caused them to view the evangelization of their personal slaves as an expression of their Christian compassion; (2) they gradually became convinced that the slave system would function more efficiently because converted slaves would likely cultivate the virtues of truth-telling, honesty, and patience, the lack of which among slaves constituted a persistent disciplinary problem. Thus, by the middle of the eighteenth century the membership of many white churches included slaves, because white slave owners were unwilling to permit racially separate associations, fearing possible slave involvement in abolitionist activity (activity designed to abolish the institution of slavery). However, most whites believed in the natural inferiority of Africans and therefore resented any semblance of equality that might be implied by slave membership in their churches. This led to the practice of relegating slaves to segregated spaces within white churches; for example, they had separate seating arrangements, received Holy Communion only after all whites had been served first, and had neither voice nor vote in matters of church governance. In spite of these restrictive conditions, however, some of the slaves gained considerable status as preachers and were praised by both whites and blacks for their oratorical excellence.

More often than not, however, special services were designed for the slaves in which the substance of the preaching consisted of the following basic tenets: (1) that the Bible admonishes slaves to obey their masters and be content with their condition in this world in the hope of eternal salvation in the world to come; (2) that slave ideas about freedom are signs of the devil's temptation; (3) that both diligence in their work and punishments for laxity are pleasing in God's sight; and (4) that forgiveness for wrongdoing lay not only with God but also with the slave owner.

Although slaves willingly participated in the worship services in order to experience some relief from the drudgery of forced labor, they were not fooled by the content of the instruction. Rather, they listened carefully and critically to the reading of the Scriptures and, in time, they discerned resources within the biblical teaching that led them to adopt an alternative understanding of Christianity to that proclaimed by the slave owners' preachers, namely, that God is the divine parent of all peoples and, hence, all are equal in God's sight.

This major turning point in the history of African American religious devotion occurred when slaves heard the biblical story of the exodus concerning Israel's deliverance from bondage. They quickly discerned that Israel's God had taken the initiative in that liberating event. The story had an indelible effect on the African slaves because it enabled them to see clearly that, contrary to the teaching of the slave owners' preachers, the biblical God identified with the Hebrew slaves and stood alongside them in opposition to their oppressors. This new understanding, which they embraced enthusiastically, portrayed God as the liberator of all oppressed peoples and opposed to all who are bent on maintaining oppressive sociopolitical systems. Henceforth, this view of God underlay the African American view of humanity.

As with the people of Israel, the exodus story has always been of paramount importance to African American Christians because it connotes a living and caring God who not only sees, hears, and knows about human suffering but willingly chooses to become actively engaged in liberating activity. The slaves gradually made the story of the exodus their own, and from one generation to the next they compared each of their major leaders to Moses and actually renamed them after him. For example, African Americans called each of the following Moses: Harriet Tubman, Sojourner Truth, Richard Allen, David Walker, and Frederick Douglass, to mention only a few.

Let us not suppose, however, that the slaves discovered this alternative understanding of Christianity under favorable conditions. Rather, their only alternative was to gather late at night for secret meetings in the brush. These meetings were subversive in nature because they provided the context in which slaves could reflect on their condition apart from the watchful eyes of their overseers. In these secret places an alternative understanding of Christianity was born, nurtured, celebrated, and proclaimed. Thus, concealed from the eyes and ears of the slave owners, the religion of African Americans emerged as a force strongly opposed to the theological and moral foundations of the slave system. Not surprisingly, in one way or another, everything that emanated from the religion of African Americans expressed their desire for freedom and their hope for a better day. Clearly, this entailed considerable ingenuity on their part, given the many severe proscriptions against such views.

The so-called spirituals, which constitute slavery's most lasting legacy to America and the world at large, tell the story of suffering and triumph, of endurance and transcendence, of history and eternity. Composed by "unknown bards" of long ago, these songs contain the substance of African American Christianity. They represent the spiritual strivings of an oppressed people in their efforts to persevere in the midst of daily threats to life and limb. The imaginative power and creative skill demonstrated in the countless spirituals manifest the transcendent capacity of the human spirit.

Ironically, the destiny of the spirituals has not been confined to the restrictive world of the slave but has become woven into the fabric of America's distinctive cultural contribution to the world. Emerging out of the spirit of an oppressed people, these songs tell the universal story of agony and pain, but not that alone. They also tell of the faith and hope of suffering souls. Through the activities of poetry, music, and song, the slaves expressed and preserved their humanity against astounding odds. Interestingly, these activities comprise some of the slaves' earliest forms of resistance to their hostile environment.

Through spirituals the slaves proclaimed their faith and hope in a God whom they believed would deliver them from bondage because this same God had also befriended and liberated the Israelites from slavery. They were confident that what God had done for the people of Israel, God would also do for them. Hence, their songs were not about suffering alone but also about their faith in a God of deliverance and their hopes for freedom both in this world and in the world to come. For obvious reasons, however, all indicators of their desire for freedom had to be concealed by the use of code words that usually conveyed more than one meaning. For example, on the one hand, the spiritual,

Go down Moses,
Way down in Egypt's land,
Tell ole Pharaoh,
To let my people go.

could be viewed as an effort to make a song out of a biblical story. Yet, on the other hand, it could be viewed symbolically as a longing for a contemporary Moses to rise and do likewise. Similarly, the spiritual

Steal away, steal away,
Steal away to Jesus;
Steal away, steal away home,
I ain't got long to stay here.

could be interpreted, on the one hand, as a meditative longing for a heavenly home. Yet, on the other hand, it could be understood as a mournful announcement of a forthcoming escape.

The slaves sang songs that spoke of ultimate justice for those who perpetrate injustice, and sometimes not without a bit of humor:

Rich man Dives, he lived so well,
When he died he found a home in hell.

Yet there were also songs that spoke of equality in heaven in such a way that the heavenly vision implied a severe criticism of the structures of injustice that shaped the daily lives of all the slaves. For example, slaves had no shoes as a rule, and robes and crowns were the inheritance of rulers alone. However, contrary to the beliefs of their slaveholders, they believed that in heaven everybody would have the freedom to walk wherever they wished and there would be no barriers of race, class, or other circumstance—everybody would have not only shoes but also robes and crowns. Why? Because all are children of God and, hence, brothers and sisters one and all. Again, the subtle humor of the slaves should not be missed as it appears in the line, "Everybody talking about Heaben ain't a-gonna there"—a double entendre unmistakably aimed at Christian slaveholders.

I've got shoes, you got shoes
All God's chillun got shoes
When I get to Heaben, gonna put on my shoes
Gonna walk all ober God's Heaben.

Refrain

Heaben, Heaben,
Everybody talking about Heaben
Ain't a-gonna there
Heaben, Heaben,
Gonna walk all ober God's Heaben.

I've got a robe, you got a robe
All God's chillun got a robe
When I get to Heaben, gonna put on my robe
Gonna walk all ober God's Heaben.

Refrain

I've got a crown, you got a crown
All God's chillun got a crown
When I get to Heaben, gonna put on my crown,
Gonna walk all ober God's Heaben.

Refrain

The themes about which the spirituals speak are numerous even as the spirituals themselves are. They cover a broad expanse of the human spirit; their imagery is rich beyond belief; their symbols are filled with experiential meaning pointing always beyond the immediate circumstances of pain and suffering to a final resting place in the divine resolution. Heaven was viewed as a place of belonging—a home—and like every genuine home, it was thought of as a place where persons are made whole in both body and soul. Yet the focus of so many spirituals on heaven should not be viewed merely as otherworldly but also as a concealed way of criticizing a present situation of pain and suffering by depicting a contrasting vision of hope and promise.

African American Christians have always been convinced that the substance of the religion of the slaves is authentic Christianity, a gospel that they believe was corrupted and rejected by whites through the practice of slaveholding. This true gospel centers on the parenthood of God and the kinship of all peoples under God. Since kinship implies the equality of persons in community, the kinship of all peoples under God implies God's opposition to those who threaten or destroy the equality of God's people. This religious vision was born in slavery; nurtured, developed, and protected in the secret meeting places of the slaves; and later institutionalized in the independent African American church movement, which began among freed slaves immediately following the American Revolution.

The religion of African Americans has constituted the one ongoing positive force in their history from the earliest times up to the present day. It has both saved the people from falling victim to fatalism and despair and given them theological grounds for their claim that suffering will end because God is on their side and desires their deliverance. Such a collective hope enables a people to dream of possible alternative worlds; such dreams formed the bedrock of black preaching from one generation to another. Clearly, all of this was implicit in the great "I Have a Dream" speech of Martin Luther King, Jr., this century's most celebrated embodiment of the African American Christian tradition.

THE INDEPENDENT AFRICAN AMERICAN CHURCH MOVEMENT

The independent African American church movement was started soon after the American Revolution by freed slaves in northern cities. The founders of these churches, unwilling at first to form racially separate organizations lest they be viewed as racists, eventually agreed that the choice to separate themselves from the white churches was not a racist act but rather a religious and moral refusal to comply with the racist practices of whites that robbed them of their human dignity in the house of God. Convinced that compliance with racism compromised their understanding of the Christian faith because it forced them to deny the parenthood of God and the kinship of all peoples, these freed slaves felt obligated both theologically and morally to separate themselves from such blasphemy and establish alternative churches that would institutionalize these principles. Thus, the independent African American churches came into existence as a prophetic response to the condition of slavery and racism. It had become abundantly clear that the white churches provided the theological and moral foundation for the degradation of African peoples. Consequently, African American Christians rebelled and their churches emerged as institutional symbols of that protest.

The African American churches suffered considerable persecution and severe restrictions during much of their existence. The most severe oppression, however, occurred during times of slave revolts, the most notable of which were the Gabriel Prosser uprising in 1800, the Denmark

Vesey revolt in 1822, and the Nat Turner rebellion in 1831. Following those insurrections, African American church meetings were banned because they were viewed as the seedbeds for sedition.

The African Methodist
Episcopal Church

The African Methodist Episcopal (A.M.E.) Church was the first independent African American denomination in the United States. It dates from 1787, when Richard Allen, Absalom Jones, and others withdrew from St. George's Methodist Church in Philadelphia because they had been forced from their knees while praying in an area of the church that was closed to blacks. In 1793, Allen bought a blacksmith shop and converted it into the Bethel Church, the first church owned by African Americans. The legal struggle to function as an independent church was formidable. Yet Allen and his supporters persisted and finally gained legal control over their property and independence over their internal affairs. From these meager beginnings, the African Methodist Episcopal denomination was formed in 1816, and Richard Allen was ordained as an elder and consecrated as its first bishop.

The African Episcopal Church

Interestingly, Absalom Jones, one of the persons who left St. George's Methodist Church with Richard Allen, was later ordained the first African American Protestant Episcopal priest. In 1794, he became the pastor of the St. Thomas African Episcopal Church. Thus, the independent African American church movement had expanded to include Episcopalianism.

The African Methodist Episcopal
Zion Church

Like the A.M.E. Church, the African Methodist Episcopal Zion (A.M.E.Z.) Church also had its origins in the late eighteenth century, when a group of African Americans, led by an ex-slave, Peter Williams, separated from the John Street Methodist Episcopal Church in New York City. Again, the separation was sparked by the discriminatory practices of the white church, which included the refusal to ordain African Americans.

The Christian
Methodist Episcopal Church

Although the circumstances of its origins differed from those of its northern predecessors, the A.M.E. and the A.M.E.Z. churches, the Christian Methodist Episcopal (C.M.E.) Church was born in the post-slavery South. Originally called the Colored Methodist Episcopal Church, this church separated from the Methodist Episcopal Church, South, after the 1844 split in white Methodism over the issue of slavery. In 1954 the denomination decided to change the term "Colored" in its name to "Christian" to retain the initials C.M.E. while also signaling its non-racial, universal character. Like its northern counterparts, the C.M.E. Church's separation from the white Methodists was a declaration of independence from the demeaning status of racial segregation within the white church.

Independent African American
Baptist Churches

During the latter half of the eighteenth century a number of independent African American Baptist churches came into existence in various northern and southern cities. The first such church in North America was the Silver Bluff Baptist Church, founded in 1787 in Savannah, Georgia.

Prior to emancipation, virtually no African American Baptist church in the South and very few in the North enjoyed full independence. Rather, they were all dependent to some extent on the patronage of white Baptists, who displayed no small amount of ambiguity toward them. On the one hand, they did not want to share equal membership with either slaves or ex-slaves; on the other hand, they did not want African Americans to have their own independent churches. It is an understatement to say that a varied and complex history attends each of these semi-independent African American Baptist churches and, especially, the story of their gradual pilgrimage toward full independence.

National Baptist Convention, U.S.A., Inc.

Being radically congregational in their church polity, these African Baptist churches soon linked themselves together into regional associations, which were characteristically abolitionist and intensely active in the so-called Underground Railroad (an effective support system for aiding and abetting slaves bent on escaping from their bondage). Various efforts to form a national convention of African Baptists eventually culminated in 1895 in the establishment of the National Baptist Convention, U.S.A., Inc., which continues to be the largest convention of African Baptists anywhere in the world. Its membership presently is estimated in excess of seven million.

National Baptist Convention of America

In 1915, the National Baptists suffered a split over an internal problem concerning the control and ownership of its publishing house. This division resulted in the formation of the National Baptist Convention of America (NBCA), which has a membership estimated at 2.5 million.

National Missionary Baptist Convention of America

In 1988 the NBCA suffered a split, with 25 percent of the membership opting to form the National Missionary Baptist Convention of America.

Progressive National Baptist Convention, U.S.A., Inc.

In 1961 the Progressive National Baptist Convention, U.S.A., Inc., came into existence as a result of a split within its parent body, the National Baptist Convention, U.S.A., Inc. This split centered on the alleged authoritarian leadership of President J. H. Jackson, who also opposed the strategies and tactics of nonviolent resistance. Under the leadership of the Rev. Dr. Gardner C. Taylor, such notable ministers and civil rights leaders as Martin Luther King, Jr., Martin Luther King, Sr., Benjamin Mays, Ralph Abernathy, and a number of others joined together to form the new convention with its motto, "Unity, Service, Fellowship, Peace." Its present membership is estimated to be 1.2 million.

The Church of God in Christ

Unlike the African Methodist and Baptist churches, the Church of God in Christ is a twentieth-century phenomenon that did not originate from a white denomination but from an interracial Pentecostal movement begun by a black minister and from which whites later withdrew. This movement was led by William J. Seymour, who conducted the so-called Azusa Street Revival in Los Angeles between the years 1906 and 1909. Out of that event emerged several Pentecostal denominations, of which the Church of God in Christ is the largest with a membership of 3.5 million. This church is now the fastest-growing African American denomination.

Black Churches within White Denominations

Many predominantly white Protestant denominations (i.e., Episcopalian, Lutheran, United Church of Christ, Presbyterian, United Methodist) along with Roman Catholicism have varying numbers of African American congregations within their denominational structures.

Women Leaders

During the twentieth century women have emerged as founders and leaders of a growing number of African American churches. Until fairly recently few African American churches permitted women to be ordained. Although the number of ordained women has steadily increased, prejudices against their leadership have not decreased appreciably. For these and other reasons, many women have founded independent churches. The most notable of these is the Mount Sinai Holy Church of America, Inc., founded by Bishop Ida Robinson in 1924 in Philadelphia. Bishop Robinson later ordained several women as vice-bishops and elders.

Protesting Racism

In spite of their denominational differences, African American churches are united by their common rejection of racism, which they consider to be the paramount sin of the white churches. Most importantly, they have never had policies of exclusion or segregation based on race or ethnicity. In fact, every independent African American church that chose to separate itself from its white counterpart, from the time of the American Revolution to the present day, did so as a religious and moral protest against institutionalized racism. By deliberately removing themselves from the public racism practiced by the white churches, African American churches gave birth to the civil protest tradition that continues to characterize their life and mission. The independent African American churches emerged especially, however, out of the desire to institutionalize Christianity in a nonracist form.

The independent African American church movement provided a place in which the people could worship God as they pleased, and in which it could serve the needs of the people in accordance with their own desires and choices. Faithful devotion to the principle of racial justice enabled these churches to construct alternative religious institutions with the unique aim of serving the well-being of African Americans in every dimension of their lives. This holistic approach and the nonracist character of the African American churches constitute the unique features of African American Christianity. Unlike any institutions in the larger white society, African American churches have made a theologically grounded nonracist principle the center of their associational life.

We must note, however, that the vast majority of African Americans have always opposed racism. That is to say, they have always abhorred any policies of exclusion based on the principle of race. This has been a predominant cultural ethos within the African American community from the earliest times to the present day. This nonracist principle has been nurtured and preserved continuously by the churches, which have been the primary societal institutions in the African American community. As such, they have been the custodians of the community's most basic values and especially its opposition to every form of white racism.

Thus, whenever African Americans become racist in attitude or practice, they betray the cultural ethos of their community and alienate themselves from it. Consequently, such leaders rarely attract much popular support.

Agencies for Social Organization
and Cohesion

The African American churches have been and continue to be the primary institutions owned and controlled by African Americans. Because no area of life is excluded from their purview, they have always exercised multifaceted roles in the African American community. Being the only independent institution dedicated to the maintenance and enhancement of the community's well-being, the role of the African American churches has been analogous to that of governments. Historically no other institution primarily served the good of the African American community. Theologically and morally legitimated by all African Americans, the churches not only founded schools, colleges, seminaries, hospitals, publishing houses, newspapers, insurance companies, banks, countless social clubs, and so forth; they institutionalized the most basic moral values of the community and provided the role models for community leadership. In fact, for generations African American churches were the training ground not only for church leaders, but also for political, civil rights, and educational leaders. Further, many professional singers, musicians, and other artists got their initial support, encouragement, and promotion from the churches. In short, throughout the nineteenth and much of the twentieth century, the African American churches had a role in virtually every good thing that occurred in the lives of their people.

Sociologists have referred to the churches as the primary agencies for social organization and social cohesion following emancipation. Clearly, one basic reason why the African American churches have flourished is their unadulterated commitment to the good of the African American community. They alone provided African Americans with opportunities for leadership, achievement, self-esteem, and racial pride. They alone enabled the people to gain a positive sense of identity as individuals and as a group. Thus, one cannot overemphasize the importance of the principles of autonomy and self-determination embodied in the African American church movement because they alone enabled African Americans to gain a significant measure of freedom from the control and domination of whites.

FOUR TYPES OF
AFRICAN AMERICAN CHURCHES

Regardless of denominational differences, African American churches can be classified in four major types based on the style of their ministry: pastoral, prophetic, political, and nationalist. It is important to note, however, that these styles are not mutually exclusive. That is to say, any particular church may exhibit the features of each style, although most likely one particular style will predominate at any given time.

The Pastoral Type

The pastoral type of ministry is the oldest, having emerged during slavery, many generations prior to the rise of the independent churches. Its function has been to proclaim the grace of God to all, regardless of circumstance, and, especially following emancipation, to assume a positive view of the nation's fundamental goodness. While condemning all forms of racism, these churches have tended to believe that the vast majority of white Americans do not approve of racism. In other words, they have tended to believe that racism is not a systemic problem but, rather, is due to the prejudicial attitudes of a few. Further, these churches have always abhorred societal conflict, which they view as the precursor of bitterness, hatred, and violence. Optimistic in outlook, they have consistently challenged blacks to be more self-respecting, industrious, honest, thrifty, self-reliant, morally virtuous, and hopeful that a better day will surely dawn because of God's providence. Accordingly, they have concentrated their energy primarily on saving souls and nurturing their people in the survival skills of patience, hope, and goodwill toward their oppressors.

The theological and moral substance of the African American churches was formed in the concealed churches of the slaves. Although the many and varied secret gatherings that comprised this concealed institution often served to aid and abet the efforts of slaves to escape, their primary purpose was to celebrate the goodness of God and to encourage one another through supportive communities in which the principal activities were praying, preaching, singing, and testifying. Clearly, these meetings concentrated on serving the intra-associational needs of the members, which, in turn, strengthened their moral and spiritual capacities. In fact, the goal of these meetings was to help the people nurture moral virtues and spiritual devotion, both of which were thought to be necessary for the preservation of their humanity. This objective has continued to characterize the ethos of many contemporary African American churches, especially those whose members are daily threatened by the devastating constraints of poverty and racism. Those whose lives are constantly being diminished need the moral support derived from close relationships with others who have had similar experiences. The character of this ministry is largely communal in nature; the people help and sustain one another as they all seek to develop the capacity to face personal suffering constructively. These churches may rightly be called "spiritual support groups." Acts of praying, singing, and testifying manifest signs of the transcendent spirit that helps them overcome adversity. This community attributes its life to the grace of God and, hence, it seemingly never ceases "praising God."

The political expression of this pastoral type of African American ministry has often been labeled accommodationist, that is, submissive to the design of racism. An alternative view is that the resiliency of the human spirit is such that African Americans constantly devised creative and subtle ways of resisting their oppressors, especially the latter's definition of them as genetically inferior to whites. As a consequence, African Americans often assumed a posture of accommodation that was more form than substance. As a defense mechanism, African Americans have tended to conceal their beliefs and feelings from whites. This tendency has often resulted in deceptive activity, such as speech and actions calculated to please their overseers while hiding their true feelings. In that way, blacks resisted the demand to participate in their own dehumanization. Hence, what might seem on the surface to be accommodationism in fact enabled many to submit partially to the racist practices while concealing alternative viewpoints.

The Prophetic Type

Prophetic ministry is characterized by its courage in proclaiming the justice of God by publicly condemning all forms of racial injustice.

Accordingly, these churches boldly criticize the white churches for straying from what they consider to be the authentic biblical understanding of humanity. Similarly, they charge that by its support of racist practices the nation has betrayed the values of its founders, as immortalized in the Declaration of Independence and the Constitution.

Although both the pastoral and prophetic traditions appeal to common sources of legitimation, that is, Scripture, tradition, and experience, those in the prophetic tradition believe that redemptive ends necessitate direct conflict with the perpetrators of injustice. As we have seen, the dominant ethos of the pastoral churches is celebrative worship expressed in dynamic preaching, vibrant song, and rhythmic music. In contrast, the dominant ethos of the prophetic churches is that of social ministry, often labeled "protest activity," in the service of enhancing social justice. Like the pastoral type, however, it also relies heavily on a liturgical pattern of powerful preaching coupled with exuberant music and song.

This prophetic church ministry originated with the birth of the independent African American church movement in the last decade of the eighteenth century. The civil rights struggles of the post-emancipation period are deeply rooted in the abolitionist tradition that was born in the Negro convention movement of the 1830s (an annual convention of all African American leaders concerned with evaluating the state of the race). Amid much debate and controversy over strategies and tactics, this protest tradition has been at the heart of these prophetic churches. In fact, the relationship between the churches and civil rights activities has been so close that many scholars have wrongly concluded that the black church is little more than a political organization promoting racial justice. Frederick Douglass, W.E.B. Du Bois, Martin Luther King, Jr., and Jesse Jackson represent some of the greatest leaders to emerge from the prophetic type of ministry. Various abolitionist societies as well as the National Association for the Advancement of Colored People, the Southern Christian Leadership Conference, and numerous other groups were virtually spawned and nurtured by these prophetic churches.

The mutual interdependence and cooperation of the pastoral and prophetic churches were graphically demonstrated in the mass rallies of the civil rights movement under the leadership of Martin Luther King, Jr. On those occasions the atmosphere was continuously charged with the testimonies and prayers of the faithful, the moving beauty of the spirituals, the guttural exuberance of the gospel music, and the persuasive oratory of dynamic preaching. These provided the means by which blacks were woven together into a harmonious whole imbued with a common mission, which they zealously affirmed. Thus folk artists and professional musicians, civil rights leaders and welfare recipients, movie stars and rural farmers, poor and middle-class people sang, prayed, joined hands, and marched together in their quest for a racially just social order. And many whites joined with blacks in that movement and thereby expressed their belief in and commitment to the struggle for a common humanity.

The Political Type

During the brief period of the Reconstruction, following the Civil War, African American churches were fully engaged in electoral politics through voter education and registration. Many clergy and laypersons were encouraged to run for political office. During the periods of exclusion from political participation, both before and after Reconstruction, the pastoral and prophetic black churches served as training grounds for the day when African Americans would assume their rightful place in electoral office.

Due to their institutional primacy in the community, African American churches have provided meeting places for virtually every forum concerning the welfare of the black community. Further, the democratic style of congregational governance in the vast majority of African American churches, together with the prudential style of pastoral leadership on matters concerning the well-being of the community, readied many African Americans for the practice of democratic politics in the nation's governments. Similarly, the long protest struggles of the churches for civil rights also prepared the way for black participation in electoral politics. Clearly, both the pastoral and prophetic styles of ministry have been and continue to be strongly supportive of black participation in elective office.

The Nationalist Type

The nationalist type of ministry stands apart from the mainstream of the African American Christian tradition. Unlike that mainstream tradition, which believes that racial justice can be realized in the nation through various kinds of reforms, the nationalists claim that America is incurably racist; hence, they believe that every attempt to rid the nation of racism is destined to failure. This implies that African Americans cannot rely on white allies in their quest for racial justice. Rather, they must rely on themselves alone. Hence, a major focus of the nationalist type of ministry is to inculcate within the people a strong sense of racial identity and self-respect that were lost as a result of slavery and its aftermath. The nationalist churches also believe that the necessary enlightenment of the race can only occur through racial separation and the development of racial pride and self-determination through a renewed appreciation for African values.

Elements of this nationalist tradition can be found in virtually every period of African American history but most clearly in the vision of such historical figures as Martin Delaney, Bishop Henry McNeal Turner, Alexander Crummell, Edward Wilmot Blyden, and Marcus Moziah Garvey, all of whom encouraged African Americans to return to Africa and aid the process of decolonization there. All of these figures claimed that the liberation of Africa was a necessary condition for the liberation of African Americans, and each advocated the importance of African American agency in Africa's liberation from colonialism. The African missionary enterprises of the independent African American churches also reflected this nationalist orientation.

Many of the marks of this nationalist type of ministry are evident in the nascent black theology movement. This movement began with the 1969 publication of James H. Cone's book *Black Theology and Black Power,* a Christian defense of the political ideology of black power and a prophetic demand that liberation from racial injustice be the goal of every authentic theology. The black theology movement initially aimed its prophetic challenge at the so-called conservative African American churches, the racist practices of the white churches, and the theological curricula of white seminaries. Its impact on the study of religion in America and abroad has been considerable, as can be seen by the number of African American religious studies courses presently offered in universities and seminaries as compared with virtually none twenty years ago.

In addition, the black theology movement has had a decisive impact on the practical life of the African churches in South Africa, where their opposition to constitutional racism (apartheid) desperately needed theological categories that would enable them to rebut the theological justification of apartheid provided by the Dutch Reformed Church. Accordingly, black theology enabled many in South Africa to construct a contextual theology with which to proclaim a prophetic message of liberation and to act courageously for its realization.

Thus, the nationalist type of ministry differs from the pastoral, prophetic, and political types by the primary importance it gives to racial identity, self-respect, African heritage, and the principle of self-determination. In short, this type maximizes the positive values implied by the distinctiveness of African heritage. Its adherents adamantly deny all accusations of advocating "reverse racism." Their principal aim has always been that of liberating the race from every vestige of racial inferiority that was bequeathed to them by white racism.

CONCLUSION

Since the social situation of African Americans has always been circumscribed by white racism, their churches have always struggled to maintain and enhance the humanity of the race by providing the necessary space for all sorts of activities in the social, economic, political, and religious spheres of life. That is to say, the internal life of the churches provided African Americans the opportunity for association and expression denied them by the white world.

More specifically, the black churches have struggled to create a world of harmony wherein the virtues of justice and respect permeate communal life. In their religious life African Americans have sought to justify the principles of freedom, liberty, and equality as harmonious with God's will. Most importantly, they have placed their trust primarily in the biblical God, whom they believed to be free from racism. Further, they have tended to evaluate all political activity in terms of its commensurability with God's nonracist will.

In short, the religion of the African American churches has always viewed freedom as both a religious and a political goal. For the most part, black churches have viewed their quest for black liberation as a contribution to the liberation of all. Although the black churches were implicated occasionally in slave revolts, in general they were committed to nonviolent resistance long before the term was popularized by Martin Luther King, Jr.

Clearly, the African American churches have enriched the nation's public realm by keeping alive issues of social justice related to public responsibility and the rights of citizenship by exposing all forms of racial hypocrisy and injustice. In this respect, they have been the conscience of the nation.

The black churches emerged on the stage of history as a response to the public issue of racism that had been firmly established both politically and religiously at the beginning of the Republic. Consequently, their life and mission have aimed at effecting alternative ways of living in a racially just world. The independent African American church movement of the late eighteenth and early nineteenth centuries represents the religious institutionalization of that aim.

The abolition of legalized racism (i.e., racial segregation and discrimination) in the 1960s marked the successful culmination of the civil rights movement, which was the political arm of the African American churches. Civil rights legislation bestowed upon African Americans their long-awaited citizenship rights. Unfortunately, a residue of cultural and psychological racism continues to function in the decision-making processes of most of the nation's institutions. In recent years, however, African American electoral politics has received strong support from the churches because its political agenda gives high priority to the role of government in protecting civil rights and effecting economic justice through full-employment policies and the abolition of poverty both at home and abroad.

POSTSCRIPT ON
NON-CHRISTIAN RELIGIONS

African American religion is no longer exclusively Christian. A number of non-Christian groups have emerged in many urban areas during this century. Of these Islam represents the largest group, with a membership estimated at one million. Various forms of Islam constitute viable alternatives to African American Christianity, especially among African American males, many of whom are readily attracted to Islam's teaching and discipline.

During the Great Depression two extraordinary developments occurred in African American religion under the leadership of two charismatic personalities, namely, the Father Divine Peace Mission Movement and Bishop Grace's (widely known as "Daddy Grace") United House of Prayer for All People. Both leaders claimed that they were divine.

In addition, various other religious groups were founded at about the same time, the most notable being Prophet Cherry's "Black Jews" (who claimed that they were the only authentic Jews) and Elijah Muhammad's "Black Muslims." All of these groups were founded by self-educated charismatic personalities who had recently migrated to the North from the southern states.

More recently various immigrants from Africa and the Caribbean have transplanted many of their traditional religions to American soil. Many of these have attracted African American members.

STUDY QUESTIONS

1. What is the "middle passage"? Why do you think that the middle passage is important for understanding the religious world of African Americans?
2. Why did few Africans become Christians during the first century of American slavery? If African slaves believed that religion is synonymous with lifestyle, what was the African slave's initial introduction to the Christianity of the white person?
3. How did African slaves maintain their religious and moral understandings of the world within the context of a new religious environment? In the contemporary African American community, do you still see "African religion" in the context of Christianity?
4. How did the "concealed church" of African American slaves differ from the white churches of their owners? What biblical message was most preached to the slaves in the white church? What was the religious message of the "concealed church"? Why might we describe this message as subversive?
5. What are the religious messages of spirituals? What symbols from traditional Judaism and Christianity are used to address the African slave's situation? What historical observations can we make about slavery by reading and listening to spirituals? Why do issues of suffering and freedom play such crucial roles in these songs?
6. Why might African American religion be considered a religion of hope? How has this theme of hope and religion manifested itself not only in the religion of African American slaves but also in this century's civil rights movement?
7. How did the independent African American church movement develop historically? What were the theological and moral underpinnings of its establishment? Name several of the founders of the independent movement. What were their specific contributions to the African American religious tradition?
8. Why has the African American church become such a critical institution in the lives of African Americans? What role has it played, and does it continue to play, in the life of the African American social community, in education, and in the business world? What contributions has the African American church made to white America, its government and its churches?

ESSAY TOPICS

Spirituals: Their History and Theology
African Religions and Their Influence on American Christianity

The African American Preacher: A New Moses
The Slave and Christianity: Paternalism or Liberation?
The Political Dimensions of African American Religion

WORD EXPLORATION

The following words play significant roles in any discussion of the religious
world of African Americans and are worth careful reflection and
discussion.

Sacred	Concealed Church	African Spirituality
Secularization	Slavery	Spirituals
Acculturation	Middle Passage	Independent African American Church

FOR FURTHER READING

Cone, James H. *Black Theology and Black Power*. New York: Seabury, 1969.
Lincoln, C. Eric, and Lawrence H. Mamiya. *The Black Church in the African American Experience*. Durham, N.C.: Duke University Press, 1990.
Paris, Peter J. *The Social Teaching of the Black Churches*. Philadelphia: Fortress Press, 1985.
———. *Black Religious Leaders: Conflict in Unity*. Louisville, Ky.: Westminster/ John Knox Press, 1991.
Raboteau, Albert J. *Slave Religion: The "Invisible Institution" in the Antebellum South*. Oxford: Oxford University Press, 1978.
Wilmore, Gayraud S. *Black Religion and Black Radicalism*. Maryknoll, N.Y.: Orbis, 1983.

4

ANDREW M. GREELEY

The Catholics in the World and in America

Catholics—they rarely use the label "Roman Catholics" of themselves and find it ever so slightly offensive—often seem to their fellow Americans to be just a little odd. They worship saints and statues; they have pictures of saints in the stained-glass windows of their often garish churches; they wear medals and carry rosaries that are superstitious charms; they obey a foreigner in Rome; they don't think for themselves but do what their bishops and priests tell them to; they're clannish; they're morally lax, given to drinking, gambling, and dancing; their politicians tend to be corrupt; and they think theirs is the only true church. There is so much pagan superstition mixed into their beliefs and practices that sometimes they seem barely Christian.

Despite all these things, individual Catholics are frequently very nice people; it's hard to understand why they remain Catholic, especially now when there is so much confusion and uncertainty in their church. You'd think they would take the opportunity to escape into a decent Christian religion.

Catholics, of course, have a different explanation of what their religion is about and a different interpretation of their practices.

WHO THE CATHOLICS ARE

Catholicism is a very old religion. It can be recognized in its present shape at least as far back as fifteen hundred years. It has penetrated, one way or another, most of the world. It has adjusted to many different cultures and appears in many different forms. It has learned much about the ways of human nature and society and hence claims a certain kind of perennial wisdom. It defines it boundaries as both extensive and permeable, including among its members anyone who has not formally left. It has at various times in its history been the only patron of arts and literature and is responsible for preserving drama, music, sculpture, painting, and literature through the troubled centuries after the end of the Roman Empire.

Yet in this country Catholicism is seen as a religion of immigrants, often poor and illiterate immigrants—more than two out of five Catholics are either immigrants or the children of immigrants. Although Catholics were among the first to explore the land that is now the United States—as such names as St. Augustine, St. Petersburg, San Antonio, San Diego, San Francisco, and Los Angeles (the Pueblo of Our Lady, Queen of the Angels) reveal—most Catholic families in the United States are descendants of immigrants who came in the last great European immigration at the turn of the present century, and half of all new immigrants today are Catholics.

Catholicism, then, is a very old, complex, and often sophisticated religious tradition in the world, but a rather new and often, it seems, rather simple religious manifestation in this country, one whose chief goal seems to be to protect the religious faith of immigrants while they are becoming successful in American society. It is sometimes hard for Americans who are familiar with the tolerant and mature Catholicism of, say, Italy or France, to comprehend how Catholicism in this country is the same religion.

About a quarter of the American population is Catholic; of this number, half attend church regularly (at least several times a month) and another quarter attend at least once a month. Fifteen percent of those who are raised Catholics leave the Church—about half of these for another religion (usually at the time of marriage) and the other half for no religion at all.[1] This loss has been canceled out by those who convert to Catholicism and by immigration. Indeed, the proportion of the country that is Catholic may be increasing slightly because of immigration.

Five major ethnic groups account for 80 percent of the Catholic population: Irish, German, Italian, Polish, and Hispanic (which includes Mexican, Puerto Rican, and Cuban, each with its own Catholic tradition).[2]

Catholics are concentrated in the big cities and suburbs of the northeast and north central regions of the country, most notably Boston, New York, Newark, Philadelphia, Baltimore, Pittsburgh, Cleveland, Cincinnati, Detroit, Chicago, Milwaukee, St. Louis, and Minneapolis/St. Paul. There is also a substantial Catholic population, much of it Hispanic, around the southern and western rim of the country—Miami, New Orleans, San Antonio, Santa Fe, Albuquerque, San Diego, Los Angeles, and San Francisco.

When Catholic immigrants first came to America, many people thought that they would never adjust to American life and become successful Americans unless they abandoned their religion and their ethnic customs. The Irish were thought to be brutal and superstitious drunks, the Italians (according to the National Immigration Commission) to be "innately criminal," and the Poles to be inherently ignorant and incapable of education. This notion of Catholic inferiority persisted for a long time and still appears occasionally in scholarly and popular articles and newspaper columns.

Despite these beliefs, shared by many of the "best minds" in America, Catholic immigrants and their descendants have been remarkably successful. The average education and income of Catholics are higher than those of Baptists and Methodists, about the same as those of Lutherans, and somewhat less than those of Episcopalians and Presbyterians. Irish Catholics are the most affluent and best-educated gentile ethnic group in America, and Italians are not far behind.

As long ago as the first decade of this century the proportion of Irish Americans who attended college was above the national average. Polish and Italian Americans caught up in the years immediately after World War II and are now also slightly above the national average. Only Jews and Episcopalians are more likely than Catholics to attend college today.

Catholics are also at the national average of 2 percent in the proportion who might be considered intellectuals: artists, musicians, writers, and scholars. Moreover, the Catholic intelligentsia attends church services not only more often than do other intellectuals but even more often than do Catholics who are not in the 2 percent that could be classed as intellectuals.

These paradoxes—a church for immigrants who are no longer immigrants, a church for the poor who are no longer poor, a church for the uneducated who are now well educated, a worldwide and complex church that has been simplified to adjust to a new society—explain not only the tensions inside Catholicism today, but also why it is often difficult for non-Catholics to understand Catholicism.

Who is Catholic anyway—the poor Mexican celebrating the Festival of Our Lady of Guadalupe or the Irish professor who makes fun of the pope but goes to mass every day? The answer is that both are Catholic, and between them there are a lot of other types of Catholics. A good rule of thumb for an outsider is that if you think you have finally figured Catholics out, you've almost certainly got it wrong.

Are younger Catholics drifting away from the Church, especially given its current internal chaos and confusion, evidenced by the obvious tendency of Catholics to obey Catholic rules selectively? It does not seem that they are. Religious affiliation and devotion for all Americans correlates with age—the rates go down in the middle and late teens, bottom out in the middle twenties, and then slowly climb to a plateau like that of the parental generation in the early forties. The curve of the relationship between age and church attendance (and prayer) is the same for Catholics as it is for others. There was a slight increase during the 1970s in the proportion of Americans with no religious identification; but that increase, a result of people marrying later or never marrying, leveled off by 1980, and Catholics were no more affected by it than was anyone else.

American Catholics indeed dissent from certain Catholic doctrines; in 1963 half accepted the Church's teaching on birth control. By 1974 that proportion had fallen to about one-tenth—for clergy as well as laity—and has not increased since then. However, this dissent, though it may have affected frequency of church attendance and financial contributions (half of what they were in 1960, adjusted for inflation), has not lessened Catholic affiliation.

In summary, American Catholics are successful urban immigrants who are loyal to their church despite some disagreement with its leaders. They have adjusted to the changes in the Catholic Church since the Second Vatican Council in 1962 with remarkable ease.

ORGANIZATIONAL CHART

According to canon (or church) law the basic unit of the Catholic Church is the diocese. Above it stands the pope and below it the parish and the people. The bishop is the key person in the Church, speaking to the local church for the universal and to the universal Church for the local. This canonical definition came into being when there was only one parish in each city, the cathedral was the parish church, and the bishop was the parish priest. In fact, from the empirical point of view of most Catholics the parish and the parish priest *are* the Church. If they like their parish priest and think he's doing a good job (especially in liturgy—that is, worship—and preaching), most Catholics are content with their church.

In many dioceses, parishes are organized into deaneries or vicariates, but the deans and vicars have little real power in comparison with the bishop. Moreover dioceses are organized into archdioceses, but the only power an archbishop has over his "suffragans" (bishops) is that he presides at their meetings. Since the Second Vatican Council, in most countries there is a national conference of bishops that holds meetings, passes laws, maintains a national bureaucracy, and tries to collect voluntary taxes from the various dioceses. But the National Conference of Catholic Bishops in the United States, for example, has no authority over what a local bishop does and can neither supervise him nor enforce its rules on him.

In most countries there is also a papal nuncio or an apostolic delegate (the former if the country has formal diplomatic relations with the Vatican, as the United States now does) who is the pope's representative and supervises in his name the Church in that country.

The papal representative, the national conference, and the individual bishops report to Rome (called *ad limina*, the "doorway" of Peter) every five years. This normally means they report to the Roman Curia, which might be thought of as both the pope's cabinet and his personal staff. There has been some debate in recent years about the relationship between the bishops and the Roman Curia. The Roman Curia's version in practice is that the bishop is a bureaucrat in their service. But others, including many bishops, hold that the pope, as Bishop of Rome, governs the whole Church together with his brother bishops (though he is not dependent upon them) and that the Roman Curia ought to work for the bishops and be responsible to them.

A Synod of Bishops was established by the Second Vatican Council to meet every three years with the pope and advise him about problems within the Church. Some bishops hoped that this Synod eventually would become the highest governing body of the Church and that the Roman Curia would be subordinate to it. In fact, however, the Synod is itself now firmly under Roman Curial control and many bishops have lost interest in it.

It must be said candidly that many American bishops, even some of the more conservative ones, privately resent the occasional and, as they see it, arbitrary interference of the Roman Curia in their work, though they would never dare to say so in public.

In addition to the diocesan structure of the Catholic Church, there are many[3] communities of men and women religious, some of whom are relatively independent of local bishops and do the specialized work of the Church, such as education, medical care, and missionizing. The most famous orders are the Jesuits, the Benedictines, the Dominicans, the Franciscans, and the Carmelites;[4] the last three include both male and female groups—indeed, many of each. They are usually governed by a "general" (now often called "president"), who may live in Rome, and by the Congregation of Religious, a part of the Roman Curia.

HOW THE CHURCH ACTUALLY WORKS

This elaborate and well-defined structure may create an initial impression of a tightly organized monolith in which orders are passed down from the pope to the local parish by a centralized power elite that has control over everything that happens in Catholicism. Nothing, in fact, could be further from the truth. Partially because of principle[5] and partially because of inefficiency, the Church leaves enormous power in the hands of the local bishop and the parish priest. Occasionally it might elect to intervene directly in the affairs of a diocese or a religious order, especially in the case of a financial scandal, though usually only after the harm has been done. Generally, however, the parish priest can do pretty much whatever he wants, if he doesn't mind an occasional complaint letter sent to Rome or an occasional phone call of reprimand from the local chancery office (the bishop's staff and cabinet).

Nothing better illustrates the radical decentralization and pluralism of the Catholic Church than its financial procedures. There is no consolidated budget for the whole Church, for the various national conferences, or even for the individual dioceses.[6] Rome does not really know what the Jesuits, for example, are doing with their money, or what the American Church is doing with its money. No one beyond the local diocese oversees its financial workings. A bishop has almost no control of how the religious orders and their institutions spend their money. Each Catholic high school and college, for example, has its own budget. Moreover, the bishops' control of the finances of local parishes is dependent upon the pastor's willingness to submit accurate reports and not keep special savings-and-loan accounts that he does not wish to report lest the chancery tax him for it.

One might say that this system maximizes local freedom and autonomy. One might also say that it is chaotic and invites corruption. One might also say that, given the flawed nature of the human condition, it works on the whole not too badly. One cannot say, however, that this is the way a highly centralized power structure works.[7]

Catholicism, therefore, is a mysterious combination of centralized control and local freedom, a system which has worked fairly well for centuries and does not seem likely to change in the near future.[8] This governance style can be illustrated by the issue of young women acting as acolytes (those who light the candles) at the Eucharist (worship service). The Vatican forbids this practice, not as a matter of Catholic doctrine, but as a matter of disciplinary practice, probably because it fears that such young women might think they have a chance to be priests someday. In the United States, however, women who may be indifferent to the possible ordination of women are often infuriated by what they take to be intolerable discrimination against their daughters. (The daughters don't particularly like it either, to put it mildly.) So the rule is evaded or ignored in many, probably most, American Catholic parishes. Some bishops, but by no means all, have written letters to their priests asking that the rule be kept. Such instructions are usually disregarded; most priests would much rather face an occasional complaint from a chancery bureaucrat than the wrath of their women parishioners.

A working compromise has emerged: there are no women acolytes (and perhaps no women distributing Holy Communion when there are enough priests available) at those times when a bishop visits the parish. That way the bishop is not personally embarrassed by being forced to witness what he knows is going on anyway, and no one can complain to the Vatican that he tolerated by his presence that which is forbidden.

Whether or not one approves of such a flexible style of governance, in which theoretical rules are sometimes interpreted out of existence to respond to local circumstances, this is the way the Catholic Church normally operates in the real (as opposed to the "organizational chart") world. For many non-Catholics this description—which you will not find in any official Catholic textbook—might come as a shock. They have always heard the "organizational chart" explanation and are astonished to hear that in reality the Catholic Church is not the massive, centralized monolith that they thought it was. They are also amazed that practices in one Catholic parish (in dealing with cases of remarriage after divorce, for example) may differ dramatically from the practices of the neighboring parish, and that Catholics now "shop" among parishes to find a parochial style and solutions that are responsive to what they think are their needs.

In fact, however, it has always been that way. What is different today is that the variety and the freedom of the local Catholic communities is more public, to the joy of "liberal" Catholics and the dismay of "conservative" Catholics. It is precisely this astonishing grassroots variety and flexibility that has enabled American Catholics to remain Catholic on their own terms during the troubling last thirty years of Catholic history. In this decision to be Catholic, but on their own terms, American Catholics (and those in the British Isles, too, for that matter) have merely caught up with how the Catholics of continental Europe have been living for years, if not for centuries. The argument here is not that this is the way they ought to live, but that this is the way they do live, for the most part with serene consciences.

A DEMOCRATIC CHURCH?

It is often said, especially by bishops who feel that they have to say it, that the Catholic Church is not a democracy. This statement is ambiguous. It describes the current organizational chart of Catholicism pretty well, though as we have seen it is less accurate in its description of how Catholicism works in practice. As a historical generalization, however, it is utterly false.

For much of the first thousand years of Catholic history bishops, including the Bishop of Rome, were elected by the vote of their clergy and people. Several popes who are also saints said that it was a grave sin for bishops to be selected any other way. Pope Leo III, for example, wrote (in elegant Latin), "He who presides over all should be chosen by all."[9] The cardinals, who were then the parish priests of Rome, would gather in St. Peter's Cathedral to nominate a new pope. They would then bring him out on the balcony for approval by the people. If the crowd cheered, he was crowned. If they booed, the cardinals would go back and try again.

Most of the great medieval orders still elect their own leaders, either for life, as in the case of the Benedictine abbot, or for limited terms (three years for a Dominican provincial). Moreover, no major statement from a pope or a council was issued without words such as "with the assent of the whole Christian people." It was even argued that such decisions were not valid without the assent of the people.

Thus the governmental structure of the Catholic Church was once far more democratic than it is today, indeed almost riotously democratic. There is no theological reason why it could not become that again. Indeed, a democratization of Catholic Church structure would return the Church to more traditional and more orthodox practice.[10]

CARDINALS AND MONSIGNORS

A word should be said about two common honorary offices in the Church: the monsignor and the cardinal.

In the United States, a monsignor is usually a priest who for one reason or another is awarded with an honorary office as a member of a papal household.[11] The office carries no special power but it does provide strikingly colorful robes. It is awarded much less frequently than it used to be.

A cardinal is technically the pastor of one of the parish churches of Rome (though in fact a vicar almost always carries out the work for him) and, in a remnant of ancient practice, is designated as one of the papal electors until he reaches his eightieth birthday. In current Church law there can be only 120 cardinals under eighty years of age.

Beyond his unimportant role as a papal elector, the cardinal theoretically has no powers besides those given to him as a bishop, Curial official, or (in a few cases) priest.[12] However, the prestige of the office, its long history, its striking robes, and the pope's frequent use of cardinals as close advisers make it potentially a very powerful position indeed.

THE CATHOLIC STORY

The crucial question with which this essay began, however, remains: Why have this large international institution in the first place? Why have popes and cardinals and monsignors and Jesuits and Dominicans and Franciscans? Why is Catholicism so different from other Christian denominations, which don't seem to need all this fancy stuff? What does it all have to do with God and human relationships to God? Wouldn't Jesus be horrified?

The answer to that question goes beyond organizational structure and theological differences to the root of religion itself. Catholicism pictures the relationship of God to the world and of humans to God differently than other forms of Christianity. Its picture is not completely different, but sufficiently so to produce a distinct approach to religious behavior.

Religion is poetry before it becomes prose. It is experience, image, story, ritual, and community before it becomes doctrine, code, and cult. Because we are rational creatures, we must reflect on our religious poetry and translate it into prose. Poetry is open to many different interpretations, so it is necessary to have some kind of community that can examine new interpretations critically to make sure they do not depart from the tradition of the story. Nonetheless, religion originates in and takes its power from its poetry, experiences, images, stories, rituals, and communities. If one wants to know why one religion is ultimately different from another religion, one must examine the different poetries of these religions. The Catholic "story" of God and humankind is somewhat different from that of other denominations. One might not like the conclusions that come from this different story and, when one hears the story itself, one might not find it particularly appealing. However, the point here is that if one wishes to understand Catholics, one ought to know the story; and if one wants to be friends with Catholics, one ought to listen to the story, not necessarily with approval, but at least with sympathetic understanding.[13]

In brief, the Catholic story (which explains such things as votive candles, rosaries, medals, saints, a large international organization, and a papacy) is that the world tells us what God is like and that we respond to the God who is revealed to the world, not merely as individuals, but as members of communities.

THE CATHOLIC EXPERIENCE

Unlike some other Christian religious denominations, Catholicism experiences the world as "grace-full." It is not afraid to say that all the creatures of the earth and all the experiences of human life are hints of what God is like. The world is sacramental in the sense that it is a metaphor for God—it gives us a hint of what God is like. Catholicism is not worried about contaminating God by comparing God to creatures and human experiences.

Perhaps the reason for this approach to God is that in its very earliest years Catholicism, filled with the optimism that came from its memory of the Easter experience, appropriated everything it thought was good, true, and beautiful in paganism and turned these adoptions to Christian purpose. If a pagan city had a special goddess to protect it, when the city became Christian it was awarded to a Christian saint whose life was thought to be a story of God's love. If a symbol told a pagan story of the return of spring (like the Brigid cross in Ireland) it was turned into a Christian symbol of Jesus the light of the world. If a pagan goddess was responsible for taking care of poets, she would be replaced by a Christian patron with the same duties (thus was the Irish goddess Brigid converted to St. Brigid). If another symbol told the story of the divinity's protection of fertility (as did the so-called Irish cross with its union of male and female symbols), then it was converted into a symbol of God's life-giving love. If washing in water was a rite of initiation into pagan cults, so baptism would come to be a rite of death and rebirth for new Christians.[14]

The argument here is not that one should accept this version of the relationship between God and world, but rather that one should understand how Catholicism tends to experience that relationship. Obviously it has its weaknesses, most notably a tendency to superstition and a mixture of Christianity and paganism that is called folk religion. But the alternatives, Catholics would argue, is a much less "grace-full" and hence a far bleaker world, a "God-forsaken world" instead of a "God-full" world.

CATHOLIC IMAGERY

Because the Catholic experience is of a world filled with God, Catholic imagery tends to be sacramental. "Grace is everywhere," as the novelist Georges Bernanos writes at the end of his classic *The Diary of a Country Priest*. The realities and experiences of human life are not exactly what God is, but they are not totally different either. God lurks everywhere, revealing goodness and love. Catholic imagery says that God is like fire and water, birth, eating and drinking, the moon, the sun and the stars, the human body, and sexual love. Such notions may seem dangerous to others because of the risk of idolatry, but to Catholics they are wonderful hints of what life means.

The Church says that some events are Sacraments with a capital "S" because they are such powerful hints of what God is like. Thus the Eucharist, a common meal eaten with friends, does not make all family meals holy. Rather it is holy and Jesus comes to us in a special way in this reenactment of his last meal with his followers because all family meals are potentially graceful and potential hints that our relationship with God is familial.

The fact that the Church has declared marriage a Sacrament does not make human sexual passion holy. Rather it is precisely because human sexual love between permanently committed partners is a hint of God's passion for us and hence enormously holy that it becomes a Sacrament.[15]

Everything is holy. Some things become especially holy because Jesus has confirmed their holiness and made them rich and deep sources of grace.[16] Hence birth (Baptism), life cycle (Confirmation, Ordination, Sacrament of the Sick), and reconciliation (Confession, or the Sacrament of Reconciliation, as it is now called) complete the list of Catholicism's seven Sacraments. But in the Catholic imagination they can become specially holy because everything is holy.

The most distinctive of Catholic symbols is that of Mary the Mother of Jesus, a hint of the mother-love of God. It tells the story of a God who loves us with the power of a father and the tenderness of a mother,[17] of a God who organizes the whole of creation and who gives life and nurturance. Catholics don't confuse God with Mary (and are astonished at the persistent argument of others that they do).[18] Rather, in Mary they see revealed the maternal love of God, and they respond to that love. Anyone who has ever been a mother or been held in the arms of a mother knows that the passionate and tender love of a mother for the child she nurses is a hint of how God loves us. Any religion that has such an image of God's love will have powerful and durable appeal to humankind. In fact, it would not be surprising if that were the most important image of the last fifteen hundred years of religious history.

Catholicism has no trouble finding hints of God in such things as devotion to the saints, statues, medals, the changing cycles of the year, art, and music. Naturally abuses of all these good and holy things is possible, but Catholicism does not reject their sacramentality merely because of the possibility of abuse.

The Catholic sacramental imagination makes the world a more lovely and reassuring place—perhaps flawed in many important ways, but not inherently evil. This imagination results in the Catholic story.

THE CATHOLIC STORY

Others may think of the world as inherently evil and of human nature as fundamentally perverse. That may be their story, and it may well more accurately describe human existence. Such a story may have a deeper sense of tragedy and a greater awareness of irony. Others may claim to stare unflinchingly at the cross of the crucified Jesus and see the only true revelation of what God is like. Catholicism claims that it too is aware of irony and tragedy in creation, but it is more aware of hope and grace. It believes deeply in new beginnings, second (and third and fourth and higher-order) chances. It knows about tragedy, but it still believes in happy endings—eventual happy endings anyway. It may seem too lighthearted a religion with all its parties and celebrations, but at least in its best moments it insists that joy and not grief, comedy and not tragedy, are the best explanations of the human condition.

Two quotations sum it up. The first is from Hilaire Belloc, an English Catholic poet of a half-century ago, in one of his "Cautionary Verses":

Wher'er the Catholic sun does shine,
There's always music and laughter and good red wine,
At least I've found it so,
Benedicamus Domino![19]

But every Catholic knows that it is not always so. Sometimes there is no laughter, the music is awful, and the wine is sour. So, from St. Teresa of Avila: "From silly devotions and sour-faced saints, libera nos, Domine!"[20]

CATHOLIC COMMUNITY

Precisely because it believes that human relations are sacramental, the poetry of Catholicism thinks that all human communities reveal God, however imperfectly. In the Catholic story, human groups do not impede our relationship with God, they enhance and support it. We relate more fully to God with the help of others than when we try to do it by ourselves. Individual prayer is necessary and wonderful, but it is far more effective when it is sustained and supported by communal prayer. Hence the Catholic community, organized however imperfectly by the Church institution, is a sacrament of God, especially in the experience of the local parish community.

This element in the Catholic story may be the most offensive to those who say that they don't need a pope, a church, a parish, or a community to relate to God. They can do it by themselves. That is clearly a very different religious story and a better one to those whose story it is. A Catholic response to this point of view (which it would think of as the most rugged of rugged individualism) is that humans don't live by themselves and don't relate to anyone else (including the most intimate lover with whom one shares life) in isolation from the rest of humankind, so it seems strange that they would prefer to deal with God in this way.

CATHOLIC RITUAL

Religious rituals re-enact the story, re-present the images, re-create the experiences, and re-new the community that is constituted by the religious tradition. Therefore Catholic rituals tend to be exuberant, at least when carried out properly. They are rituals of grace, of a present God rather than an absent one, of sacramental imagery, and of stories with hopeful and hence happy endings.

For many this exuberance is too much. They prefer sober, restrained, self-controlled, even somber rituals (Catholics might call them dour). They believe that life is much too serious a business for all the celebration (especially when the celebration is mixed with paganism as at Christmas and Easter). They are entitled to that taste if it is more in keeping with their own religious story, but they should realize that Catholics have a different religious story and rituals that are consistent with that story.

CONCLUSION

What seems so strange to many other Americans about Catholic doctrines, organization, behavior, and practices is not the result necessarily of ignorance, superstition, idolatry, or perversion, but rather of a slightly different religious story. Like all other Christians, Catholics believe in God and Jesus and the Bible. That they may approach these beliefs in a somewhat different fashion is the result of the fact that they tell the Christian story from a somewhat different perspective.

Whether it is a better or worse, richer or poorer story is for everyone to decide for themselves. In order to understand Catholics, however, you must know they have this slightly different story. And to be friends with Catholics it helps to try to hear this story as they hear it, from the inside.

NOTES

1. This rate has not changed since 1960.

2. Of the other groups, the largest are the French Canadian, either in New England or as "Cajuns" of Louisiana and Texas, and the Portuguese in New England (including immigrants from the Azores and the Cape Verde Islands). In addition to the "Roman" Catholics, those whose "rite" (customs, especially the format of the Mass) follows that of the Church of Rome, there are other "Eastern" or "Greek" or "Uniate" Catholics whose rites follow ancient customs different from those of Rome but who remain in communion with the Roman rite. In the United States the largest group are the Ukrainian Catholics, whose churches were suppressed by Stalin but restored by Gorbachev. At one time their Eucharist (Mass) was in Old Slavonic and married men were ordained as priests. Now the liturgy is in English and somewhat different in format (as well as longer) than the Roman Mass. In the United States the ordination of married men is not permitted, much to the offense of the Ukrainians. A patriarch presides over each of these rites, the pope being the patriarch of the Roman rite.

3. The joke used to be that there were three things God didn't know: what a Jesuit is thinking, how much a Dominican has learned, and how many religious orders of women there are in the Catholic Church!

4. Founded, respectively, by St. Ignatius of Loyola, St. Benedict, St. Dominic, St. Francis of Assisi, and St. Simon Stock.

5. The Catholic social principle of "subsidiarity" says that nothing should be done in any human organization at a higher level that cannot be done just as effectively at a lower level. This principle has been enshrined by name in the charter of the European Community, though it now seems to be ignored by most American Catholic social theorists, who are committed to ever-more government intervention.

6. Not consolidated in the sense that the various high schools, colleges, universities, religious orders, and hospitals (for example) are included.

7. What, it may be asked, about the vast wealth of the Vatican? In fact, the Vatican's endowment is not any larger than that of a small-sized Catholic university such as Georgetown. Despite its income from the annual Peter's Pence collection (which is reportedly diminishing each year), the Vatican has been forced to operate at an ever-increasing budget deficit. Should it sell all its "treasures," including the Vatican Museum and the Sistine Chapel? Income from such sales would not notably enhance the Vatican's endowment, and it is not clear what the worth of Michelangelo's frescoes would be, even if they could be peeled off the walls of the Sistine. As for St. Peter's Cathedral, doubtless its replacement value would be in the billions of dollars, but it is currently a "loss leader"; the income from the votive candle shrines does not even pay for the upkeep of the building. And what would a buyer do with it? Subdivide it into condominiums?

What about all the Catholic property in the big cities? Some of the empty parish "plants" (from which Catholics have moved to the suburbs) may look rich and might cost large sums of money to replace. But their resale value is minimal because no one has any use for a secondhand Catholic church. In fact, subsidies to keep the buildings from falling apart and the school open (for a heavily non-Catholic student body) mean that the "plant" has no real value and indeed is a negative asset—it costs a lot more than the income it produces.

The Catholic Church may look rich; it may even seem to be rich to some of its leaders. In fact, it is poor, poorer perhaps than it ought to be given its size and, in the United States, anyway, the relative affluence of its membership.

8. It must be remembered that the style of Catholic governing dates to an era before the Transatlantic cable and the railroad, to say nothing of television and jet aircraft. The second American bishop was never installed as auxiliary because it took five years for the papers confirming his election (lost twice) to make their way from Rome to Baltimore. John Carroll, the first American bishop, required more time to journey from his mother's home at Rock Creek (Washington, D.C., of today) to Baltimore, than it takes his successor to

journey from Washington to Rome. However, the style of the Catholic governance is still strongly effected by the former era.

9. "Qui praesidet super omnes, ab omnibus eligatur." The Latin verb *eligo*, it should be noted, is the root from which the word *elect* comes.

10. Having had an opportunity to observe and compare the two Chicago mayors named Richard Daley and two Chicago cardinals, the present writer would endorse the wisdom of democratic ways.

11. A fact which has led some priests, usually not monsignors, to say that their empurpled colleague is nothing more than a papal broom sweeper.

12. Some men who were not priests have been named cardinals in the past. It is even possible, according to some, for a layman to be named a cardinal. A laywoman? Not yet anyway!

13. Catholicism shares this story with Orthodox Christianity and to some extent with Anglicanism.

14. Catholicism in its best moments has always had the courage to adapt foreign cultures to its religious poetry. At other times, it has turned its back on such adaptation, most notably in the sixteenth and seventeenth centuries on adaptations in China, India, and Ethiopia.

15. The Church has had and continues to have its hang-ups about sexual love, as does the rest of our culture. Nonetheless, in its best moments, especially in the marriage rituals through the ages, it has always insisted on the sacramental nature of human passion and that the appealing body of the beloved discloses to us the seductive appeal of God.

16. Note that this is "pre-theological" talk, poetry before prose. Precise theological reflection on the poetry of the Sacraments can be found in any standard Catholic theological book.

17. The image of God as mother as well as father has always been part of the Catholic tradition and was expressed again recently by Pope John Paul I.

18. Catholics wish that others would listen to them when they talk about the Mother of Jesus, instead of imposing their own preconceptions on that devotion.

19. "Let us praise the Lord!"

20. "Deliver us, O Lord!"

STUDY QUESTIONS

1. List four or five characteristics that you believe best describe Catholicism. Compare with a classmate. Have you agreed or disagreed with this chapter?
2. Which major ethnic groups account for the make-up of American Catholicism? How is such diversity considered a contributing factor in what the author describes as the religious "paradox" of American Catholicism?
3. What is the organizational structure of the Catholic Church? Is the structure hierarchical? How so? What roles do persons in the organization play? Which role does the author believe is most representative of the Church? Why?
4. What disagreements have begun to take place between American Catholicism and Catholic doctrine coming from Rome about the role of women in the Church? About birth control? How, in light of such differences, can American Catholicism remain Catholic?
5. What are the roles and functions of the two honorary offices, cardinals and monsignors, in the American Catholic Church? How do these roles relate to the priestly positions in other religious traditions with which you are familiar?
6. What does "sacramental" mean in the Catholic religious tradition? How does the sacramental experience inform the ways in which Catholics relate to the world? Name the seven sacraments of the Catholic Church. What functions do they play in defining social order for Catholics?

ESSAY TOPICS

Women in the Catholic Church
The Historical Development of the Papacy
The Development of Catholicism in the United States
American Catholicism and Native Americans
American Catholicism and American Politics: John F. Kennedy, the First
　　Catholic President

WORD EXPLORATION

The following words play significant roles in any discussion of Catholics in America and are worth careful reflection and discussion.

Ritual	Pope	Rome
Madonna	Canon Law	Sacraments
Priest	Parish	Religious Orders

5

JUSTO L. GONZÁLEZ

The Religious World of Hispanic Americans

A LONG AND VARIED TRADITION

Can you name the four countries in the Western Hemisphere with the largest Spanish-speaking populations? Mexico is clearly the largest. Then come Argentina, Colombia, and . . . the United States! Yes, this country has the fourth largest Spanish-speaking population in the Western Hemisphere, and it is about to become the third. Thus, if you yourself speak Spanish, or if you have several classmates who do, you are not an exception. On the contrary, if you live in an area where you never hear Spanish, you are indeed an exception. The 1990 census recorded just over 22 million Hispanics in the United States out of a total population of 249 million. Of these, roughly 64 percent had traditional ties with Mexico, 10 percent with Puerto Rico, 5 percent with Cuba, and 21 percent with other countries.

How did this come about? Obviously, in recent years there has been a great wave of immigration. But the story is much longer than that. In fact, the first European language to be spoken in what is now the United States was not English but Spanish. As you know, the Englishman Sir Walter Raleigh tried to found a colony in Virginia in 1584, but it failed. Jamestown Colony was founded in 1607. And the Pilgrims arrived at New England in 1620. By that time, the Spanish had explored much of the continent and had even founded cities that are now part of the United States.

Naturally, the explorers came first. Juan Ponce de León landed in Florida in 1521. Between 1539 and 1543 Hernando de Soto reached the

111

Mississippi River and crossed Arkansas and part of Oklahoma. In 1540 Francisco Vásquez de Coronado led an expedition that explored much of what is now Texas, Oklahoma, and Kansas. A few years later, another expedition from Mexico reached Oregon.

Then came the settlers. After a number of failed attempts by other Spaniards, some as far north as the Carolinas, Pedro Menéndez de Avilés founded St. Augustine, Florida, in 1565. Santa Fe, now the capital of New Mexico, was founded in 1610. If you ever visit one of those cities, you will be able to see many signs of their Spanish heritage.

At first, the United States did not include any permanent Spanish settlements, only the thirteen former British colonies on the eastern seaboard. However, as the country expanded, it came to include many people whose language was Spanish. For a long time, there were tensions between the United States and Spain over Florida. In 1819, the United States finally bought Florida from Spain. At that time most Spanish-speaking people living in Florida chose to leave and settle in Cuba, but some remained.

The largest geographical expansion of the United States into Spanish-speaking territories, however, took place at the expense of Mexico. First was the independence and eventual annexation of Texas. One of the conditions on which Mexico insisted before granting independence to Texas, and to which the United States agreed, was that Texas would remain an independent republic and would not become part of the United States. In 1845, however, through a joint act of Congress, Texas was made part of the United States.

That also was the year when the famous phrase "manifest destiny" was coined, to refer to the historic task of the United States to encompass all the land "from sea to shining sea." This involved occupying Oregon, whose possession the British disputed, and all Mexican territories directly west of the original thirteen colonies. The Oregon matter was settled through diplomatic channels; the other, by force of arms. The war with Mexico did not last long. It ended in 1848, through the treaty of Guadalupe Hidalgo, which stipulated that for $15 million the United States would purchase from Mexico the present states of New Mexico, Arizona, California, Utah, Nevada, and part of Colorado. Also, by the same treaty, Mexico agreed to accept the annexation of Texas by the United States.

Even after the treaty of Guadalupe Hidalgo had moved the border to the Rio Grande, Mexicans continued their age-old tradition of moving freely north and south across the river. They had families on both sides of the border, so they would cross back and forth in order to find jobs, or simply to go visiting. Then, around 1880, as railroads established closer links with the East, the territories that the United States had acquired became part of the national economy and began requiring a larger labor force. This in turn meant that more people moved from Mexico to the United States than the other way around.

Although you may have heard much about the patrolling of the border and about immigration laws, the main factors governing Mexican and other Latin American migration have been the relative economic and political conditions on both sides of the border. When things have been good in the United States and bad in Mexico, there has been a veritable flood of immigration, no matter what the law may have said or what the border patrol may have done. When things have been good in Mexico and not so good in the United States, immigration has practically stopped.

Between 1909 and 1929, it is estimated that about one million Mexicans—roughly one-tenth of the entire population of Mexico—migrated to the United States. This was the time of the Mexican Revolution, which caused great hardship for many people. It was also a time of economic expansion in the United States. Then came the Great Depression, and Mexicans ceased coming to a country where there was no work. Furthermore, throughout the Southwest there was a widespread sentiment that "Mexicans" were taking jobs that belonged to "Americans," and as a result almost half a million "Mexicans"—many of whom were born in the United States—were deported. Later the situation changed again. Farmers in the United States needed laborers, and arrangements were made so that farm workers could come from Mexico. Although in theory they were allowed to come to the United States only temporarily, many stayed. Eventually this program was legally discontinued. Whenever there was a shortage of farm laborers, however, other similar means—some legal and some not—have been found to provide farmers with the laborers they required by bringing them across the border. More recently, when vast reserves of oil were discovered in Mexico and the price of oil was high, immigration into the United States slowed to a trickle, only to accelerate again when the price of oil dropped and the Mexican economy came to the verge of collapse.

Similar factors have also governed immigration from other Spanish-speaking places. Puerto Rico became an American territory in 1898, and its inhabitants became American citizens in 1917. Therefore, they can travel freely between Puerto Rico and the mainland without passports or other documents. After World War II Puerto Ricans began migrating to the mainland in vast numbers. As in the case of Mexico, those numbers have depended mostly on the economy of the island.

The case of Cuba is similar. In the second half of the nineteenth century, when Cuba was still a Spanish colony, many Cubans went into exile in Tampa and Key West, and their descendants still live there. Since Cuba's independence in 1898, migration to the United States—particularly to Florida—has depended on the political and economic conditions in Cuba. Large numbers of Cubans fled to southern Florida after the revolution of 1959, led by Fidel Castro.

More recently, as war, unrest, and economic collapse have shaken countries in Central America and elsewhere, immigrants from those countries have come to the United States in large numbers. In the late 1970s and early 1980s, for instance, economic conditions in the Dominican Republic became desperate and many Dominicans settled in New York and neighboring areas. By the mid-1980s, civil war and human rights violations in El Salvador and Guatemala uprooted hundreds of thousands of people, and more than half a million settled in southern California.

In short, Hispanics in this country are both recent immigrants and descendants of people who have been here for centuries. The ancestors of some Hispanics were here even before the country itself existed. In many cases, they did not come into the country; rather, the country engulfed them. Although many are recent immigrants, almost three out of four Hispanics are native citizens of the United States. At the same time, they are preserving their language and cultural identity. Thus, three out of four Hispanics, even those whose families have been here for centuries, still speak Spanish, although most also speak English.

THE RELIGION OF THE
EARLY SETTLERS

Obviously, the Spanish language is no more native to this land than is English. Both languages are here because of a long history that involves immigrants coming here from Europe and, in the case of Hispanics, also from other Spanish-speaking countries in the Western Hemisphere. Elsewhere in this book you have studied how this affected the original Americans, who lived here long before Columbus; you have also studied how the English language and the religious traditions of Britain were brought here. Now, in order to understand the traditions and religious life of Hispanics, we must say a word about the Spanish who first came to these lands.

These people came from Spain to the Western Hemisphere—to what is now both Latin America and the United States—for a number of reasons.

Many were following dreams and legends: Ponce de León came to Florida in quest of the "fountain of youth," and the early explorers of the Southwest were looking for the Seven Cities of Cibola. Some hoped to get rich through mining or trade; others were simply curious. But in almost every case, even among those who were dreaming of youth, gold, and power, there was also a strong religious motivation. That is why so many of the cities they founded bear names of saints: San Antonio, San Agustín, San Francisco, Santa Mónica, Santa Paula, San Juan, and so on. (You may wish to look in the index to an atlas of the United States to see how many names of cities and places begin with "San" or "Santa.")

Spain was a deeply religious country. Isabella and Ferdinand, who ruled there at the time of Columbus, were given the title of "Los Reyes Católicos"—the Catholic Sovereigns. Their Catholicism, however, was of a very special kind. In 711 Spain had been invaded and conquered by the Moors, who were Muslims. Soon, however, small Christian kingdoms had emerged in the north. For several centuries Christians, Muslims, and Jews had lived together. There were frequent wars between various rulers, Christian as well as Muslim; but in such wars religion seldom played a crucial role. Indeed, quite often a Christian ruler would make an alliance with a Muslim counterpart in order to make war against another Christian neighbor. Even El Cid, the famous warrior who later was depicted as a great Christian champion, on occasion fought on the side of the Moors and against other Christians—his very title, "Cid," comes from an Arabic word meaning "lord."

Then, shortly before the time of Columbus, things changed. The northern Christian kingdoms—particularly Castile—decided to undertake a great crusade against the infidel, who must be expelled from the peninsula. In their view it was the task of Christians in Spain to unify the country under one crown and one faith. They would look back at their history and see it, not as it had really been, but as a great "Reconquista"—reconquest—against the Moorish invader. They felt God had given them this task, and in order to accomplish it they had to be faithful to God and to the Christian religion.

In 1492, just a few months before Columbus sailed, the last Moorish stronghold in Spain, Granada, had fallen to the armies of Ferdinand and Isabella. The terms of surrender included a number of guarantees for the Moors and their customs. But these were soon forgotten, and by 1502 all Moors living in Spain were ordered to either convert to Christianity or leave the country. In 1492, just about the same time that Columbus sailed, some 200,000 Spanish Jews had been forced to leave under similar circumstances. It mattered little that these Muslims and Jews considered themselves Spanish, or that they had lived in Spain for generations. (Remember, the Moors had been in Spain roughly twice as long as English-speaking people have lived in what is now the United States.) They were not Christians, and there was no place for them in Spain, whose "manifest destiny"—especially after the birth of Protestantism a few years later—was to uphold true, pure, Catholic Christianity.

This combination of Catholicism and nationalism was also the main reason why the Inquisition became so powerful in Spain. It was feared that some Muslims or Jews who had declared themselves Christian and accepted baptism might in fact be practicing the old religion in secret. Anyone who did not eat pork was suspect. In Seville, an officer of the Inquisition would climb to the top of the cathedral tower on Saturdays and take note of any chimney where no smoke could be seen—perhaps the inhabitants were Jews keeping the Sabbath and should be investigated.

Then God seemed to place a new challenge before Spain. Across the "Ocean Sea," vast new lands were "discovered"—lands ripe for conquest, exploitation, and Christianization. These three motives, conquest, exploitation, and Christianization, went hand in hand. At times, it is difficult to distinguish among them. When Spanish explorers met a native ruler, they were supposed to read to him a strange document called the *Requerimiento*—a Spanish word whose meaning is somewhere between a request and a demand. This document claimed that Christ had been made absolute ruler over the entire world, that he had given his authority to the pope as his representative on earth, and that the pope in turn had given these lands to the Spanish crown. Those who heard the *Requerimiento* were invited to accept these facts and submit to their new masters. If they refused—or if they simply did not understand what was being said, usually in Spanish—they became rebellious subjects, and therefore those reading the document to them were free to take military action against them, to take their lands, and to enslave them. Strange as it may seem, the regulations regarding the reading of the *Requerimiento* were enacted by well-meaning people who thought they were protecting the rights of the native inhabitants of these lands!

Another indication of the manner in which Christianity was brought to these lands is the system of *encomiendas*. The word *encomendar* means "to entrust." Therefore, an encomienda was a group of natives who were "entrusted" to a Spanish settler in order to be taught the rudiments of Christianity. In exchange for that service, which they had not requested, and for their keep, which they could easily earn in their traditional occupations with much less work, the natives were to work for the settler—the *encomendero*. Again, those in Spain who issued laws regarding the encomiendas thought that they were doing what was right and apparently believed that through this system they were truly serving and protecting the "Indians," as Native Americans were mistakenly called.

Needless to say, both the *Requerimiento* and the encomiendas were very much abused. In theory, they were means to make certain that the native inhabitants of these lands were treated justly. In fact, they functioned as excuses for violence and exploitation.

Most Spanish settlers, and even most religious leaders, were convinced that this was a proper and just way to do things. They were used to judging everything by European standards, and therefore they had very little appreciation for the native people, their culture, or their family lives, all of which were being destroyed.

There were, however, others who saw things very differently. At first these were mostly Dominicans, and later also Jesuits and Franciscans. These are all religious orders whose members have vows of poverty—they cannot own anything. For that reason, they were often used as the vanguard of missionary work. Many lived among the native people (as you may have seen in the movie *The Mission*), so they could understand the tragic side of the conquest—that people were dying, families were being broken up, and entire tribes were being wiped out. Some missionaries endeavored to go out into Native American territory far ahead of the soldiers and settlers, to help the people organize themselves into towns that they hoped would provide a greater chance of survival. That was the origin of many of the "missions" in the West and Southwest. Others responded by raising their voice of protest.

These voices of protest in Spanish (and Portuguese) America are one of the bright points in the history of the Christian church. At a time when most people, including just about all the top leaders of both church and state, were convinced that Spain was leading the world in doing God's will, these people thought otherwise and said so quite plainly, even at great personal risk. Antonio de Montesinos, a Dominican priest in Hispaniola (the island that is now Haiti and the Dominican Republic), preached the first sermon on this topic. Among many other very harsh things, he said:

Tell me, by what right do you wage such detestable wars on these people who lived mildly and peacefully in their own lands, where you have

117

consumed infinite numbers of them with unheard-of murders and desolations? Are they not men? Do they not have rational souls? Are you not bound to love them as you love yourselves? How can you lie in such profound and lethargic slumber? Be sure that in your present state you can no more be saved than the Moors or Turks who do not have and do not want the faith of Jesus Christ.[1]

Hundreds of others protested similarly. Probably the most famous is Bartolomé de Las Casas, of whom you may have read elsewhere, who spent a lifetime traveling back and forth between Spain and the colonies. He would lobby in Spain to have laws enacted for the protection of the Native Americans and then would come back to the colonies to try to have them enforced. When the settlers found a way to get around the new laws, he would hurry back to Spain and try to plug whatever loopholes there were. Others voiced their protest by refusing to give communion to those who had taken lands from the native people—which was just about everybody who owned any real estate. These dissenters persisted even when they were ordered by higher church authorities to give communion to the settlers. Many were silenced and sent back to Spain. Others were murdered. But still the protest continued. Eventually, even in the famous University of Salamanca, in Spain, there were some who questioned the legitimacy of the conquest. Some say that Charles V himself, moved by all these voices of protest, for a while considered canceling the entire colonial enterprise. Whether that claim is true or not, its very existence is an indication of the extent of the protest against the injustices that were being committed.

Thus, the Christianity that came to Spanish America was marked by contrasts that today we find striking. It was intolerant and authoritarian. It found ways to justify wanton war, cruelty, and exploitation. Yet many within it raised voices of protest and criticized the entire colonial enterprise with a firmness that had no parallel in the British colonial enterprise—or, later, in the United States' continued conquest of Native Americans' lands, which destroyed and uprooted entire tribes.

A MIXTURE OF CULTURES
AND TRADITIONS

There was much more contact between Europeans and Native Americans in the Spanish colonies than in the British colonies of North America. There were many reasons for this. For example, the Spanish came earlier and settled in the areas where gold and precious metals were most abundant. They needed the native inhabitants to work in the mines. In contrast, British settlers in North America came later, and they came to farm. In order to farm, they needed land; therefore, the native inhabitants were simply pushed farther and farther west. Also, very few women came from Spain in the early stages of the conquest, so there was more intermarrying of races. As the native population dwindled in many areas and slaves were brought from Africa, the practice of mixed racial unions continued. Later immigrants came to Latin America from various parts of Asia—especially China and Korea—and their genes too were added to the pool. Today's Hispanics in the United States represent that entire history. Therefore, today you may find some Hispanics who look like Africans, some who look like Europeans, some who look like Native Americans, some who look like Asians, and many who look like a mixture of two or more of these. What makes them "Hispanic" is not race but the Spanish language and the culture and traditions that have resulted from all this mixture.

This mixture of cultures can also be seen in the field of religion. Most of the early Spanish missionaries thought that whatever religion was already here was of the devil and should be entirely rejected. Yet matters were not that simple. Native peoples had dances and other ceremonies for just about every occasion—planting, harvest, building, birth, puberty, marriage, death, rain, drought, and so on. The missionaries saw that they could use some of those traditions to communicate and teach their faith. Thus developed hundreds of religious customs in which to this day one can see the mixture of the native and the European.

For example: When Queen Isabella heard that the "Indians" in the Caribbean bathed every day, amid much shouting and celebration, and seemed to make a ritual out of it, she gave instructions that such an ungodly custom should be stopped. (What she objected to was not so much the ritual as the bath itself. It is said that she once took a bath, and felt that it was a terrible sin!) But then the island of Puerto Rico was consecrated to St. John the Baptist, and on his feast day it was customary to reenact the baptism of Jesus. The native people took that as an opportunity to practice their tradition of communal public bathing, which had always had religious significance for them. To this day, on the feast day of St. John the Baptist, thousands of Puerto Ricans wade into the sea, even with their clothes on, in a celebration that may look like a wild party but has religious overtones that go back for centuries.

Naturally, Native Americans also played an active role in combining their traditions with those of the newcomers, sometimes even hoodwinking the missionaries. In a city in Bolivia, for example, the parish priest of a small church dedicated to Saints Peter and Paul commissioned one of his parishioners to make statues of these two saints. After several weeks, the man arrived with two statues. They were so large that they could not be put inside the church, so they were placed at each side of the entrance. The priest was delighted to see people flocking to pay their respects to Peter and Paul. It is only recently that scholars have discovered that "Peter and Paul" were in fact ancient images of local deities, which the supposed sculptor had taken from their original setting and moved to the church. No wonder so many people came to pay their respects. Eventually, even in the minds of those who knew the true origin of the statues, the two Christian saints became confused with the ancient gods.

Another example of the same phenomenon: In several places, altars built with native labor have been found to contain images of ancient gods, which the workers apparently hid there when the church was being built, so that they could continue coming before such altars and worshiping in good conscience.

A similar pattern developed with the coming of slaves from Africa. They too brought their religion with them. It was part of their identity and an important means of psychological survival. When they were forced to become Christians, they often did so by equating their traditional gods with Christian saints. In some areas, the ancient god of entrances was equated with St. Peter, who was always depicted with keys. St. Barbara, the patron saint of artillerymen, became the same as Changó, who ruled over thunder. The old practices of healing with herbs and potions continued and, because some of them seemed to work, slowly made their way among people who were not necessarily of African descent. (That is why to this day, in some areas of Miami and New York, you may find *botánicas*—stores where medicinal herbs are sold jointly with all kinds of ingredients for potions that are supposed to have medicinal and even magical powers.)

Independence from Spain came for most Latin American countries in the early nineteenth century. With independence came the Protestants, mostly from Britain and the United States. A few came as immigrants, but most came as entrepreneurs or as missionaries. The entrepreneurs built railroads, factories, and various sorts of trade and industry. The missionaries brought new ideas, not only about the meaning of Christianity, but also about how the church and the society ought to be organized. Many were convinced that Protestantism and democracy were two sides of the same coin. As they saw it, Latin America's worst problems stemmed from its Roman Catholic tradition. To them, Roman Catholicism was obscurantist, authoritarian, and reactionary. To some degree they were right, for by that time much of Latin American Roman Catholicism had indeed become reactionary. (It is important to understand that the nineteenth century was a time of great upheavals in politics, as well as astounding scientific discoveries that challenged many traditional notions. While Protestantism tended to go overboard in accepting many "modern" ideas, Roman Catholicism tended to reject them. In more recent times, both traditions have taken a more balanced approach.) In contrast to what they saw as an authoritarian and antiquated Catholicism, Protestant missionaries insisted on people reading the Bible for themselves, on freedom of expression, and on a more democratic form of church government—although many of the missionaries who spoke of such a democratic ideal were rather reluctant to give up their own power in the churches they had founded.

Protestants also came to what is now the American Southwest, especially after the area became part of the United States. At that point, most major Protestant denominations decided that God was "opening a door" for their missionary work in the area, and they began work among the Hispanic population there. What was done there was similar to what took place in Latin America, except that it was done in an area where Hispanics were rapidly losing control of the land, the economy, and their own future.

Protestantism came to the Hispanic world claiming to be a purer form of Christianity than Catholicism. Any practice that could not be found in the Bible was to be rejected—at least that was the theory. What in fact happened was that anything that was not practiced by Protestants in the countries where the missionaries came from was declared to be "Roman" and "unbiblical." Candles, robes, incense, and crucifixes were out. So was the practice of wearing black for mourning, or of *novenas* for the dead—the custom of meeting for nine days after someone's death to remember them and to pray for them. Even Ash Wednesday and Lent were often decried as unbiblical. But pianos, pews, and Christmas trees were acceptable, and no one seemed to remember that they too are not in the Bible.

Finally came the great Pentecostal wave. Stemming mostly out of a great "revival" that took place at a church in Azusa Street in Los Angeles early in the twentieth century, it rapidly spread throughout the world, but especially into Latin America and among Hispanics in the United States. The movement has taken many shapes among Hispanics and Latin

Americans. In some countries, it has resulted in independent denominations with hundreds of thousands of members. There are also thousands of small independent churches. Some tend to be very otherworldly and shun any social or political activity. Others are very much involved in organizing their communities for self-improvement, and for empowering the people to oppose various systems of oppression. Therefore, any generalization would be wrong.

Pentecostalism clearly has hit a nerve among Hispanics. Today, Pentecostals form the second-largest religious group among Hispanics in the United States, after Roman Catholics. Although some Pentecostal Hispanics are members of North American denominations, many are members of denominations that began in Latin America and then spread to the United States. Even many of those who belong to American denominations have been converted through their connections with Latin America. This is true, for instance, in the greater metropolitan area of New York, where several of the largest Pentecostal churches were founded by pastors or by members moving to the United States from Puerto Rico.

RELIGION AND IDENTITY

Today in any major city in the United States one can find a variety of religious practices and traditions among Hispanics. On the surface these practices and traditions may seem to have very little in common, but they are fundamental to the identity of a people who have often wandered in exile, and whose identity has sometimes been denied by the dominant culture. At the same time, however, these religious expressions also reflect much of the dominant culture. Thus, while from the perspective of that culture they may seem alien, something brought from Latin America, from the perspective of Latin America they often seem very much influenced by North American culture and religious traditions.

You may find, for instance, Spanish-speaking synagogues. In some of those synagogues you will find Sephardic Jews—descendants of those who were expelled from Spain in 1492—who still speak Spanish very much as it was spoken back then. You will also find other Jews who went to Latin America from central Europe or from Germany, many fleeing from Nazism, and who have now come to the United States. A number of these Jews consider themselves both Jewish and Hispanic; they are also very much citizens of the United States and participants in much of the common culture of this nation.

You will also find a number of Catholic traditions and practices that are closely tied to people's identities. Among these are the *posadas* and the devotion to the Virgin of Guadalupe.

The posadas—literally, "lodgings"—are an ancient tradition that became quite popular in Mexico and in what is now the American Southwest, and is still practiced in various parts of the United States. Traditionally, they begin on the evening of December 16 and continue for nine evenings in a row until Christmas Eve—although there are now many variations on this. Each evening, people set out with Mary and Joseph, seeking lodgings. "Mary and Joseph" may be an actual young girl riding a donkey, with an actual young man leading it, or they may be statues that the people carry. The procession goes from house to house, asking for lodging in traditional songs and being told, also in song, that there is no room. Finally, they arrive at a prearranged place, where they are told that there is lodging. They all go in, and there is a celebration that usually includes food, songs, prayers, a rosary (a prayer to the Virgin Mary), and often a piñata. The crowds grow larger each day, so that the posada on Christmas Eve is often a big affair that ends at the church or at some public place that can accommodate a large crowd.

The posadas are lots of fun. But more than that, they have become very important for people who have had to move repeatedly looking for work, many of whom do not have legal papers for residence in the United States, while others, even those who are citizens by birth, are often told in many different ways that they are foreigners. In such a situation, it is comforting and strengthening to remember that Jesus too had difficulty finding a place, that he was born away from home, and that thereafter he was an exile in Egypt.

The veneration of the Virgin of Guadalupe celebrates a story that takes place shortly after the conquest of Mexico by the Spaniards. The story, in a nutshell, tells of a poor Indian, Juan Diego, and his conflict with the learned and powerful bishop of Mexico. According to the story, the Virgin Mary appeared to Juan Diego and gave him some instructions for the bishop, who refused to pay any attention to what the Indian had to say. After repeated attempts by Juan Diego to instruct the bishop, the Virgin provided proof that Juan Diego was telling the truth by imprinting her own image on the apron in which Juan Diego was carrying flowers to the bishop. When the bishop saw the miraculous image, he repented and did as Juan Diego told him. A large church was built where the Virgin had appeared, and the miraculous apron was enshrined in it.

Some may see in this nothing but superstition. Yet what we have here is the story of the vindication of Juan Diego and others like him, to whom people of power and prestige, like the bishop, pay no attention. For that reason, among Catholic Hispanics, especially those of Mexican or Mexican American descent, the Virgin of Guadalupe—who is understood to be the Virgin Mary as she appeared to Juan Diego—has been a sign of empowerment and vindication for the oppressed native inhabitants of these lands, and in general for all the poor and the downtrodden. Her image was on the first national flag of Mexico. For the same reason, when Mexican American farm workers and others began a long struggle for the right to unionize, the Virgin of Guadalupe was one of their most powerful symbols.

Many such celebrations and stories contain much that is Native American in origin. Indeed, the hill of Tepeyac, where the Virgin of Guadalupe is said to have appeared to Juan Diego, was also a place where an ancient goddess was worshiped—and there are elements of those ancient traditions in much that is done today at Tepeyac in celebration of the Virgin.

In recent times, a reform has taken place in Roman Catholic worship. Until a few years ago, the mass had to be said in Latin, even if the people did not understand a word of what was being said. With the new directives of the Second Vatican Council, the mass was translated into the languages of the people, including Spanish. In ancient cathedrals such as those in San Antonio and Santa Fe, where Spanish had long been the language of the people, the mass was said in Spanish for the first time. This renewed people's interest in the mass. A number of Hispanic musicians began composing new music for the mass, exploring some of the ancient native traditions to see how they could be related to Catholic worship. The result has been astounding. If you want to go to mass at the church of San Juan de los Lagos, in San Antonio, you had better arrive early or you will not be able to get in. Once in, you may be surprised to hear mariachis playing tunes that are typically Mexican and that convey the meaning of the mass with amazing freshness and vigor. You may be even more surprised to see a group of dancers wearing costumes that look very much like those of the ancient Aztecs, decorated not only with plumes, but also with images of the Virgin of Guadalupe. Above all, you will notice that, although the mass has lost the somber tone it had when it was said in Latin, it has become a very significant and enriching worship experience for those who participate.

In other sections of the Hispanic American community, you may hear drums beating in rhythms that are clearly African. If you approach, you may find yourself in a *bembé*—a religious celebration that has deep roots in

Africa. Most everybody will be dancing to the rhythm of the drums, which will be so catchy that you will have difficulty standing still. There may be religious symbols about. If you do not come from that tradition, you may recognize some Christian symbols, such as the cross or perhaps the image of a saint, but others will be quite foreign. In some cases, you may see offerings of grain and animals. People will dance, and dance, and dance—sometimes for three days and nights without stopping. If you attend these rituals often enough, you will come to recognize that different rhythms are used for different occasions. If you stay long enough in one of them, you may see someone who "gets the saint": that person will fall to the ground in spasms, roll his or her eyes back, and perhaps speak words of wisdom on his or her own behalf or on the community's. Then the person will be so exhausted that he or she will have to be carried to another room to rest.

If you think you are a little sophisticated, you may look upon all this with a bit of disdain, telling yourself that it is primitive and has no place in the modern world. But if you stop to think about it you may realize that these people are trying to come to grips with the mystery of life; that they are celebrating rituals that somehow connect them with a distant past that is half forgotten and has been denied them; that they are celebrating their common heritage and mourning their common lot; that they are making a statement that religion has to do not only with the soul and the mind, but also with the body; that rhythm and music, just as much as logic and speech, are God-given and may be used to worship God.

In the same city where you find a Spanish-speaking synagogue and a bembé, and where Catholics celebrate the posadas, you probably can also find a Hispanic Pentecostal church. Even if you do not belong to this tradition, you will again find much that will be familiar from other experiences, especially if you understand the language. The church will look like most Protestant churches, though perhaps less ornate. There will be no images, usually no stained-glass windows, and probably no organ—depending mostly on the financial resources of the church. There will be pews, a railing, and a pulpit that will be the focus of attention. Perhaps there will be a few scriptural verses inscribed on the wall—a custom that may remind you of some Jewish synagogues or Muslim mosques. There will be music—lots of music, with pianos, guitars, tambourines, maracas, and synthesizers. If you have attended an evangelical church you will recognize many of the hymns whose lyrics have been translated from English. Others may be quite different, with rhythms that sound like something you would expect in a secular setting. People will sing loudly, clapping and swaying to the rhythm of the music. At times, the place may seem as noisy as a baseball stadium during a World Series. Some people may be shouting, "Alleluia" and others "Amen," while still others may be praying their own prayers out loud.

If you are an outside observer, you will probably conclude that there is much here that is similar to what you could see in a synagogue or in a Catholic church—especially as far as the words are concerned—but that there is also much that reminds you of the bembé: the rhythm, the noise, the willingness to release oneself to the consciousness of the group. If you are used to more sedate worship services, you may even be shocked and decide that this is not true worship at all. If so, you may try conveying that opinion to one of the members, and she might respond that she does not understand how you can get so excited over a football game but then hear the story of Jesus and not jump up and down. Perhaps she has a point worth considering.

She might also tell you that in order to understand what the people there are celebrating, you have to listen to their "testimonies." Testimonies, in which people stand up and give an account of what God has done for them, are an important part of most Hispanic Pentecostal services. In this particular service, this woman would tell you, you might hear the testimony of a young man who had been unable to free himself from his drug addiction until he came to church. Now, through prayer and with the support of the rest of the community, he can finally say that he is free of his habit. Another may speak of how her child was ill, and how she had no money for medicines; but the congregation prayed for the child and it was cured. Still a third would speak of how he was unemployed, and how through prayer and the support of the community he was able to survive and then to find a job. In short, these people, many of whom have found themselves in desperate situations, are celebrating a newly discovered life. This new life is not only spiritual, but also communal, and in many cases even economic. As with the other places you would have visited, you would be witnessing religion at work in affirming people's identity and empowering them to deal with the adversities of life.

WHAT MAKES IT
ALL HISPANIC AMERICAN

By now you may be wondering if there is any unity at all to the Hispanic American religious life and experience. What is it, after all, that allows us to speak of "Hispanic American religious life," as if there were something common to it? In this chapter, we have met Jewish, Catholic, and Protestant Hispanic Americans, as well as some whose religious practices still reflect much of their African ancestry. If there had been more space to go into further details, you would also have met Hispanics with many other beliefs.

Obviously, the most important element common to all Hispanics, no matter what their particular religion, is the Spanish language and cultural tradition. People are Hispanic not because of their race but because of their culture and traditions. Genetically, Hispanics are various mixtures of European, African, Native American, and even Asian ancestry. It is the language and all the traditions and social conventions that go with it that make us Hispanic. It is also the history, for we all somehow partake of the history of the original inhabitants of America, of the Spanish invaders, and of slaves who were brought from Africa. That is why some Hispanics speak of themselves as "the race that is not a race," while others prefer to speak of a *raza cósmica*—a "cosmic race."

Once you begin to understand that common history and culture, you may also begin to see commonalities cutting across many of the varying religious practices that we have been discussing. I have already mentioned that the writings on the walls of a Pentecostal church are reminiscent of many ancient synagogues and mosques in Spain. And there is much similarity between the mood of a Pentecostal service and that of a bembé—or even a mariachi mass.

In some cases, ancient traditions lead to religious practices that cut across denominational lines. For instance, for most Hispanics, Catholic or Protestant, Christmas Eve and Epiphany (January 6) are much more important than Christmas Day. If you grew up in a non-Hispanic Christian household in the United States, Christmas probably was the big family day, and much of the excitement of Christmas had to do with Santa Claus and presents. Among Hispanics, both Catholic and Protestant, the big family day is Christmas Eve, when the family gets together for a late meal. Many traditional Catholic families then attend a midnight mass at which they celebrate the birth of Jesus.

The other important day is January 6, which in the Christian calendar is usually called "Epiphany" but in most Hispanic households is called "Kings' Day." That is the day the "Three Kings"—the three wise men— bring gifts to children. Hispanic Christian children know the Three Kings by name and await them as eagerly as many other children await Santa Claus. Some households leave out straw for the Kings' camels. Many set up nativity scenes a few days (often nine days) before Christmas Eve, with figures depicting Mary, Joseph, the shepherds, angels, and all the animals at the manger. The Child is not placed in the manger until Christmas Eve. Slowly, the wise men appear on the horizon, until they arrive on January 6. That morning children get up to find the goodies that the Kings have left, under the bed or in some other convenient place.

This is one of the many traditions that make us *Hispanic* Americans. But we are also Hispanic *Americans*. We are part of a society and a culture that has its own traditions. In the old days, after going to mass late on Christmas Eve, we could sleep late on Christmas morning. Santa Claus never came to Latin America, or to the American Southwest, until commercial interests got him there. Now, however, Santa is also part of our common tradition, and we no longer get to sleep late on Christmas morning! But the children are the winners, for they get presents on Christmas *and* on Kings' Day!

This is a symbol of what it means to be a Hispanic American. Hispanics belong to a tradition that has deep and long roots in this country. As Americans, we share in a wider culture that draws from many a tradition. Sometimes these two seem to be in conflict. Most of the time, however, they enrich each other.

As to the wide variety of religious expressions among Hispanics, perhaps that too is part of what it means to be an American. In the Spain of Ferdinand and Isabella, none of those various religious expressions would have been tolerated. Here in the United States, they are all tolerated and celebrated. Some may think that this is because religion is not important, that it makes no difference. But the opposite is true: The reason why we tolerate and even celebrate such a variety of religions is precisely because religion is so important, because it touches each of our lives so deeply, and because its contributions to society are so valuable. If we do not allow all to bring their contributions we shall all be the losers.

NOTES

1. H. McKennie Goodpasture, *Cross and Sword: An Eyewitness History of Christianity in Latin America* (Maryknoll, N.Y.: Orbis, 1989), 11–12.

STUDY QUESTIONS

1. How did Spanish-speaking people come to reflect such a large percentage of the American population? Be sure to name several significant events in American history that brought this about, and to distinguish between recent immigrants and descendants of persons who have been here for centuries.

2. What influence did Spain have on the development of the religion of the earliest Spanish-speaking settlers in America?

3. What role did the Spanish-speaking church and its priests play in resisting the "conquest, exploitation, and Christianization" by Spain of the Americas? Why does the author call this resistance one of the "bright points in the history of the Christian church"? How did the priests who practiced such resistance suffer?

4. Why was there more contact between Europeans and Native Americans in the Spanish colonies than the British colonies of North America? What effect did this mixture of cultures have on the religious development of the colonies? Give two examples of how Native Americans made Spanish Christianity acceptable to their own religious traditions.

5. What conflicts developed between Catholicism and Protestantism soon after the Spanish colonies established independence from Spain? Describe several details of this conflict.

6. What is the "Pentecostal wave" that began in Los Angeles in the early twentieth century? What was its impact on Hispanic Americans?

7. Why is it wrong to assume that Hispanics belong to any particular religion? Why is such an assumption often made?

ESSAY TOPICS

The History of Pentecostalism in the Hispanic Church
The First Spanish Missions in the Americas
The Religious World of Hispanic America: Unity and Diversity
Spain and the Christianization of America
Religious Story: The Virgin of Guadalupe

WORD EXPLORATION

The following words play significant roles in any discussion of the religious world of Hispanics in America and are worth careful reflection and discussion.

Hispanic
Manifest Destiny
The Catholic
   Sovereigns
Moors

El Cid
Bembé
Requerimiento
Encomiendas

Latin America
Posadas
Virgin of
   Guadalupe

FOR FURTHER READING

González, Justo L. *Mañana: Christian Theology from a Hispanic Perspective.* Nashville: Abingdon, 1990.

Romero, C. Gilbert. *Hispanic Devotional Piety: Tracing the Biblical Roots.* Maryknoll, N.Y.: Orbis, 1991.

Valdez, Margarita, ed. *Tradiciones del Pueblo: Traditions of Three Mexican Feast Days in Southwest Detroit.* Detroit: Casa de Unidad Cultural, 1990.

6

JAROSLAV PELIKAN

Orthodox Christianity in the World and in America

Their onion-domed churches dot the hills of Pennsylvania coal country and the mill towns of New Jersey and Ohio; in Tarpon Springs, Florida, their Greek priests bless the fleet of the sponge fishermen in the colorful ceremonies for the annual opening of the season; and, about as far away from Tarpon Springs as anyone can go and still be in the United States, Kodiak and Sitka, Alaska, are connected by way of their traditions, which date to the Russia of the Czars, to the Judeo-Christian traditions shared by most other Americans. There are about four million Eastern Orthodox Christians in the United States, with ties of varying firmness binding them to mother churches in Greece, the Middle East, and the Slavic lands of Eastern and Central Europe. They have a long and turbulent history of their own in the New World, and they are increasingly visible as a vital force within American religion.

The first time some of you encountered Orthodox Christianity may have been through the luminous discourses of Father Zossima in Dostoyevsky's *Brothers Karamazov*, or through the liturgical pageantry in the coronation scene of Modest Mussorgsky's *Boris Godunov*, or through the haunting faces and figures of icons from Mount Athos or icons by Andrey Rublyov (ca. 1350–ca. 1430) in a book on art history. Or perhaps you read a spy novel in which a Western operative in Moscow, despite his flawless Russian, blew his cover at the dinner table, by making the sign of the cross Western-style, from left to right rather than from right to left ("always ending at the heart," as my late mother used to say). But as Orthodox Christianity throughout the United States has finally begun to emerge from its various language ghettos, its system of religious belief and practice has also begun to claim its proper share of serious attention from other American religious groups, from the American public, and sometimes even from the American media.

Depending on how one elects to count them and on how seriously one takes their recurrent schisms, past and present, there are as many as twenty-five or more jurisdictions of Orthodox Christians in the United States. The very names of the American denominations of Orthodox Christianity, as usually listed in standard almanacs, are instructive echoes of their immigrant origins. Of these, the major ones are, in alphabetical order: the Albanian Orthodox Diocese of America; the American Carpatho-Russian Orthodox Greek Catholic Church ("Carpatho-Russian" or "-Rusyn," from what was once called Ruthenia, part of Czechoslovakia between World War I and World War II, and now forming western Ukraine); the Antiochian (formerly Syrian Antiochian) Orthodox Christian Archdiocese of North America; the Bulgarian Eastern Orthodox Church; the Coptic Orthodox Church; the Diocese of the Armenian Church of America; the Greek Orthodox Archdiocese of North and South America; the Orthodox Church in America (formerly Russian Orthodox Greek Catholic Church of North America); the Romanian Orthodox Episcopate of America; the Serbian Eastern Orthodox Church; the Syrian Orthodox Church of Antioch; the Ukrainian Orthodox Church in America; and the Ukrainian Orthodox Church in the U.S.A.

This bewildering, almost kaleidoscopic array of names, some of which have changed over the years, and the ongoing disputes between the groups in both ecclesiastical and secular courts indicate the quest for religious identity that persists among American Orthodox. It also indicates the continuing struggle to achieve some sort of unity within Orthodox America before being able to work on the problems of unity with other Christians or even with Orthodoxy throughout the world. It would be unfair, however, to exaggerate this problem, because about three-fourths of all the Orthodox believers in the United States belong to either the Greek Orthodox Archdiocese of North and South America or to the Orthodox Church in America.

THE HISTORICAL ORIGINS OF ORTHODOX CHRISTIANITY

Orthodoxy was called "a new and unknown world" by an outstanding Russian Orthodox poet and lay theologian of the nineteenth century, A. S. Khomyakov (1804–1860). But as Khomyakov was the first to insist, this "new world" is in fact very old, and it deserves to be better known in the West. For Eastern Orthodox Christianity is, in a very real sense, as old as Christianity itself. At the first Pentecost in Jerusalem fifty days after Easter, described in the second chapter of the Acts of the Apostles and often called "the birthday of the Christian Church," many nations of the Mediterranean world were represented among the converts: "Parthians, Medes, Elamites; inhabitants of Mesopotamia, of Judaea and Cappadocia, of Pontus and Asia, of Phrygia and Pamphylia, of Egypt and the districts of Libya around Cyrene; visitors from Rome, both Jews and proselytes; Cretans and Arabs" (Acts 2:9–11). Almost every one of these (with the major exception of Rome, of course), indeed almost every Christian center referred to by name anywhere within the pages of the New Testament, belongs to Eastern Christendom—Jerusalem, Antioch, Alexandria, Athens, Corinth, and many others (many of them now bearing other names as a result of later conquests, especially by Muslims). In each of those centers, moreover, Orthodox Christianity has had a more or less unbroken history since the first century C.E.

During the centuries of Christian history when Eastern and Western Christendom were still maintaining some sort of communion with each other, moreover, the religious and spiritual balance of trade—liturgically, culturally, and theologically—was predominantly from East to West. Most of the major Christian theologians before Augustine (d. 430) wrote in Greek (as did, for that matter, most of the major heretics): Ignatius of Antioch, Irenaeus of Lyons, Clement of Alexandria, Origen, Athanasius, Basil of Caesarea, Gregory of Nazianzus, Gregory of Nyssa, Cyril of Jerusalem, and Cyril of Alexandria, to name only a few. All seven ecumenical councils of the "undivided Church" were held in Eastern territory: the First Council of Nicaea (present-day Iznik, Turkey) in 325; the First Council of Constantinople (present-day Istanbul, Turkey) in 381; the Council of Ephesus in 431; the Council of Chalcedon (present-day Kadiköy, Turkey) in 451; the Second Council of Constantinople in 553; the Third Council of Constantinople in 680–681; and the Second Council of Nicaea in 787. Christian monasticism began in the East and only eventually moved West, and the same was true of Christian mysticism, Christian philosophy, and much of Christian art. And Greek was the language not only of Paul's epistles to the Greek cities of Corinth, Philippi, and Thessalonica, but also of his epistle to Rome. Even the sayings of Jesus, which originally were probably spoken in Aramaic, a Semitic language, were written down and preserved in the Gospels through the medium of Greek, from which they have been translated into nearly two thousand languages (including Semitic languages). "Ex Oriente lux," according to the Latin proverb: the light rises from the East (sometimes the proverb has been amplified with the addition, "ex Occidente lex": law comes from the West).

It was appropriate to put the phrase "undivided Church" into quotation marks in the preceding paragraph, because implicit and explicit forms of disunity can be found regardless of how far back in time our historical study goes. The official schism between East and West, with its fateful consequences for both, did, however, change things in a fundamental way. Like most divorces, it was a consequence of estrangement, which turned into alienation, which turned into hostility, which turned into separation. When the official and legal separation finally did come, the idea of a unified Church had long since died among the people. Textbooks of history, including Edward Gibbon's *History of the Decline and Fall of the Roman Empire,* have traditionally dated the schism from 1054, when spokesmen for the two churches exchanged writs of excommunication. Others have marked the date earlier, to the ninth century. At the beginning of that century, on Christmas Day in the year 800, the pope crowned the king of the Franks, Charles (Charlemagne), as Roman emperor, despite there already being a Christian Roman emperor in Constantinople, who claimed authority also over the upstart West. As has happened so often, and not only in East–West relations, this political schism had its counterpart in the ecclesiastical schism. Later in the ninth century, as we shall note in greater detail later, East and West clashed over the mission to Moravia of the two brothers, Saints Constantine-Cyril and Methodius, in 862.

For my part, I have always been inclined to accept the view of many Orthodox scholars that the real break came in the year 1204, when the Western Christian armies on the Fourth Crusade, ostensibly bent on the liberation of the Holy Land and the Holy Places, sacked Christian Constantinople, establishing a Latin empire (until 1261) and forcibly "reuniting" the Latin and Greek churches, though in fact they were dividing them, perhaps permanently. Temporary reunions, notably the one at the Council of Florence in 1439, have all proved to be short-lived. The attendance of Orthodox clergy at the ecumenical Stockholm Conference of 1925, however, marked a gradual change in attitude on both sides, and such significant gestures as the embrace of Ecumenical Patriarch Athenagoras and Pope Paul VI at their meeting on the Mount of Olives in 1964 have reawakened hopes that someday there may still be a reconciliation between Eastern and Western Christendom after so many centuries of bitter conflict.

Above all, however, it has been in America that Orthodoxy has come to play a significant ecumenical role, partly because of its new situation in the New World and partly because of the ecumenical rediscovery of other Christians that has played a large part in the history of almost every denomination in the twentieth century, especially on American soil.

HOW EASTERN ORTHODOXY
CAME WEST

Eastern Orthodoxy came to the Western Hemisphere by traveling east. Although the very first Orthodox believers to arrive in colonial America were probably the members of a Greek colony in Florida in 1768, the institutional beginnings of Orthodox Christianity came a few decades later and many thousands of miles away, on Kodiak Island, Alaska, in what was then Russian territory. It was in Alaska that the Divine Liturgy of the Orthodox Church was celebrated, apparently for the first time anywhere in the Western Hemisphere, by naval chaplains of the Russian Orthodox Church on July 20, 1737. With the establishment of partial control of the Czar over Alaska, permanent settlements of Orthodox Russians came to Alaska. There was a growing conviction among some of them, partly for commercial and political reasons but also partly for spiritual reasons, that their Christian and Orthodox faith should be brought to the natives of the region. The Metropolitan of the Russian Orthodox Church for Novgorod and St. Petersburg, Gabriel Petrov, commissioned ten Russian monks to undertake the Kodiak mission. The monks landed at Kodiak on September 24, 1794, which is observed as the founding date of American Orthodoxy.

The Orthodox mission in Alaska nourished two of the earliest Christian saints of any denomination in America. One was the monk St. Herman of Alaska, who worked there for forty years until his death in 1837. The other was Bishop Innocent, whose name as a layman had been Ivan Venjaminov, bishop of Sitka (1840) and eventually of Moscow (1868); his saint's day is observed according to the calendar of the Orthodox Church on October 6. As Paul D. Garrett, historian of American Orthodoxy and biographer of Innocent, has said of him, he was "a true 'Renaissance man' " who "traveled widely for fifteen years in Unalaska and Sitka, personally helped the people build churches, mastered their languages (translating and writing in Aleut), and provided the first detailed scientific description of the region," before being called back to Russia. (I once had the unforgettable experience in Alaska of attending an Orthodox liturgy celebrated by an Aleut priest with a Tlingit congregation and choir, who chanted the responses in Church Slavonic—although I was the only Slav in the room!) Alaska Orthodoxy continued after the purchase of the territory by the United States in 1867; thus Orthodox Christianity can lay claim to a history in North America that has persisted, though not without serious interruptions, for almost exactly two centuries.

These origins are extremely important for the self-definition not only of the Orthodox believers in Alaska who are Native Americans, such as Eskimos, Aleuts, and Tlingits, but also for that of all Orthodox Christians in North America whatever their ethnic origins may be. Nonetheless, the majority of the Orthodox population in the Western Hemisphere must, of course, trace their own roots to far more recent arrivals. This is not the place to recount the entire history of the immigrations from Eastern Europe to America during the nineteenth and twentieth centuries, except perhaps to point out that even in a time that celebrates "cultural diversity" most history books continue to be preoccupied with the English-speaking population of America and to manifest an interest in other groups primarily after they, too, become English-speaking. As a result, the vast body of historical source material in languages other than English, including the several languages of Eastern Orthodox Christianity, remains largely unknown even to many scholars.

It was especially in the thirty years or so prior to World War I, and as a result of the political and economic upheavals in Russia and the Balkans, that Orthodox Christians began to come to America in large numbers from Russia, Greece, Serbia, Romania, Austria-Hungary, and the Near East. As sociological-historical studies with such titles as *Has the Immigrant Kept the Faith?* (Gerald Shaughnessy, 1925) have repeatedly shown, it has been true of immigrant religious groups as widely separated, both geographically and spiritually, as Sicilian Catholics and Finnish Lutherans that "when you leave the language, you leave the church." But Orthodox Christians in America have experienced their own special version of this phenomenon. Because they had no centralized authority anywhere in the world that could legislate their organizational and liturgical life for them—even in the Old World, much less in the New World—Orthodox Christians were free to evolve here, particularly after their separation from their original countries in the aftermath of World War I into the linguistic and jurisdictional Tower of Babel evidenced by the catalog of denominations listed at the beginning of this chapter. The great-grandchildren of Greek, Russian, and Syrian immigrants now find themselves united in their Orthodoxy but separated from their fellow

Orthodox by the bonds of their ancestral language, which has increasingly become a foreign tongue for them also. That situation becomes all the more ironic in the light of the Orthodox emphasis on celebrating the Divine Liturgy in the language of the people, in contrast to the traditional Western Catholic insistence on the use of Latin in the mass.

The traumatic effects of the Bolshevik Revolution of October 1917 made themselves felt with dramatic force in the Orthodox Christianity of the New World. After the fall of Constantinople to the Seljuk Turks in 1453, Moscow had increasingly assumed a place of importance and influence, becoming a patriarchate in 1589 by the action of the Ecumenical Patriarch of Constantinople, Jeremias II. Moscow was sometimes called "Third Rome"— superseding Old Rome as the "First Rome," which fell to heresy, and New Rome (Constantinople) as the "Second Rome," which fell to Islam—which serves to symbolize a considerable shift of Orthodox power to Muscovite Russia. But with the ascendancy of the atheistic Communists, Moscow was in the control of the avowed enemies not only of Orthodox Christianity but of all religions, including Judaism and Islam. There was, consequently, a new wave of emigration of Orthodox Christians to the West.

A unique feature of this emigration, by comparison with earlier ones, was that these refugees included many artists and intellectuals, and among these many scholars and theologians. Through their work in such cultural and intellectual centers as Paris, Prague, and Oxford the knowledge of the Orthodox artistic and literary heritage, as well as its liturgical and theological heritage, was broadly disseminated in the West for the first time. Of special importance for us has been the work of Orthodox émigrés on American soil, above all that of Georges V. Florovsky (1893–1979), who left Russia in 1920, taught in Prague from 1922 to 1926, and then in Paris at the Orthodox Theological Institute of Saint Sergius from 1926 to 1948, before coming to America. While teaching at Saint Vladimir's Orthodox Seminary (1948–1955), Harvard Divinity School (1956–1964), and Princeton University until his death, Father Florovsky became for many American scholars (including myself) a mentor and guide to Orthodox history, theology, and spirituality; and by his books (see "For Further Reading" at the end of this chapter) he continues to instruct others.

DISTINCTIVE FEATURES
OF ORTHODOX CHRISTIANITY

Throughout its history, Orthodox Christianity has had certain qualities by which it continues to be identified by its adherents and by outsiders. To those Americans who are accustomed to being able, at best, to recognize some of the major differences between Roman Catholicism and Protestantism, or perhaps even some of the differences among some of the bewilderingly many species of Protestantism, Orthodox Christianity poses a particularly challenging problem. As has already been noted, Rome is the one significant exception to the historical observation made earlier, that most of the major centers of early Christianity are now identified with Eastern Orthodoxy; and that exception has often been taken to be the defining principle of Orthodoxy. To many Americans, whether Jewish, Christian, or secular, therefore, Orthodox Christianity is to be defined as a Christianity that is somehow neither Roman Catholic nor Protestant. In fact, of course, this is neither fair nor accurate, for reasons that should become clear to anyone after even a brief examination of a few of the distinctive features of Orthodox Christianity.

Orthodox Worship

The most imposing of these features is undoubtedly Orthodox worship. Within Judaism, "Orthodoxy" refers chiefly to matters of religious observance; within Protestantism, to matters of doctrine, especially perhaps to the doctrine of the inspiration of the Bible. Neither of these criteria, particularly the second (though with the emphasis on the Trinity and the Incarnation, rather than on biblical inspiration), is altogether absent from the definition of Eastern Orthodoxy, but neither of them is exclusive. One of the roots of the name "Ortho*doxy*," the Greek word *doxa*, may sometimes mean "opinion, teaching," but it also means "glory." In the Slavic word for Orthodoxy, "Pravo*slavie*," *slava* means "glory," too, so that Orthodoxy/Pravoslavie means the proper method of rendering glory, right worship, and consequently the right way of teaching about the One to whom the glory is rendered. This, for Orthodox dogma, is what is meant by the doctrines of the Trinity and the Incarnation.

According to an ancient chronicle of Kiev (capital of modern Ukraine), when a delegation of pagan Slavs came to Constantinople in the tenth century and visited the massive Church of Hagia Sophia (Holy Wisdom), which had been constructed by Emperor Justinian in the sixth century, they reported: "We knew not whether we were in heaven or on earth. For on earth there is no such splendor or such beauty, and we are at a loss how to describe it. We only know that God dwells there."

Already a century earlier, in 862, the two previously mentioned brothers, Saints Constantine-Cyril and Methodius, originally from Thessalonica, had come from Constantinople to the Slavs of Moravia. Unlike the Western missionaries, who in Christianizing most of Europe brought with them the Latin Mass instead of creating a form of worship in the language of the people, these "apostles to the Slavs" translated the Divine Liturgy into Slavonic, inventing an alphabet in the process; the present-day alphabet of Eastern Slavs such as Russians, Ukrainians, Bulgarians, and Serbs is still called "Cyrillic," though it was probably not the alphabet that St. Cyril created, which is usually called "Glagolitic" (from *glagol*, the Old Slavic word for "word"). The Slavonic liturgy of Cyril and Methodius occasioned a bitter conflict with German Catholic missionaries, who had been working among the Slavs in Latin, and the case was appealed to Rome. The pope confirmed the legitimacy of the appointment of Methodius as archbishop of Moravia, but despite an initial friendliness to the Slavonic liturgy Rome ultimately decreed that Latin must be used.

The Slavic Christian world, alone among the major ethnic groupings, was thus divided into two camps, with consequences that are still visible, for example, in the present-day conflicts between Orthodox Serbs and Croatian Catholics in the former Yugoslavia. On the one side were those Slavs who accepted the authority of Rome and surrendered the Slavic liturgy (Poland, Bohemia, Slovakia, Croatia); on the other side were those who adhered to the Slavic liturgy but lost the tie to the pope (Russia, Ukraine, Byelorussia, Serbia, Bulgaria). This ancient liturgy, whether in Slavonic, Greek, or Arabic, has constituted the form of Orthodox worship.

Immediately upon stepping into an Orthodox church building, of whichever tradition it may be, the visitor will be struck by how different in atmosphere it is from any other house of worship, Christian or non-Christian. To begin with the most obvious difference from other Christian church buildings, there are no pews (although chairs are often provided for the elderly and infirm), so that even during a very long service, such as the Easter vigil of several hours' duration, worshipers are expected to remain standing. If such a visitor witnesses a church service, even a wedding or a funeral, the difference of atmosphere will become much more pronounced. From its beginning the Orthodox Christian liturgy has sought to emphasize simultaneously two opposite poles of faith: God's distance and majesty, and God's nearness and accessibility. God the Almighty is transcendent over heaven and earth and humanity—indeed, transcendent over all the language, including the language of Orthodox liturgy and doctrine, with which mortals seek to describe the awesome mystery of the Holy One. At the same time, the Holy One is near and accessible to us through the ultimate mystery of the Incarnation of the Son of God, "God the Word," in the birth, life, death, and resurrection of Jesus

Christ, and therefore through the "mysteries" (the Orthodox term for "sacraments") celebrated by the Church in its liturgy. As the divinely chosen instrument of the Incarnation, the Virgin Mary occupies a unique place also in the liturgy: she is *Theotokos*—"the one who gave birth to the one who is God"—and in that sense, though only in that sense, "the Mother of God." The Council of Ephesus decided in 431 that it was inadequate to call her only *Christotokos*, "bearer of Christ," as though she were not the mother of the entire person of the incarnate God-man, divine as well as human.

Worship and song are inseparable in many religions, but the ancient Byzantine chant—in Greek or Church Slavonic, but now also in English—dominates Orthodox worship, there being no service that is only spoken. Although song is so central to Orthodox worship, most Orthodox churches do not include musical instruments. Igor Stravinsky (1882–1971), though an Orthodox Christian, composed a Roman Catholic Mass in Latin because, as he explained to Robert Craft, "I wanted my *Mass* to be used liturgically, an outright impossibility so far as the Russian Church was concerned, as Orthodox tradition proscribes musical instruments in its services." Although many Protestant theological seminaries have been able to carry on their work of training clergy for centuries without having a professor of church music on their faculty, that would be unthinkable at an Orthodox seminary. So powerful is the Church Slavonic chant of the Russian Orthodox Church that in the twentieth century it has become part of the secular concert repertoire, with several choirs in Europe and the United States, including choirs completely made up of non-Slavs, carrying it far beyond the sacred precincts of the church to the music hall and the recital stage. That process has been abetted by the popularity of masterpieces by several composers in the Russian Orthodox tradition, notably the *Vespers* of Sergey Rachmaninoff (1915) and various sacred works of Dmitry Bortnyansky (1751–1825) and Pyotr Ilich Tchaikovsky (1840–1893).

Orthodox Tradition

Another characteristic of Orthodox Christianity, evident in its liturgy but expressed throughout its faith and life, is its profound sense of tradition. It is true of all Christians, perhaps of all believers everywhere, that when they pray they do so with an awareness of the presence and power of all who have believed before them, sharing in what one ancient Christian creed calls "the communion of saints." For an Orthodox Christian, that awareness is heightened by a church calendar on which every day is dedicated to a particular saint, and by a liturgy in which not only the saints of Israel and of the New Testament, but also the ancestors of the faith throughout Christian history, are remembered and honored. Upon stepping into an Orthodox church, moreover, that casual visitor we spoke of will see pervasive evidence of the communion of saints in the icons—characteristically Eastern pictures of Christ, of the Virgin Mary, and of other saints—prominently featured on the "iconostasis," a wall dividing the two main parts of the church.

There was, in the "iconoclastic controversy" of the eighth and ninth centuries, severe religious and political conflict over the legitimacy of employing such pictures, in the light of the prohibition against images in Exodus 20:4 (which Orthodox Christians, together with most Protestants, count as the Second Commandment, although Roman Catholics and Lutherans do not): "Thou shalt not make unto thee any graven image, or any likeness of any thing that is in heaven above, or that is in the earth beneath, or that is in the water under the earth." The outcome of the controversy, at the Second Council of Nicaea in 787, was the reinstatement of the icons. This took place through a characteristic combination of political and religious forces, but the rationale for it was the argument that the coming of the very Son of God in human flesh had fundamentally altered the meaning of the Second Commandment. What was now pictured in an icon was not an idol of pagan mythology, but part of the history of Jesus' sojourn on earth, either during his own human lifetime or in the careers of his disciples and saints. Significantly, the anniversary of that reinstatement is observed as the "Sunday of Orthodoxy" at the beginning of Lent.

Orthodox Doctrine

The Orthodox reverence for tradition, moreover, comes to voice not only in liturgy but in doctrine. This reverence is expressed in the opening words of the most important creedal affirmation of Christian faith about the relation between the divine and the human in the person of Jesus Christ, an affirmation shared also by most Western Christians, adopted at the Council of Chalcedon in 451: "Following the holy fathers." This formula could serve as the motto for much of what Orthodoxy is and does, for how it prays, what it teaches, and how it lives in the world. Again, while it is probably true that every religious group affirms the authority of tradition—even if it is only the tradition of formally rejecting the authority of all tradition!—Orthodox Christianity is based on a special form of such authority. On the one hand, there is no central figure in the Orthodox hierarchy whose office possesses the right to speak on behalf of the entire Church, as the Bishop of Rome does in the Roman Catholic Church. On the other hand, Orthodoxy does not reject that centralized structure in the name of the Protestant principle (as the seventeenth-century Anglican, William Chillingworth, formulated it) that "the Bible, and the Bible alone, is the religion of Protestants." To Orthodox Christian believers, supreme authority attaches to the Bible only as it has been interpreted by tradition. Specifically, tradition has been set down for all time in the doctrines decreed by the previously mentioned Seven Ecumenical Councils of the Church, which took place between 325 and 787. To be on the same level with the decrees of those councils, a doctrine would have to be in harmony with that tradition and would have to be legislated by a body of comparable authority. The political situation of twentieth-century Orthodoxy, with all of its ancient patriarchates and most of its other major centers in the control of governments hostile to it, has sometimes all but paralyzed its capacity to respond to opportunities or to crises, as well as its ability to formulate "the faith once delivered to the saints" (Jude 3) against the major heresies of the time, such as Marxist dialectical materialism.

It is in the intersection of liturgy and doctrine that one of the most persistent differences between Eastern and Western Christendom appears. To the words of the Nicene Creed, "[We believe] in the Holy Spirit . . . who proceeds from the Father," the West added: "and from the Son," in Latin *ex Patre Filioque.* In one way, this difference may well seem, even to a sympathetic observer, to represent an unwarranted prying into the impenetrable mystery of the inner life of God. Therefore, such an observer might conclude that both sides are wrong if they claim to understand that mystery which is denied to mortals, indeed to all creatures and even to the angels.

At another level, however, this Western addition to the original text of the Creed as shared by all is taken by Orthodox Christians as manifest proof of the tendency of the Western Church to ignore both the authority of ancient tradition and the collegiality of the Church as a whole, with all its bishops, in contradiction also to the explicit statement of Christ in the New Testament (John 15:26): "the Spirit of truth, which proceedeth from the Father."

At yet another level, the two theological theories may be said to involve two distinct ways of affirming (and safeguarding) the oneness of God in the face of the Christian doctrine of the Trinity: either by saying that both the Son of God and the Holy Spirit proceed from the Father, who is thus the single Source of both (the Eastern version); or by saying that the Holy Spirit, in proceeding both from the Father and the Son, unites them in the single Godhead (the Western version). The need to protect the oneness of God against an interpretation of the Trinity as teaching "three Gods" is affirmed by all: the Nicene Creed opens with the formula "We believe in one God" before it goes on to say anything about either the Son or the Holy Spirit.

Another difference of doctrine is considerably less abstract, and it is, as so often in Orthodoxy, expressed more in the language of worship and prayer than in theological speculation. Although both Eastern and Western Christians believe, with all Christians, that the human race was saved through the works performed by Jesus Christ, crucified and risen, there is between East and West a difference of emphasis so profound as to become substantive. In speaking about how Christ saves, the West has used the metaphors of sacrifice (Christ as the Lamb of God, who takes away the sin of the world) and of vicarious atonement (Christ as the one whose sinless death satisfies the violated justice of God over human sin). The Orthodox way of speaking and praying about Christ as Redeemer, while also invoking the biblical concept of sacrifice, emphasizes instead the theme of "Christ as Victor": sin, death, hell, and the devil hold the human race captive, until Christ the Son of God, coming as a human being through the Incarnation, engages them in conflict through his death on the cross and triumphs over them through his Resurrection. "Thou hast," the Liturgy of St. John Chrysostom prays, "trampled down death and overthrown the devil and given life to the world." To attend one of the Easter services in an Orthodox church is to see in action this emphasis on Christ as Victor and to sense its difference from Western ways, a difference that is not an official matter of dogma but that deeply touches the life of Orthodox Christian faith.

Orthodox Church Organization

As is already clear from its definition of doctrinal authority, the conception of church organization in Orthodoxy is also distinctive. Like Roman Catholicism—indeed like ancient Christianity in both East and West until the Protestant Reformation—it affirms a hierarchical structure of deacons, priests, bishops, archbishops, metropolitans, and patriarchs. But that structure is not seen as a pyramid in its design, with one bishop at the apex. Rather, as Bishop Kallistos Ware has phrased it, "the Orthodox Church is a family of self-governing Churches. It is held together, not by a centralized organization, not by a single prelate wielding absolute power over the whole body, but by the double bond of unity in the faith and communion in the sacraments."

Within the family of Orthodox churches, a special position of honor is accorded to the Patriarch of Constantinople, who carries the title of "Ecumenical Patriarch," and a special position is accorded also to the other ancient Patriarchates of Jerusalem, Alexandria, and Antioch; but these are positions of honor rather than of jurisdiction. The clash between the Eastern and the Western churches over the Moravian mission in the ninth century, described earlier, was indeed provoked by the issue of liturgical language; but coming when it did in the already stormy history of relations between Rome and Constantinople, it quickly became an issue also of jurisdiction and authority. The same Council of Chalcedon in 451 whose phrase "Following the holy fathers" has served here as an epitome of the Orthodox view of tradition in matters of doctrine also spoke, in its famous (or infamous) Canon 28, on the question of jurisdiction: "Following in all things the decision of the holy fathers [from the Council of Constantinople in 381] . . . we also enact and decree . . . equal privileges to the most holy throne of New Rome [Constantinople] . . . with the old imperial Rome." Old Rome and its bishops never accepted that canon, despite its having been solemnly legislated by an Ecumenical Council. The gradual development of papal monarchy in the Middle Ages, combined with the loss of all four Eastern Patriarchates to Muslim conquest, helped to bring about the estrangement, separation, schism, and mutual excommunication recounted earlier.

The large Orthodox churches of Greece, Russia, Ukraine, Romania, Serbia, and Bulgaria all have administrative self-rule, as do the smaller churches of Albania, Cyprus, and Poland, and even the tiny Church of Sinai (whose membership may be as small as one hundred). This feature of Orthodox church administration—especially in combination with the emphasis on using the language of the people in the liturgy—has enabled each Orthodox church to develop its own special relation with its national culture and to avoid homogenizing all the Orthodox churches into a single organization.

But that great advantage has been transformed into a distinct disadvantage in the New World, as the catalog of Orthodox denominations in the United States indicates. Orthodox observers themselves have noted, with a rather grim sense of irony, that the flexibility that allows the Orthodox Church of Sinai to have its own local control does not seem to apply to the thriving Orthodoxy of the United States and Canada. Part of the same irony is that, although Orthodoxy for more than a millennium had differentiated itself from Roman Catholicism by worshiping God in the languages of its several peoples rather than in the language of ancient Rome, Orthodox congregations in the Western Hemisphere went on worshiping in the languages of ancient Greece, Syria, or Moravia—and this at a time when, as a result of the "Constitution on the Sacred Liturgy" of the Second Vatican Council (1962–1965), Roman Catholic congregations in America and elsewhere had begun to use English and other vernaculars. In the New World, ancient forms and ancient languages can constitute an obstacle for the generations born in the United States. The jurisdictional question of self-determination and the liturgical question of the language of worship were obviously connected, so that the establishment of the Orthodox Church in America in 1970 out of the former Russian Orthodox Greek Catholic Church of North America entailed also the transition from Old Church Slavonic to English. In the parishes of the Greek Orthodox Archdiocese, moreover, and despite the canonical rupture occasioned by the creation of the Orthodox Church in America, bilingual services have been evolving, though not (or at any rate, not yet) a wholly English liturgy.

The Question of Church and State

Throughout much of the history of Orthodoxy, the question of ecclesiastical jurisdiction has been closely related to the question of church and state. The existence of Constantinople as the capital of a Christian empire, indeed the name itself, testified to the historic importance of the conversion of the emperor Constantine (d. 337). For more than eleven hundred years, the Christian emperor and the Christian church maintained there a relation that was sometimes amicable and sometimes adversarial, but was always close. A similar pattern of coexistence has characterized the Orthodox relation to the state in the Kingdom of Greece and in most of the Orthodox churches in Czarist Russia, the Kingdom of Serbia, and the Kingdom of Bulgaria. But when conquest from without or revolution from within put an end to one or another of these political regimes, this coexistence meant that the national church, too, was in jeopardy. During the many centuries of its dependence on a Christian monarch, Orthodoxy had not developed the patterns of self-government—an independent canon law, an international organization, and a long-range strategy of political activity—that had come to characterize Roman Catholicism. Already in the seventh century, the Patriarchates of Jerusalem, Antioch, and Alexandria had come under Muslim rule; in 1453 Constantinople itself followed, and then Athens in 1503. But the Orthodox pattern of church–state relations and the very way of life and faith identified as Orthodox was to face an even graver threat in the twentieth century.

ORTHODOXY AT THE CLOSE OF THE TWENTIETH CENTURY

A religion whose central features are liturgy, tradition, and dogma and whose organizational structure has tied it closely to the political regime must seem a museum piece to many, especially to activist American Christians, one of whom, Walter Rauschenbusch (1861–1918) identified sacramentalism, asceticism, and dogma (all three of them typically Orthodox) as the three forces that "deflect" Christianity from its primary responsibility for "Christianizing the social order." Therefore, when the Bolshevik Revolution of 1917 declared war on all religion, but in particular on Orthodox Christianity, there were more than a few voices heard who said, in effect, that Russian Orthodoxy was only getting its just reward. Though less shocking than the indifference of American Christians to the events that were to take place in Nazi Germany two decades later, this dismissal of Orthodoxy became standard in American textbooks and sermons. From time to time, as accounts of the terror reached the West, above all in the three volumes of Aleksandr Solzhenitsyn's *Gulag Archipelago, 1918–1956*, readers also received glimpses of the heroism and faith of Orthodox believers, both clergy and laypeople. With the overthrow of communism, however, the picture of those seven decades is becoming clearer. Although there is practically no Orthodox believer alive in Eastern Europe who was baptized before the Bolshevik Revolution, and although the sacramental life and the religious instruction of the Orthodox Church have operated under enormous handicaps even during those times when they were not being subject to overt persecution, Orthodoxy has survived.

Through the patient but stubborn continuity of what Russians sometimes call "the church of the grandmothers," Orthodoxy has demonstrated that it does not need to be sitting in the lap of a friendly "Christian" government to promote the obedience of faith, and that the qualities denounced as "reactionary" by its critics, both Christian and non-Christian, are the ones that can sustain it in a time of troubles and can outlast its persecutors. Meanwhile, the decades of communist oppression have also been responsible for a generation of what are now being called in Russian "neo-martyrs," who showed themselves to be worthy successors of the Three Men in the Fiery Furnace (Daniel 3) and of the Martyrs of the Catacombs. Such revolutionary changes in the Orthodox world, especially in combination with the radically altered ecumenical climate, must have far-reaching effects on American Orthodoxy at the close of the twentieth century.

The new situation in the former Soviet Union presents the Orthodox here with an opportunity similar to that envisioned by Winston Churchill when, speaking on June 4, 1940, he looked to a future in which, "in God's good time, the New World, with all its power and might, steps forth to the rescue and the liberation of the Old." Material relief and spiritual solidarity, books and liturgical needs, exchange students and communications technology—all of these are elements of that new opportunity for American Orthodox. Conversely, the fall of communism has evoked the less than edifying picture of various Western denominations scrambling for Russian and Eastern European proselytes, instead of looking for ways to support and strengthen those who have survived difficult times.

These opportunities would seem to add new urgency to the imperative for American Orthodoxy to put its own house in better order. To quote Paul D. Garrett, "the essential unity of the Orthodox church, in spite of conflicts and paradoxes, is still evolving. But if unity comes and the false accretions finally fall away, it will be in America." And now that Orthodoxy is more free in other countries than it has been for generations, American Orthodoxy faces the prospect of recovering a unity across national boundaries to match the unity across the centuries that has always been one of its most priceless treasures.

STUDY QUESTIONS

1. How do you explain the rich diversity of Orthodox Christianity in America, particularly in light of the various names of the American denominations of Orthodox Christianity?
2. Why does Orthodox Christianity lay claim to being as old as Christianity itself? What connection does Orthodox Christianity have to the New Testament church?
3. According to the author, did the schism take place between Western and Eastern Christianity? What were the causes of the split?
4. What were the reasons for Orthodox Christianity's spread to America? Trace its historical development and growth.
5. What are the characteristics and functions of the following distinctive features of Orthodox Christianity? (a) Orthodox worship; (b) Orthodox tradition; (c) Orthodox doctrine; (d) Orthodox church organization; and (e) Orthodox church and state relations.
6. What differences in practice and doctrine do you see between Orthodox Christianity, Catholicism, and Protestantism?

ESSAY TOPICS

The Schism between East and West
The Religious Art of Orthodox Christianity
Elements of Worship in Orthodox Christianity
Settlement in Alaska: The First Orthodox Christians in America
Emperor Justinian and the Church of Hagia Sophia

WORD EXPLORATION

The following words play significant roles in any discussion of Orthodox Christianity in America and are worth careful reflection and discussion.

Schism	Christotokos	Iconography
Hagia Sophia	Christ as Victor	Theotokos
Orthodoxy	Constantinople	Mass

FOR FURTHER READING
AND REFERENCE

For some of the reasons already pointed out, the number of works in English about Orthodox Christianity has lagged significantly behind those dealing with other major religious traditions in America. Nevertheless, it is possible to go a long way toward acquiring a solid grasp of the issues and developments described here, even if one does not read Greek or Russian.

There are several general introductions to Orthodoxy in English, each of which has a bibliography for deeper and more detailed reference. Among these, Kallistos [Timothy] Ware, *The Orthodox Church* (Harmondsworth: Penguin Books, 1964), is especially useful and accessible. Alexander Schmemann, *The Historical Road of Eastern Orthodoxy*, translated by Lydia W. Kesich (New York: Holt, Rinehart & Winston, 1963), and John Meyendorff, *The Orthodox Church: Its Past and Its Role in the West Today*, 3d ed., translated by John Chapin (Crestwood, N.Y.: Saint Vladimir's Seminary Press, 1981), analyze the problems and opportunities in the light of Orthodox history. John Meyendorff, *Byzantine Theology: Historical Trends and Doctrinal Themes* (New York: Fordham University Press, 1974), and Jaroslav Pelikan, *The Spirit of Eastern Christendom (600–1700)* (Chicago: University of Chicago Press, 1974), which is Volume 2 of the five-volume *The Christian Tradition: A History of the Development of Doctrine*, cover the development of Orthodox thought and teaching in the period of its transition from the history it shares with the West to the emergence of the modern period. For that modern period, the most authoritative treatment in any language is now available in English: Georges Florovsky, *Ways of Russian Theology*, translated by Robert L. Nichols, Volumes 5 and 6 of his *Collected Works* (Belmont, Mass.: Nordland Books, 1979–1987). Florovsky discusses all the major thinkers, placing them into the context of Russian intellectual, literary, and religious history. The pages of *The Greek Orthodox Theological Review* and *Saint Vladimir's Quarterly* are an ongoing documentation of American Orthodoxy as it works to define itself.

The best brief introduction to the history of Orthodoxy in America is the succinct but substantial essay by Paul D. Garrett, "Eastern Christianity," in *Encyclopedia of the American Religious Experience*, edited by Charles H. Lippy and Peter W. Williams (New York: Charles Scribner's Sons, 1988), 1:325–344. Garrett has also written *Saint Innocent, Apostle to America* (Crestwood, N.Y.: Saint Vladimir's Seminary Press, 1979). The broader context of the work of St. Innocent is outlined in Gregory Afonsky, *A History of the Orthodox Church in Alaska (1794–1917)* (Kodiak, Alaska: Saint Herman's Theological Seminary, 1977). Constance J. Tarasar and John H. Erickson have edited *Orthodox America, 1794–1976: Development of the Orthodox Church in America* (Syosset, N.Y.: Orthodox Church in America, 1975). The cultural, literary, and religious significance of the Russian emigration after the Bolshevik Revolution is described by Nicholas Zernov, *The Russian Religious Renaissance of the Twentieth Century* (New York: Harper & Row, 1963).

There are histories of most of the major and minor Orthodox groups on American soil. George Papaioannou, *From Mars Hill to Manhattan: The Greek Orthodox in America under Athenagoras I* (Minneapolis: Light and Life, 1976), concentrates on the experience of the Greek immigrant community. Gerald J. Bobango, *The Romanian Orthodox Episcopate of America* (Jackson, Mich.: Romanian-American Heritage Center, 1979), is an introduction to one of the lesser-known groups. Jaroslav Pelikan, *Confessor between East and West: A Portrait of Ukrainian Cardinal Josyf Slipyj* (Grand Rapids: Wm. B. Eerdmans, 1990), is a portrait of the largest group of Eastern Rite Catholics in America. The essays in Volumes 8 and 9 of the *Collected Works* of Georges Florovsky (see above), *Ecumenism: A Doctrinal Approach* and *Ecumenism: A Historical Approach,* both published in 1989, benefit from the author's personal experience as the leading Orthodox participant in the ecumenical movement and from his scholarship on all periods of Orthodox history. His thought and work have been treated with great sympathy and understanding in a monograph-length article by George Huntston Williams, "Georges Vasilievich Florovsky: His American Career," *Greek Orthodox Theological Review* 11 (1965):7–107.

7

JACOB NEUSNER

Judaism in the World
and in America

I grew up three things: (1) a boy in West Hartford, Connecticut, and therefore a New Englander; (2) a native-born American, son and grandson of native-born Americans, and therefore very patriotic; and (3) a Reform Jew. The toughest moment of my young life, therefore, came when I discovered that the Pilgrim Fathers about whom we studied in third grade—founders of the first three towns of Connecticut, Hartford, Windsor, and Wethersfield—weren't Jewish; they attended a church, which wasn't the same thing as our Temple on Farmington Avenue (which I thought the most beautiful building in the world, where surely God lived), and didn't even take Hebrew class when they went to Sunday school the way I did. But I got used to the idea that I was different from other kids in some ways; I remained a proud New Englander—America was the only country I could imagine—and I made my peace with the fact that the Congregationalists who founded Connecticut had ample place for me too. I decided I liked things as they are, and me as I was—and am.

American Jews make their peace with lots of things; they are different in religion but the same as other people in most other ways of life. They are Jewish, but not so Jewish that they can't be as American as everybody else. In a country with a Christian majority, where the celebrations of Christianity divide the year, American Jews respect their neighbors and enjoy their good will as well. The secret of the Jews in America and Canada is that, although they are different, they love being exactly what they are.

You probably have Jewish neighbors and friends. In the United States nearly six million Jews (more than half of all the Jews in the entire world) live in all fifty states, adding up to 2.5 percent of the American people. Close to half of the Jewish population is found in the Northeast, with large populations in the South and the Far West as well. Wherever you live in this country, you are likely to know Jews and realize that Judaism is widely practiced.

Most American Jews live pretty much the way other Americans do. It is estimated that, because of intermarriage between Jews and non-Jews, 8.2 million Americans live in households in which there is at least one Jewish member. Recent studies have shown that 28 percent of married Jews are wed to non-Jews (called "gentiles"), and another 4 percent are married to converts to Judaism. A very high proportion (88 percent of Jews surveyed) said that they would accept the marriage of their child to a non-Jew. About 72 percent of Jews live in homes that are entirely made up of Jews, and about 28 percent in mixed households.

Jews come in all shapes, sizes, and colors, so just by looking at a person you cannot tell whether or not he or she is Jewish. Jews do not form a single racial group or ethnic group. There are black Jews—Sammy Davis, Jr., and Whoopi Goldberg among the more popularly known—and black Jews generally find a welcome in synagogues. (The State of Israel recognized as authentic Jews the dark-skinned "house of Israel" of Ethiopia and undertook heroic efforts to save nearly the entire community from massacre during the wars there.) There are blond Jews and brown-haired Jews, rural Jews and urban Jews, rich Jews and poor Jews. American Jews live in most localities and are found in all social and economic groupings.

It is not easy to tell a Jew from a gentile, except in one important way: most Jews believe in one religion—Judaism. Of the nearly six million Jews in the United States, about three-quarters, or about 4.5 million, define being Jewish as a matter of religion. So while Judaism is not the religion of a single people, the Jews are a people with a single religion. But you should not take for granted that because someone you know is Jewish, that person practices Judaism. There are also many Judaisms in North America, just as there are many Christianities, and the differences between Reform, Orthodox, Reconstructionist, and Conservative Judaisms are as real as the ones that separate the Catholic from the Protestant, or the Latter-day Saint or Mormon from a member of the Unification Church.

And clearly, there are many Jews who do not identify "being Jewish" with "being religious" or practicing a Judaism. Jews form a set of ethnic groups, and those Jews who practice a Judaism form a religious group. But if you practice Judaism the religion, you automatically have a place among the Jews, an ethnic group. So Judaism is the religion of one people, although not all Jews belong to one and the same religion, Judaism, or to any religion at all.

Most Christians know three things about Judaism. First, it is the religion of the Old Testament. Second, it is the religion into which Jesus Christ was born, in which he lived, and which he practiced to the day of his death. Third, Jews do not "accept" Jesus, meaning they are not Christians. These three statements are true, but they are only part of the story. Left out of the picture of Judaism is most of what Jews believe, since the prevailing portrait is negative—they don't believe this, they don't do that—and misses what makes Judaism a living religion for millions of Americans.

The three things that make Judaism a living religion are represented in the words *God, Torah,* and *Israel.* These are the native categories of Judaism. To put it differently, the name, in Judaism, for the religion of Judaism is "the Torah." "The Torah" is given by God to "Israel," which is not the contemporary State of Israel but the Israel that is holy and loved by God. Israel is made holy by the Torah and defined by the Torah. Clearly, just as there are Jews who are ethnic and Jews who are ethnic and also religious, so the word "Israel" stands for both a worldly, political fact, and also for the children of Abraham, Isaac, and Jacob, to whom God through Moses gave the Torah: a holy people, comparable to the Church as "the mystical body of Christ." This problem of understanding the ambiguity of the word "Israel"—which refers to several things, not some one thing—will be discussed in a moment.

GOD, TORAH, AND ISRAEL

The God of Judaism is the one and only God, who created heaven and earth, who governs our lives with mercy and justice, and who revealed the Torah to Moses at Mount Sinai.

The "Torah"—a Hebrew word taken to mean "revelation"—of Judaism is God's will and word to humanity. The Torah includes the Ten Commandments (Exodus 20) as well as many other commandments that God has given to Israel, the holy people.

God's word comes to "Israel." Who, and what, is this "Israel"? In Judaism, "Israel" is defined as the children of Abraham, Isaac, and Jacob, who assembled before Mount Sinai to receive the Torah from God, and their descendants through all time, including all of those, anytime and anywhere, who join them at Sinai by accepting the Torah. The word

"Israel" also refers to a particular land, which in Judaism is called "the land of Israel," and which today corresponds to the State of Israel, created in 1948. The "Israelites" of the ancient Hebrew Scriptures or Old Testament bear two other names, Hebrews and Jews. Hebrews take their name from the Hebrew language; Jews are the descendants of that part of ancient Israel that survived the destruction of the Northern Kingdom of ancient Israel in 722 B.C.E. In general, "Israelites," "Hebrews," and "Jews" may be used interchangeably, but in this country most are comfortable with the designation "Jews." The citizens of the present-day State of Israel are called "Israelis," to keep them distinct from the ancient Israelites of Old Testament times.

As a living religion—not merely a naysayer to some other religion—Judaism thrives in American homes and synagogues. The first American synagogue was built in New York City in 1654, when Jews fleeing from Brazil and the Spanish Inquisition reached American shores. In our own day, Judaism also draws Jews from home and synagogue to pilgrimages to distant lands as well. Judaism makes life meaningful for millions of Americans.

WHERE JUDAISM LIVES:
HOME, SYNAGOGUE, PILGRIMAGE

To understand the religion of Jewish Americans, you have to go to the home and the synagogue, and you also have to travel with Jews to distant places, because that is where Judaism lives: at home, in the synagogue, and on pilgrimages.

Home

Some of the most important moments in the life of Judaism take place in the home. In the United States and Canada nearly all Jews celebrate a festival meal at Passover. At the festival of Passover, which coincides with the first full moon after the vernal equinox, Jewish families gather around their tables for a holy meal. At this meal Jews, seeing themselves as the contemporary "Israel" of whom the Scripture speaks, retell the story of the exodus from Egypt in times long past. With unleavened bread and sanctified wine, they celebrate the liberation of slaves from Pharaoh's bondage. What is important is that Jews don't merely recount an event from their ancestors' remote history. They see themselves today as personally freed by God from the slavery of Egypt:

For ever after, in every generation, *every Israelite must think of himself or herself as having gone forth from Egypt* [italics added] ... We were slaves of Pharaoh in Egypt and the Lord our God brought us forth from there with a mighty hand and an outstretched arm. And if the Holy One, blessed be he, had not brought our fathers forth from Egypt, then we and our descendants would still be slaves to Pharaoh in Egypt. And so, even if all of us were full of wisdom, understanding, sages and well informed in the Torah, we should still be obligated to repeat again the story of the exodus from Egypt.

Another passage of the Passover liturgy says:

This is the promise which has stood by our forefathers and stands by us. For neither once, nor twice, nor three times was our destruction planned; in every generation they rise against us, and in every generation God delivers us from their hands into freedom, out of anguish into joy, out of mourning into festivity, out of darkness into light, out of bondage into redemption.

This sense of being "Israel" in the here and now, the representatives in today's America of the Israel to whom God spoke at Sinai, is made explicit:

For ever after, in every generation, *every Israelite must think of himself or herself as having gone forth from Egypt* [italics added]. For we read in the Torah: "In that day thou shalt teach thy child, saying: All this is because of what God did for me when I went forth from Egypt." It was not only our forefathers that the Holy One, blessed be He, redeemed; us too, the living, He redeemed together with them.

Why does Passover mean so much to American Jews? The Jews are a minority, small in numbers. They are different, and difference can be difficult to take. To be different—whatever the difference—requires explanation; it may provoke resentment or create tension demanding resolution and pain requiring remission. Treating difference as destiny, Passover celebrates the family of Israel and is celebrated by the families of Israel.

The Passover rite is not the only occasion on which your Jewish friends and neighbors turn their homes into holy places. The rite of circumcision—in Hebrew, *berit milah*—commonly takes place in the home. This covenant of circumcision involves the surgical removal of the foreskin of the penis of male Jews eight days after birth in commemoration of the covenant made by Abraham with God. The marriage rite happens as often at home as in a synagogue. The festival of Tabernacles—in Hebrew, *Sukkot*—commemorating the first full moon after the autumnal equinox, is celebrated at home by building a temporary shelter covered with leafy boughs, under the stars, and eating meals there. The December festival of dedication—in Hebrew, *Hanukkah*, the feast of lights—in remembrance of the salvation of Israel in the time of the Maccabees in the second century B.C.E. when pagans tried to destroy Judaism, takes place through the lighting of candles in the home.

There are dietary laws, observed by some Jews at home, fewer of them outside of the home, involving the food laws given in the book of Leviticus (not eating pork, shellfish, and eating only meat that has been humanely slaughtered). These laws identify food that is *kosher*, or fit and suitable for Jews. Keeping these laws is another way in which the home is made into a holy place, where God is worshiped and where God's will, in the Torah, governs.

Synagogue

The synagogue (or temple) is the other location in which Judaism takes place. Synagogue buildings in the United States take many forms, from New England colonial, as in Worcester, Massachusetts; to Moorish, as in San Francisco; to Gothic, as in the Temple Emanu-El in New York City. But if you walk into any synagogue in the world, the first thing you will see is the holy ark, in which the scrolls of the Torah are kept. That fact tells you how the place of worship is made holy: through the public reading of the scrolls of the Torah, which takes place on the Sabbath, the day of rest (Saturday), and (in abbreviated form) Monday and Thursday as well. In an Orthodox, Conservative, or Reconstructionist synagogue you will notice that men and boys cover their heads with a skullcap, called in Hebrew a *kippah*, and in Yiddish a *yarmulke*. This covering of the head is a sign of humility and respect in worship. Many Orthodox males keep their heads covered at all times.

The synagogue in any American town or city is a place of study of the Torah, a place of prayer in community, and a place of gathering. Study of the Torah translates into "Jewish education." Most synagogues maintain schools for young people that meet on Sunday morning and several afternoons a week as well; many also maintain ambitious adult education programs. All synagogues conduct Sabbath and festival prayer, and many have daily worship too. All synagogues bring people together for occasions of meeting and renewal. Israel, the Jewish people, form a strong community; Jews enjoy one another's company and share concerns, commitments, and responsibilities. Associating with other Jews forms an important part not only of the life of the Jews as an ethnic community, but also of the expression of their religion. (In contemporary European

Judaism, that is the main function of the synagogue. In the United States there are Jewish community centers, in addition to synagogues, which brings together all elements of the Jewish community, whether religious or secular.)

The synagogue fills to capacity during the New Year (in Hebrew, *Rosh Hashanah*) and the Day of Atonement (in Hebrew, *Yom Hakippurim*), a period of ten days in the autumn that marks the beginning of the holy season three weeks prior to the autumnal equinox. The holy season comes to a climax in the Festival of Tabernacles. During this season, the community assembles for rites that are, in fact, intensely personal and private. The New Year and Day of Atonement define a penitential season, a time of stocktaking, when, in the language of the faith, God judges each person and decides on the future of us all. The prayers that are said speak of what happens to me, but use the language of "we" and "us" and speak about the entire holy people, Israel, which stands before God for judgment.

The prayers recited in the synagogue define the individual and holy Israel together; a pilgrim people, seeking to worship the God of all humanity. On the New Year, which is called "the birthday of the world," God asserts sovereignty, as in the New Year Prayer:

> Our God and God of our Fathers, Rule over the whole world in Your honor . . . and appear in Your glorious might to all those who dwell in the civilization of Your world, so that everything made will know that You made it, and every creature discern that You have created him, so that all in whose nostrils is breath may say, "The Lord, the God of Israel is king, and His kingdom extends over all."

Since people have been told what God requires of them, they are judged:

> On this day sentence is passed upon countries, which to the sword and which to peace, which to famine and which to plenty, and each creature is judged today for life or death. Who is not judged on this day? For the remembrance of every creature comes before You, each man's deeds and destiny, words and way.

The liturgy creates a dramatic moment. These are strong words for people to hear. As life unfolds and people grow reflective, the Days of Awe seize the imagination: I live, I die, sooner or later it comes to all. The call for inner contemplation implicit in the mythic words elicits deep response.

We see that Judaism, a religion of one holy people, presents a vision of all humanity; it is not particular but universal in its concerns. It also is very personal, dealing with sin, atonement, and reconciliation. The most popularly practiced public rite of Judaism is the rite of atonement, which takes place in the autumn and occupies what are called in this country "the High Holy Days" and in Judaism, "the Days of Awe." The most personal, solemn, and moving of the Days of Awe is the Day of Atonement, *Yom Kippur*, the Sabbath of Sabbaths. It is marked by fasting and continuous prayer. On it, the Jew makes confession:

> Our God and God of our fathers, may our prayer come before You. Do not hide yourself from our supplication, for we are not so arrogant or stiff-necked as to say before You. . . . We are righteous and have not sinned. But we have sinned.
>
> We are guilt laden, we have been faithless, we have robbed. . . .
>
> We have committed iniquity, caused unrighteousness, have been presumptuous. . . .
>
> We have counseled evil, scoffed, revolted, blasphemed.

The Hebrew confession is built upon an alphabetical acrostic, as if by making certain every letter is represented, God, who knows human secrets, will combine them into appropriate words. The very alphabet bears witness against us before God. Then:

> What shall we say before You who dwell on high? What shall we tell You who live in heaven? Do You not know all things, both the hidden and the revealed? You know the secrets of eternity, the most hidden mysteries of life. You search the innermost recesses, testing men's feelings and heart. Nothing is concealed from You or hidden from Your eyes. May it therefore be Your will to forgive us our sins, to pardon us for our iniquities, to grant remission for our transgressions.

A further list of sins follows, again with a line beginning with each letter of the alphabet. Prayers to be spoken by the congregation are all in the plural: "For the sin which we have sinned against You with the utterance of the lips. . . . For the sin which we have sinned before You openly and secretly. . . ." The community takes upon itself responsibility for what is done in it. All Israel is part of one community, one body, and all are responsible for the acts of each. The sins confessed are mostly against society, against other people; few pertain to ritual laws. At the end comes a final word:

> O my God, before I was formed, I was nothing. Not that I have been formed, it is as though I had not been formed, for I am dust in my life, more so after death. Behold I am before You like a vessel filled with shame and confusion. May it be Your will . . . that I may no more sin, and forgive the sins I have already committed in Your abundant compassion.

While much of the liturgy speaks of "we," the individual focus dominates throughout. The Days of Awe speak to the heart of the individual, telling a story of judgment and atonement. So the individual Jew stands before God; possessing no merits, yet hopeful of God's love and compassion. The power of the Days of Awe derives from the sentiments and emotions aroused by the theme of those days: What is happening to me? Where am I going?

Answers to these questions come not only from the synagogue, but also from the home. But just as the home forms a principal setting in which the public life of Judaism takes place, so the synagogue makes ample place for events in personal life. The most important is the celebration of the maturing of young women and men. At the advent of puberty the community, along with the family, celebrates the young person's becoming responsible, specifically, for keeping the Torah, in Hebrew, *bar mitzvah* (for males) or *bat mitzvah* (for females); *mitzvah* means one who is responsible to carry out religious duties. The religious rite is simple. At any synagogue service, when the Torah is read aloud to the community, various persons are called to say a blessing before each reading. On the occasion on which a young person reaches the age of religious responsibility, that person is called to the Torah and says the blessing. In addition, the bar or bat mitzvah will also be given the honor of reciting the *haftarah*, which is a passage from the Prophets (the Old Testament books of Joshua, Judges, Samuel, Kings, Isaiah, Jeremiah, Ezekiel, or the Twelve Minor Prophets). Family assembles from far and wide, and, in North America, chances are many Christian and other gentile friends of the young person and family will participate in the celebration.

Pilgrimage

A journey undertaken for religious reasons, to a holy place, or a place rich in memory, is called a *pilgrimage*. In ancient times, Judaism called upon people to leave their homes and come to the holy Temple in Jerusalem, where animal sacrifices were prepared, as set forth in the Torah in the books of Leviticus and Numbers; the fat was burned on the altar, and the meat was eaten by the pilgrim. Three times a year, on Passover, Pentecost (in Hebrew, *Shavuot*, held fifty days after Passover to commemorate the revelation of the Torah to Moses at Mount Sinai fifty days after the exodus from Egypt), and Tabernacles, people would leave their villages and make the trip to Jerusalem, a vast assembly of holy Israel in its holiest place. The Temple was destroyed in 70 C.E. by the Romans, who then controlled the Land of Israel (later on called "Palestine") and suppressed a Jewish rebellion against their rule. The destruction of the Temple brought an end to animal sacrifice as a form of worship in Judaism. It also canceled the possibility of pilgrimage. Three generations later, in 135, in subduing a second war against their rule of the Land of Israel, the Romans even prohibited Jews from entering Jerusalem, their holy city.

Events in our own century have once more made pilgrimage into a major expression of Judaism. The most important was the reestablishment of the Jewish state in the Land of Israel in 1948. This was the work of Zionism, a political movement begun in 1897 to bring all Jews who needed a home and a refuge together in the ancient Land of Israel and there to found the State of Israel. In half a century Zionism succeeded in its goals. But between 1948 and 1967, Jerusalem was divided between the State of Israel and Jordan, with the Judaic holy places in Jordanian hands. At the end of the Six Day War, when the Arab countries surrounding the State of Israel tried to destroy the Jewish state, the Israelis retook the eastern sector of Jerusalem from the Jordanians and reopened the holy places of Judaism (as well as of Christianity and Islam) to everybody. From that time onward, the western wall of the ancient Temple of Jerusalem, which had survived the destruction in 70, became the principal center of pilgrimage for Jews throughout the world. Many American Jews have made the pilgrimage to the wall, and most American Jews take a deep interest in the welfare of the State of Israel and its people. That concern, political as much as ethnic and religious, persuades American Jews to accept their share of responsibility for sustaining the State of Israel as the refuge for all Jews who need a home.

For some Jews in recent times the pilgrimage to Jerusalem takes a detour through Poland and other places in Central and Eastern Europe. To understand the route you have to remember that the State of Israel came into being because of the Holocaust, the systematic, well-organized, and efficient murder of millions of Jews in Europe as part of Germany's war effort in World War II, particularly from 1941 through 1945. In the recent past, therefore, one form of the expression of Judaism has called people to visit sites at which Jews were murdered. The Germans built death factories, in which thousands of people were gassed and their bodies then cremated, day after day, so people—including many Germans today, who have sincerely repented the crimes of World War II—come to pray, remember, and cry. From Auschwitz, near Cracow, in Poland, where millions of Jews died only because they were "Israel," the holy people, the pilgrims' path ascends to Jerusalem.

Many American Jews are descendants of those who came in the mass migration between 1880 and 1920 from the lands of Eastern Europe, Poland, Russia, White Russia, Ukraine, Hungary, Bohemia, Moravia, and Slovakia, as well as Germany. When the immigrants came to America, many changed their names in order to cut ties to the past and start anew. As a result, many American Jewish families cannot even name the victims of the Holocaust to whom they were personally related. But all identify with the experience of Holocaust and the heroism of emerging from death camps to found a state; that is why the age of pilgrimage opens roads that lead from Cracow to Jerusalem.

So much for the life of Judaism in the world today. Now to define the faith in its classical and normative writings: the Torah.

DEFINING JUDAISM:
WHAT IS THE TORAH?

You now know that Judaism is the account of the way of life and the worldview set forth by (1) God in (2) the Torah given to Moses at Mount Sinai to (3) Israel, the holy people. So you may define "Judaism" as God's will conveyed in the Torah to Israel. From the viewpoint of Judaism, when the Torah is properly explained, people who practice Judaism, who are called "Israel," therefore know what God has to say to them and wants them to do. If you look in the Old Testament or in other holy books of Judaism, however, you will not find the word *Judaism*. When the faithful wish to refer to the faith, they use the word *Torah*. Torah refers to God's revelation to the holy people, Israel, through Moses at Mount Sinai, which is described in the Old Testament book of Exodus. Judaism teaches that this revelation of the Torah at Mount Sinai was in two forms, one written and one oral.

The Written Torah

Included in the Torah is, to begin with, the Pentateuch or the Five Books of Moses: Genesis, Exodus, Leviticus, Numbers, and Deuteronomy. In addition, the written Torah comprises two other parts: the Prophets (listed earlier) and the Writings, which are Psalms, Proverbs, Job, Song of Songs, Lamentations, Qohelet ("Ecclesiastes" in the Christian Old Testament), Ruth, Esther, Daniel, Ezra, Nehemiah, and Chronicles.

The Oral Torah

Judaism maintains that the Torah was given ("revealed") by God not only in the written form—that is, in what the Christian world now knows as the Old Testament—but also in oral form. The oral tradition was handed on from master to disciple, from Moses to Joshua, and onward to the sages who flourished for centuries to come. The Torah therefore stands for an enduring revelation by God to Israel, the holy people who stood at Sinai. When the scroll of the Torah—the Five Books of Moses—is read in worship services, a blessing prior to the reading says, "Blessed are you, Lord, our God, ruler of the world, who has chosen us from among all peoples and has given us the Torah. Blessed are you, Lord, who *gives* the Torah."

The story of the oral Torah is contained in a few words of a document called the *Sayings of the Founders* (in Hebrew, *Pirqé Avot*), a writing of about 250 C.E. read in the synagogue, chapter by chapter, as a principal part of Torah study. *Avot* 1:1–2 tells us,

> Moses received Torah at Sinai and handed it on to Joshua, Joshua to the elders, and the elders to the prophets. And the prophets handed it on to the men of the great assembly. They said three things: "Be prudent in judgment. Raise up many disciples. Make a fence for the Torah." Simeon the Righteous was one of the last survivors of the great assembly. He would say: "On three things does the world stand: On the Torah, and on the Temple service, and on deeds of loving kindness."

This statement is striking for three reasons. First it claims that there is a tradition from God's revelation to Moses at Sinai that continues beyond the figures we know in the Holy Scriptures of ancient Israel ("the Old Testament"), specifically, Joshua and the Prophets. The "men of the great assembly" and Simeon the Righteous stand in the chain of tradition from Sinai, but they are not figures out of the Old Testament. It follows that there is another part of the Torah that is orally formulated and orally transmitted. The second claim is that this other Torah comes down through the relationship of master to disciple, who then becomes a master. The third striking fact is that what is stated is not a citation of Scripture but a saying that stands on its own. Simeon's saying is part of that Torah from Sinai, for example, but it does not refer to or quote Scripture.

Certainly the single most important figure in the chain of tradition from Sinai onward is Hillel, a sage who flourished at about the same time as Jesus, and to whom is attributed a statement strikingly like the Golden Rule: "What is hateful to yourself, do not do to anybody else. That is the whole of the Torah. All the rest is commentary. Now go learn." Both the teaching of Hillel and that of Jesus in the Golden Rule—"Do unto others as you would have them do unto you"—state in other language the commandment of the Torah at Leviticus 19:18: "You shall love your neighbor as yourself," and many great sages of Judaism have maintained that that statement summarizes the whole of Judaism. A further statement in Hillel's name (*Avot* 1:13) forms the foundation of the morality of Judaism:

> If I am not for myself, who is for me? And when I am for myself, what am I? And if not now, when?

The collection of sayings gathered in the *Sayings of the Founders* appears now as part of the most important holy book of Judaism after the written Torah, the Mishnah, a philosophical law code written down about 200 C.E.

Scripture, which Judaism calls the written Torah, and the Mishnah, which Judaism knows as the first document of the oral Torah, received extensive commentaries. Books of the written Torah, such as Genesis, Exodus, Leviticus, Numbers, and Deuteronomy, were given extensive commentaries, called in Hebrew *midrash* (plural: *midrashim*). The Mishnah too was given its extensive commentary, called in Hebrew a *talmud* (plural: *talmudim*). There are two *talmudim*, the Talmud of the Land of Israel (ca. 400 C.E.) and the Talmud of Babylonia (ca. 600). The fact that the written Torah and the Mishnah are treated in precisely the same way— that is, are read in a close and careful manner so as to discover their meaning for the world today—proves that the Mishnah enjoyed a unique position as part of the Torah. The two *talmudim* then provided an authoritative explanation of what the oral part of the Torah meant and how it was to be observed.

To sample the kind of religious writing we find in the Mishnah, let's consider the single most important statement of that book. What makes this statement important is that it defines who is, and who is not, "Israel"—that is, who does or does not gain "a portion in the world to come," meaning the resurrection of the dead and eternal life beyond the grave. Judaism has its dogmas, for example, that God is one and that God gave the Torah. Here is how "Israel" is defined, together with some of its key dogmas:

Mishnah-tractate Sanhedrin 11:1–2

A. All Israelites have a share in the world to come,

B. as it is said, "your people also shall be all righteous, they shall inherit the land forever; the branch of my planting, the work of my hands, that I may be glorified" (Is. 60:21).

C. And these are the ones who have no portion in the world to come:

D. He who says, the resurrection of the dead is a teaching which does not derive from the Torah, and the Torah does not come from Heaven; and an Epicurean.

Here is the rule of the Mishnah that defines who is, and who is not, a Jew, that is, "Israel, the holy people." It does so by explaining who belongs and who does not: "All Israel" will not die but will rise from the dead at the end of days; then those who do not "have a portion in the world to come" will not be part of Israel in the resurrection. Excluded are those who deny the resurrection of the dead, or deny that the Torah teaches that the dead will live, those who deny that the Torah was given by God ("does not come from Heaven"); and those who deny the principles of the faith ("an Epicurean").

The notions of "the world to come" and "the resurrection of the dead" clearly refer to the end of time; the Torah teaches that in the end of days, God will rule over all humanity, and life as we know it will be succeeded by eternal life. The belief that Jesus Christ was raised from the dead corresponds to this conviction and was taken by his followers to indicate that the end of days was at hand and the rule of God ("the Kingdom") beginning. This passage asserts that every Israelite has a share in the world to come, meaning that each will rise from the dead and live forever in the Holy Land.

The Babylonian Talmud to this passage begins with two questions in mind: Is the rule of the Mishnah fair? How, on the basis of the written Torah, do we know the fact taken for granted by the oral Torah, namely, that the resurrection of the dead will take place and that the Torah itself says so? First comes the justification of God's way:

Babylonian Talmud Tractate Sanhedrin
Folio Pages 90A–B

I.

A. [With reference to the Mishnah's statement, *And these are the ones who have no portion in the world to come:*] Why all this [that is, why deny the world to come to those listed]?

B. On Tannaite authority [it was stated], "Such a one denied the resurrection of the dead, therefore he will not have a portion in the resurrection of the dead.

C. "For all the measures [meted out by] the Holy One, blessed be he, are in accord with the principle of measure for measure."

What someone denies shall be denied to that person; hence, it is only fair that someone who does not believe in the resurrection will not live when the dead are raised up. But where in Scripture do we find that fact? The Talmud proceeds to many pages of proofs, among which the following provide a taste of the discussion:

IV.

A. It has been taught on Tannaite authority:

B. R. Simai says, "How on the basis of the Torah do we know about the resurrection of the dead?

C. "As it is said, 'And I also have established my covenant with [the patriarchs] to give them the land of Canaan' (Ex. 6:4).

D. " 'With you' is not stated, but rather, 'with *them*,' indicating on the basis of the Torah that there is the resurrection of the dead."

V.

A. *Minim* [believers, sectarians, sometimes identified as Jews who believed in Jesus as the Messiah, hence, Christian Jews] asked Rabban Gamaliel, "How do we know that the Holy One, blessed be he, will resurrect the dead?"

B. He said to them, "It is proved from the Torah, from the Prophets, and from the Writings." But they did not accept his proofs.

C. He said to them, "From the Torah: for it is written, 'And the Lord said to Moses, Behold, you shall sleep with your fathers and rise up' (Deut. 31:16)."

D. They said to him, "But perhaps the sense of the passage is, 'And *the people* will rise up' (Deut. 31:16)?"

E. He said to them, "From the Prophets: as it is written, 'Thy dead men shall live, together with my dead body they shall arise. Awake and sing, you that live in the dust, for your dew is as the dew of herbs, and the earth shall cast out its dead' (Is. 26:19)."

F. They said to him, "But perhaps that refers to the dead whom Ezekiel raised up."

G. He said to them, "From the Writings, as it is written, 'And the roof of your mouth, like the best wine of my beloved, that goes down sweetly, causing the lips of those who are asleep to speak' (Song 7:9)." ...

L. [The *minim* would not concur in Gamaliel's view] until he cited for them the following verse: " 'Which the Lord swore to your fathers to give to them' (Deut. 11:21)—to *them* and not to you, so proving from the Torah that the dead will live."

We see how the Talmud of Babylonia has faithfully expounded the Mishnah's teaching, so forming an expansion and explanation of the oral Torah's claim. What it tries to do in particular is explain the faith, and its particular point is to show that the teachings of the oral part of the Torah—for example, about the resurrection of the dead—derive from and are validated by the written part of the Torah. That is why so many verses of Scripture, the written part of the Torah, are cited in this passage.

We see that Judaism sets forth a number of theological dogmas of fundamental importance. The first concerns the belief that the Torah is revealed by God ("comes from heaven"), that there is the world to come, and that the resurrection of the dead will take place at the end of time. Another concerns the unity of God. A third maintains that God is made manifest in the Torah. A fourth is that God wants humanity's love ("You will love the Lord your God with all your heart"), and a fifth is that Israel, the holy people, is made holy by various religious obligations, or commandments, that God has assigned to them. Living the holy life in this world will lead in time to the advent of the Messiah, the end of days, and the resurrection of the dead. These theological dogmas, set forth in the Mishnah and the Talmud, come to expression in the prayers that are recited in the synagogue as much as in the documents of the Torah that are studied in the schoolhouse. They define Judaism.

JUDAISM IN AMERICA
OR AMERICAN JUDAISM?
SEGREGATION AND INTEGRATION

If you asked your Jewish friend or neighbor, Do you believe in the resurrection of the dead? chances are that the answer will be negative. For what the books say and what the people actually believe are two different things. Just by reading the books of the Torah, you cannot describe Judaism as it flourishes in North America, even though Jews refer to those holy books and revere them. Religions don't live in books but in the lives of people working together, so if you want to describe a religion, you can't just find out "what Judaism believes," but have to ask, "What do people do, because they practice Judaism?"

If you know Jews, you probably realize that different families observe Judaism in different ways. Chances are that in your community there are Conservative synagogues and Reform temples, and there may be an Orthodox *shul* as well. All three words refer to the same thing, a building where people gather for prayer, study, and fellowship. But each word speaks of a different kind of Judaism. In fact, there is no single, uniform Judaism here or anywhere else in the world. Like Islam and Christianity, Judaism comes to everyday expression in more than one way. Just as we know about Roman Catholic and Protestant and Orthodox Christianity or Sunni and Shiite Islam, so we recognize that there are Reform, Conservative, Reconstructionist, and Orthodox forms of Judaism, and within Orthodox Judaism there are many subdivisions as well. To make sense of them all, you have to start with a single question, which every Judaism answers. When we know the answers, we can make sense of the differences.

Segregationist and Integrationist Judaisms

The question that allows us to sort out different Judaisms is, Should Jews live not only among gentiles, but also with them, or should Jews live all by themselves? The Jews who believe that they should be fundamentally different from everyone else segregate themselves in as many ways as they can. Those who believe that Jews should be fundamentally like everybody else, except for some specific, religious differences, integrate themselves.

For many centuries Jews believed that they should live entirely in their own framework, in line with the prophecy of the gentile prophet, Balaam, "For from the top of the mountains I see him, from the hills I behold him; lo, a people dwelling alone, and not reckoning itself among the nations" (Num. 23:9). Living throughout Europe, North Africa, and the Middle East, speaking the languages of the countries where they dwelled, most Jews preferred a segregated existence. Long before Christian Europe imprisoned Jews in ghettos, where they were required by law to live, Jews preferred to live in Jewish streets or neighborhoods, near synagogues for example, since traveling long distances on the Sabbath is forbidden. In 1787, the American Constitution accorded to all white males full rights of citizenship; in 1789, the French revolution proclaimed the same. Jews then had to decide whether or not they wished not only to live among gentiles, but also with them as part of a nation other than holy Israel, God's people.

Segregationist Judaisms

From that time to the present, some Jews have freely chosen to live a life that, in most ways, separates them from everybody else. They choose to speak a Jewish language, in the United States preferring Yiddish, a language based on medieval German with many Hebrew, Polish, and Russian words in it spoken only by Jews. Their sense of the holiness of

Israel required them to wear clothes that were distinctively Jewish; to eat only food that was kosher in a very strict sense, and hence not to eat at a gentile's table under any circumstances; to live in mostly Jewish neighborhoods; to study only the sacred books of Judaism; to buy goods and services only from other Jews; and, in general, to live that wholly segregated life that much of Israel, the Jewish people, had lived for many centuries. In the world today, such Jews are numerous in most of the largest cities of the United States and Canada—New York City (especially Brooklyn) and Montreal, for instance—some major cities in Europe (Antwerp is one), and in the State of Israel (Jerusalem and Bené Beraq, for instance, as well as in neighborhoods of every Israeli city).

All segregationist Judaisms are Orthodox in their fundamental affirmations, but not all Orthodox Judaisms are segregationist. What makes a Judaism Orthodox is the belief in the literal truth of the Torah, written and oral, and the commitment to practice the requirements of the Torah in every detail, both the ritual and the ethical teachings, as the way of carrying out God's will. Segregationist Judaisms believe that the only way to carry out the Torah is to live separate from both other Jews and also gentiles. Integrationist Orthodox Judaism, as well as all other integrationist Judaisms, maintains that Jews can live by the Torah and also share the common life of modern society.

Hasidic Judaism. Segregationist Jews do not agree among themselves on numerous important questions. Some of them belong to groups that are called "Hasidic." Others reject the basic doctrines and practices of that subset of Judaisms. A Hasidic Judaism believes that a holy man, or *tsaddiq* in Hebrew, stands in a special relationship to God, and takes shape around a particular holy man, believed to convey God's special blessing to his followers. The most important Hasidic Judaism is Lubovitch Hasidism, with its center in Brooklyn and with followers in every Jewish community throughout the world. Believing that its leader, the Lubovitcher rebbe, is a holy man, the Lubovitch disciples live wholly in accord with the rules that all Orthodox Judaisms follow, which derive from the written and oral Torah as interpreted for all Jews through time. But they revere, in addition, teachings of their own group, and especially those of their rebbe. In his service they call on Jews who are in prisons; they find their way to the most remote places of the world where Jews are located and try to win them to the service of God in the way in which they serve God. They are the single most successful Judaism when it comes to winning formerly secular or isolated Jews to the Judaic religion as they define it.

168

Yeshiva Judaism. Not all segregationist Judaisms fall into the classification of Hasidic. Another type altogether is centered on *yeshivas,* or places in which people spend some or all of the day studying the Torah, and particularly the Talmud. These communities flourish in North America, Europe, and the State of Israel. The segregationist Judaism formed around a yeshiva will focus on the study of the Talmud of Babylonia, its commentaries and codes, and will involve its members in intense relationships of study and prayer. Some members of the community will devote their entire lives to Torah study, and others—very often, their wives—will support them to do so. Like monastic communities, the yeshivas, with their masters and disciples, will aim at forming centers of holy living, quite distinct from the world outside. Such yeshiva communities flourish in Boston, New York City, Baltimore, Chicago, Los Angeles, and elsewhere in the United States, and in Montreal and Toronto, in Canada, among many places.

Integrationist Judaisms

Integrationist Judaisms include Orthodox, Reform, Conservative, and Reconstructionist groups. Broadly divided among themselves in both theology and practice, all integrationist Judaisms concur that the Jews can and should live lives like those of their neighbors, differing only in some ways. All maintain that Jews should study secular as well as religious books. All agree that Jews may wear the same kinds of clothing as gentiles, pursue the same kinds of careers, speak the same language, and in most (though not all) ways, live the same kinds of lives. True, there may be some "insider-words," often from Yiddish, such as *kosher* or *maven*. But these words circulate everywhere and end up in common use. In that way, all integrationist Judaisms differ from all segregationist ones. But to know one integrationist Judaism from another, we have to turn from questions of how Jews are supposed to live their lives to those concerning what Jews are supposed to believe. Differences of doctrine separate one integrationist Judaism from another.

Orthodox Judaism. Among Jews who live integrated lives among gentiles, a small number observe the rules of the Judaism of the dual Torah precisely as these are kept by all of the segregationist Judaisms. If you live in a big city, Los Angeles, Chicago, or Miami, for instance, you probably know Jews who go to school with you but bring their own, kosher food; who play baseball with you but will not travel to games from sundown on Friday through sundown on Saturday. If you go to France, England, or Germany, you will find that most Jews in those countries identify with Orthodox synagogues. The leading voice of Judaism in Great Britain is the Chief Rabbi, who is the leader of Orthodox Judaism, as well as a major figure in British religious life.

These Jews call themselves "Orthodox." (The word *orthodox* means "right doctrine.") They will belong to Orthodox synagogues, where the prayers are said entirely in Hebrew, where women and men sit apart from one another, and where the classical writings of the Torah are expounded in terms familiar through the ages. But they are integrationist in that they do not center their lives on a yeshiva, or on a rebbe, and so they may be distinguished from those who do. Orthodox Judaism is diverse and includes segregationist and integrationist, Hasidic and non-Hasidic, and yeshiva-centered and synagogue-centered types. But all Orthodox Judaisms concur that the entire Torah, oral and written, comes from God, in exactly the words in which we now have it, and that everything in the Torah happened exactly as it is said to have happened.

Orthodox Judaisms, whether segregationist or integrationist, enjoy the support of less than 10 percent of Jews in the United States. The majority of American Jews are integrationist: 35 percent are Reform, 43 percent Conservative, and 2 percent Reconstructionist. When we add to these the fair number of integrationist Orthodox Jews as well, more than 90 percent of American Jews count themselves as assimilated in important ways into everyday life in this country. The largest synagogues in most Jewish communities are Reform or Conservative; the Orthodox ones, though numerous, are smaller in membership. The reason for this is that the vast majority of Jews in America have formed for themselves a Judaism that is distinctively American. It is thoroughly integrationist, so that few Jews keep the dietary laws, and fewer still keep them in such a way that they cannot eat with gentiles. While Jews in numbers attend synagogue services on Friday evening or Saturday morning, they drive to synagogue, so that they are not limited to homes within walking distance of a synagogue. Nearly all Jews provide their children with a secular education, and most of them send their children to public or secular schools, not to yeshivas or to Jewish parochial schools that combine religious and secular education as Roman Catholic or Lutheran parochial schools do. So the vast majority of Jews in America want to be Jewish in a way that permits them, also, to be an integral part of the American society and culture (however these may be defined).

Reform Judaism. Reform Judaism is the most important Judaism in the United States, and the most successful of the integrationist Judaisms. It is on the basis of total integration that Reform Judaism sets forth its reading of the Torah. In matters of doctrine and practice, Reform Judaism affirms that the Torah is holy, but reads it as the work of people of a given time and place. The holy way of life taught in the Torah is binding, with special reference to what is relevant to the everyday world in which Jews live. Above all, what God wants is for us to "do justice, love mercy, and walk humbly with God," that is, ethics takes the highest priority in Judaism.

The American Reform rabbis, meeting in Pittsburgh in 1885, issued a clear and accessible statement of their Judaism. The initial, forthright formulation of Judaism as integrationist and not segregationist still holds true, not only for Reform, but in its ideal of integration, for most American Jews today:

> We recognize in the Mosaic legislation a system of training the Jewish people for its mission during its national life in Palestine, and today we accept as binding only its moral laws and maintain only such ceremonies as elevate and sanctify our lives, but reject all such as are not adapted to the views and habits of modern civilization. . . . We hold that all such Mosaic and rabbinical laws as regular diet, priestly purity, and dress originated in ages and under the influence of ideas entirely foreign to our present mental and spiritual state. . . . Their observance in our days is apt rather to obstruct than to further modern spiritual elevation. . . . We recognize in the modern era of universal culture of heart and intellect and approaching of the realization of Israel's great messianic hope for the establishment of the kingdom of truth, justice, and peace among all men.

The Pittsburgh Platform takes up each component of the system in turn. Who is Israel? What is its way of life? How does it account for its existence as a distinct, and distinctive, group? Israel once was a nation ("during its national life") but today is not a nation. It once had a set of laws that regulated diet, clothing, and the like. These no longer apply, because Israel now is not what it was then. Israel—in America at least—now forms an integral part of Western civilization. The reason to persist as a distinctive group was that the group had its work to do, namely, to realize the messianic hope for the establishment of a kingdom of truth, justice, and peace. For that purpose, the nineteenth-century founders of Reform Judaism held that "Israel"—meaning the people—no longer constitutes a nation. It now forms a religious community. Long before the creation of the State of Israel in 1948, Reform Judaism redefined its views and affirmed that the Jews form not only a religious group but a "people." For instance, in 1937 the Reform rabbis, meeting in Columbus, Ohio, reframed the notion of "Israel" to make room for Zionism, the movement that saw the Jews as a nation and that ultimately created the State of Israel. At the same time, the Reform rabbis affirmed the basic conception that Jews live not only among gentiles, but with them. This formulation of Judaism today speaks for the largest group of American Jews.

Conservative Judaism. Most communities of Jews are divided between Reform temples and Conservative synagogues. The differences do not strike outsiders as very weighty. On most basic questions, members of Reform temples and Conservative synagogues concur. Differences on religious observance among ordinary folk, not rabbis, will be trivial. Their rabbis may differ, since Conservative Jews who do not observe dietary laws or the Sabbath and festivals expect that their rabbis will, while Reform Jews do not. Indeed, Conservative rabbis will refer to the Talmud of Babylonia and the later commentaries and codes for precedents on questions of Jewish observance, and they make every effort to keep the faith in a manner not strikingly different from the way in which Orthodox rabbis and some Orthodox laypeople do. Consequently, some suppose that Conservative Judaism is best described as Orthodox rabbis serving Conservative synagogues made up of Reform Jews, and that formulation is not unfounded. Conservative Judaism was the most numerous and influential Judaism in the United States in the middle of the twentieth century, but at the end of the century, Reform Judaism has replaced it.

Reconstructionist Judaism. A distant third in numbers, after Reform and Conservative Judaism, Reconstructionist Judaism emphasizes a naturalist theology, meaning a theology that defines God entirely in this-worldly terms ("God is the power that makes for salvation," so "what makes for salvation is God"). Reconstructionism is the most ethnic of Judaic religious systems, because it treats the Jewish people as the center of interest, and the values and beliefs of the people as the source of authority. It took shape in America as a naturalist, this-worldly Judaic system, originally within Conservative Judaism. Only in the recent past has it attained recognition as a distinct Judaism.

Gentiles and Judaism

Anti-Semitism

Whether segregated or integrated, Jews find themselves the object of hatred. The murder, by Germany and its allies, of nearly six million Jews in Europe between 1933 and 1945 points toward the persistence of hatred of Jews called "anti-Semitism." That hatred is a form of racism that attributes negative traits to all Jews. For many centuries, the New Testament's picture of the conduct of Jews in the time of Jesus and Paul—themselves also Jews—led people to call Jews "deicides," or "Christ-killers." In the aftermath of the murder of European Jewry, the Christian churches have repudiated that charge.

The National Socialists, or Nazis, claimed that the Jews bore racial traits that accounted for the evil in the world and should be murdered ("exterminated" like vermin), and this was called "the final solution to the Jewish problem." In this country, some maintain the stereotype that Jews love money (more than most people) or that they are "excessively clever." Imputing to an entire group of people traits such as these is seen by most people as unfair, untrue, and unintelligent, so for most Jews anti-Semitism is not an everyday problem. They find themselves accepted, and a mark that they are right is the very widely held agreement— approximately 88 percent—among gentiles that they would accept the marriage of a child of theirs with a Jew or that they would "vote for a Jew for president." Specific incidents of anti-Semitism notwithstanding, American society accepts Jews as normal and entirely ordinary members of society.

Gentiles in the Life of Judaism

Since most Jews in the United States opt for an integrated life, and since most gentiles accept this, we cannot find it surprising that many gentiles find a place within the Jewish community. Sociologist Barry A. Kosmin comments, "There is integration into American society that makes inter-marriage more possible. On the other hand, a more tolerant, pluralistic society allows you to continue to maintain your traditions even in an intermarriage." In families in which all members are Jews, 86 percent attend a Passover seder; where there is a mixed marriage, 62 percent do. Only 18 percent of families in which both parents are Jewish will have a Christmas tree, whereas 80 percent of those in which one is a Jew and the other a gentile will have one. Where both parents are Jewish, 41 percent of families belong to synagogues; where there is an intermarriage, 13 percent do. Since 1985, 52 percent of Jews to marry have married gentiles; before 1954, the figure was 9 percent. This does not mean Judaism is done for in America. It means that Judaism is changing under conditions of integration.

Jewish Americans or American Jews: Neither or Both?

When we study Islam or Buddhism in America, what we learn about is Islam and Buddhism; these world religions have only recently arrived on the American scene, and we do not yet know much about how the challenges and opportunities of life in this country will shape these ancient religions. And although Protestant and Roman Catholic Christian religions have shaped America, so has America shaped them. Hence we learn as much about America as we do about Christianity when we study about Protestant and Roman Catholic Christianity in America. Judaism falls somewhere in between.

Most Jews in the United States see themselves as Jewish Americans—a Jewish species of American, different in religion alone. A smaller number regard themselves as American Jews—that is, a particular kind of Jew, but not different in any important ways from other Jews. Both are deeply American in their loyalties and commitments, but each has a quite distinctive theory of what it means to be an American. In the climate of a country open to difference but united in political institutions and loyalties to "one nation, under God, indivisible," American Judaism flourishes in diverse forms—segregationist and integrationist alike—because America accepts and even nurtures diversity. So the very diversity of American Judaism itself expresses the character of the shared life and social dreams of this country. But that diversity is possible to begin with because America stands on foundations of a national consensus. And one plank in the American platform is that there is room for every religion the world has known, and every version of that religion. That is what "one nation, under God" means.

STUDY QUESTIONS

1. What do you think the author means when he says that "while Judaism is not the religion of a single people, the Jews are a people with a single religion"?
2. What are the three things that make Judaism a living religion? How does each function within Judaism?
3. What roles do home, synagogue, and pilgrimages play in the religion of Jewish Americans? What religious functions take place in each of these locations and activities? How would you compare these "places" of religion in Judaism to "places" of religion in other traditions you have studied?
4. What is the difference between the written Torah and the oral Torah? Is it an important distinction? Why?
5. What do you see as the relation between the Torah and the Christian Old Testament? How are they similar? How do they differ?
6. Compare and contrast segregationist Judaism with integrationist Judaism? What are the reasons for Jews choosing to embrace either policy? Are there religious disagreements among members within each tradition? Why does such diversity within traditions suggest strength of commitment as opposed to fragmentation?
7. Why do you think anti-Semitism exists? What stereotypes should we avoid to help us avoid anti-Semitism? What evidence suggests that Jews and gentiles within the United States are developing even closer and more harmonious relations?

ESSAY TOPICS

The Relationship between Conservative, Orthodox, Reform, and Reconstructionist Judaism
The Role of the Torah in Judaism
The Holocaust and the Jewish Religion
The Religious Dimension of the Synagogue: Design and Function
Sacred Days of Judaism: Origin and Function

WORD EXPLORATION

The following words play significant roles in any discussion of Judaism in America and are worth careful reflection and discussion.

Jews	Bar Mitzvah	Hebrew
Temple	Yahweh	Yom Hakippurim
Scroll	Torah	Mitzvah
Yarmulka	Synagogue	Shavuot
Rosh Hoshanah	Holocaust (Shoa)	Anti-Semitism
Yom Kippur		

8

GERALD JAMES LARSON

Hinduism in India and in America

PEOPLE OF INDIA IN THE WORLD TODAY

People from India live in all fifty of the United States and now represent the fourth largest Asian ethnic minority (after Chinese, Japanese, and Filipinos). According to the 1990 Census, there are 815,447 "Asian Indians," people from India or people of Asian Indian descent, living in the United States. The largest concentrations of Asian Indians are in the states of New York (140,985) and California (159,973) and in such major urban areas as New York City, Chicago, Los Angeles, Houston, Philadelphia, and the San Francisco Bay area.

Most of the people from India who have settled in the United States are highly educated and prosperous and have become prominent in such areas as medicine, law, engineering, aerospace research, business, and the arts. More than five thousand Asian Indians in America hold faculty positions (especially in the sciences and engineering) in American colleges and universities, and many have become department chairs or directors of programs.

There are also sizable populations of Asian Indians elsewhere in the world today, including Canada, the United Kingdom, Europe, the Caribbean, South America, the Middle East, Africa, the Indian Ocean islands, and elsewhere. Asian Indians, in other words, can be found almost everywhere in the world.

India itself has a population of 843,930,861, according to the Census of India for 1991, making it the second most populous nation in the world after China.[1] Given the present growth rate and the relative youthfulness of India's population (40 percent under the age of fifteen), the population of India may surpass that of China early in the next century.

When speaking about Asian Indians, therefore, we are speaking about a sizable percentage of the population of our planet (currently 16 percent, but rapidly advancing toward 20 percent). We are also speaking about people of great diversity and remarkable contrasts. Whereas Asian Indians living in the United States and other industrialized Western nations (and to some extent those living in the Persian Gulf region) are for the most part highly educated and prosperous, the same does not hold true for Asian Indians elsewhere in the world, for example, in South Africa, Malaysia, or, of course, in India itself.

India is made up of twenty-five states and seven Union Territories, ranging from Jammu and Kashmir in the far north (in the cold foothills of the Himalayas, bordering Tibet and China on the east and Pakistan on the west) to Tamil Nadu in the far subtropical south (almost reaching to Sri Lanka). Eighteen official languages are recognized in addition to English. Hindi is spoken by about 40 percent of the population, mainly in those highly populated northern states sometimes referred to as the "Hindi Heartland." English is spoken by about 3 percent of the population.

The Anthropological Survey of India has identified the staggering number of 4,599 distinct communities in India, and as many as 325 languages in 12 language families and 24 different scripts. Nevertheless the survey also found that an "all-pervasive sense of Indianness prevails through the linguistic, cultural and ecological diversities of the communities of the country."[2]

At this point you may well be thinking, What about religion? Why aren't you telling us about Hindus and Hinduism? My answer is that I have been writing about Hindus and Hinduism. The most important thing to learn about Hindus and Hinduism is that being religious for Hindus has very little to do with what they think or believe; put another way, it has very little to do with "orthodoxy," or correct belief and doctrines. There are, of course, some common beliefs or characteristics that pertain to most Hindus, which we will look at later in this chapter, but there is overall a remarkable freedom and tolerance for almost all religious points of view (including agnosticism and atheism). Being religious for the Hindu, rather, has much more to do with behavior and action, or what is sometimes called "orthopraxy"—correct action. The Hindu has basic duties and responsibilities in terms of personal cleanliness (ritual bathing), eating habits (what kind of food is to be eaten, who prepares it, and with whom it can be eaten), family relations (obligations to siblings and parents), marital practices (when and whom one can marry), regional associations (including caste associations), and the manner in which one can choose and interact with friends. In other words, Hindus are engaging in a kind of "religious" talk when they tell you about their family, their occupations, the regions in India from which they come, the groups to which they belong by birth or choice, the native languages they speak, and the sorts of food they eat. Moreover, as your Hindu friends describe all of this, you will be struck not only by how different their views and ideas can be, but also by the great range of differing duties and responsibilities that they follow depending upon the regions and groups from which they come. The rules are by no means the same for everyone. While you will come to realize that there are many ways of being "Hindu," you will also note an "all-pervasive sense of Indianness." This somewhat strange juxtaposition of radical diversity or tolerant pluralism along with an "all-pervasive sense of Indianness" is basically what it means to be a Hindu.

HINDU, HINDUNESS, INDIAN, AND INDIANNESS

At this point you might be tempted to think that "Hindu" simply means "Indian" or "Asian Indian." In other words, you might be tempted to think that Hinduism is the name of a culture, civilization, or ethnic identity rather than a religion as such. To some extent, you would be right—much of what it means to be Hindu is related to the simple fact that one has been born in India into a Hindu family. However, such a simple equation of Hindu or Hinduness with Indian and Indianness is not by any means the full picture, for there are many Asian Indians who are not Hindu and deeply resent being called Hindus. The Sikhs, for example, refuse to be absorbed into Hinduism, and Indian Muslims make up a significant minority. The actual breakdown of major religions in India, according to the population totals of the 1991 census, is roughly as follows:

Hindu	83.0%	700,000,000
Muslim	10.9%	92,000,000
Christian	2.4%	20,000,000
Sikh	2.0%	16,000,000
Buddhist	0.7%	6,000,000
Jain	0.5%	4,000,000
Other	0.5%	4,000,000

The "Other" category includes Parsees, Jews, Animists, and other traditions, all of which together are only one-half of 1 percent. There is, thus, a clear overlap between Asian Indian and Hindu, but it is equally clear that we cannot equate the two.

THE DEVELOPMENT
OF HINDUISM IN INDIA

Unlike most historic religions, such as Christianity, Islam, and Buddhism, Hinduism has no human founder and no datable beginning in time or history. In an important sense, one might well say that Hinduism has no beginning; it just emerges out of the ancient earth of South Asia. If you have ever seen a banyan tree with its aerial roots that grow down from its branches into the soil to form additional trunks, thereby spreading in all directions in a bewildering complexity of formations, then you have a good metaphor for thinking about Hinduism.

The development of Hinduism occurs over many centuries and is incredibly dense and complex, so it may be helpful if we identify certain distinct periods in order to organize the discussion. Altogether it is useful to identify six such fundamental periods for the development of Hinduism: the *Indus Valley Period* (ca. 3000–1500 B.C.E.), the *Brahmanical Period* (ca. 1500–600 B.C.E.), the *Buddhist and Shramana Period* (ca. 600 B.C.E.–300 C.E.), the *Classical Hindu Period* (ca. 300–1200 C.E.), the *Muslim Period* (ca. 1200–1757 C.E.), and the *Modern Period* (ca. 1757–present).

The Indus Valley Period
(ca. 3000–1500 B.C.E.)

The Indus Valley civilization flourished from the third through the first half of the second millennium B.C.E. in the region of the Indus valley and in the area known as the Punjab. It was a sizable civilization, covering as much as half a million square miles (including what is now Pakistan and much of northwest India as well). Very little is known about the origins of this civilization or about its end.

Excavations of the two large urban sites, Mohenjo-daro and Harappa, have yielded some intriguing clues about the culture and religion of the Indus Valley civilization. Each city, for example, had a large artificial hill or citadel with what appear to be sizable official buildings (possibly governmental or religious, or both). There was also in Mohenjo-daro what appears to be a large, rectangular bathing area in the main part of the citadel area with steps leading down into it, suggesting some sort of ritual bathing practice (not unlike the ritual bathing "tanks" connected to Hindu temples in later Indian culture). The cities themselves are rather sophisticated in design, with carefully planned streets and houses facing away from the street.

In terms of artifacts, archaeologists have uncovered what appear to be phallus-shaped stones and crude terra-cotta female figurines, suggesting some sort of fertility cult and belief in a Mother Goddess. The Indus Valley language has not yet been deciphered, so scholars can only guess what this civilization's religion and culture were like. But it is intriguing to entertain the possibility that prominent features in later Hinduism may indeed be traceable ultimately all the way back to the third millennium B.C.E., and possibly earlier to the village cultures that go back to time immemorial.

The Brahmanical Period
(ca. 1500–600 B.C.E.)

Sometime in the early part of the second millennium, seminomadic warrior tribes who had been living in the steppeland that ranges from Eastern Europe to Central Asia began to undertake extensive migrations. These migrations may have been occasioned by famine, some sort of natural disaster, or an epidemic. Whatever the reasons, some tribes migrated west, finally finding their way to Europe and becoming the ancestors of the Greeks, Romans, Celts, and Teutons. Other tribes remained in the steppeland region, becoming the ancestors of the Baltic and Slavonic peoples. Still others migrated south and east, moving first into Persia and then into present-day Afghanistan, and Baluchistan (a desert region in western Pakistan), and finally into the Indus Valley region. The tribes conquered local peoples as they moved, intermarried with the indigenous population, and developed into a ruling elite. They called themselves Aryas or Aryans (meaning "noble ones"), and those Aryan tribes that reached ancient Persia and India are known as Indo-Iranians or Indo-Aryans. These migrations did not occur all at once. There were probably waves of migrating Indo-Aryan tribes over a period of some years.

In the middle of the second millennium (ca. 1500 B.C.E.) these Indo-Aryan nomadic tribes brought with them into India a number of cultural characteristics that were to determine the development of later Indian civilization and Hinduism: (1) a form of the Sanskrit language called simply Old Indic (or Vedic Sanskrit), later to develop into the classical language of India known as classical Sanskrit; (2) a patrilineal system of organization that centered around the three social functions of priests (Brahmins), warriors, and food-gatherers, later to develop into what we now know as the caste system; (3) an elaborate ritual system of sacrifice on open-air altars involving offerings of milk, honey, clarified butter (ghee), and animals, together with imbibing a sacred drink that brought about hallucinogenic effects; and (4) the worship of an elaborate pantheon of sky, atmospheric, and earth gods.

In order to perform the ritual sacrifice, the Brahmins had to master an extensive body of what can be called sacred "utterances," including hymns, chants, and ritual instructions. These liturgical utterances (not yet written texts, since writing was not extensively used until many centuries later) are referred to as the Vedas, from the root meaning "to know." In other words, the Vedas are what the Brahmins had to know in order to perform the ritual sacrifice. Originally there were three basic ritual collections. Somewhat later a fourth set of sacred utterances was added.

The purpose of the ritual sacrifice was to propitiate and "feed" the gods. In return the gods would assist their Indo-Aryan devotees with long life, much cattle, and earthly happiness. This reciprocity between gods and Brahmins maintained the cosmic order. Interestingly enough, in this early Brahmanical Period, gods other than Vishnu and Shiva, who nearly a millennium later would emerge as principal gods in classical Hinduism, were preeminent. The tendency in this Brahmanical Period was to move away from personal gods in the direction of speculative abstractions, which put ever greater emphasis on the importance of the Brahmins both for the performance of ritual and for the interpretation of its meaning.

Over the next thousand years the Indo-Aryan nomadic tribes spread over all of north India, intermarrying with the indigenous population and becoming a settled agricultural people. During this thousand-year period many important changes occurred. The sacrificial ritual became much more complex and came to be divided into two basic types: (1) great public rituals involving as many as seventeen priests and three sacred fires and lasting for several days and in some instances up to two years; and (2) home-based oblations into a single fire in the domestic hearth. Also related to the domestic rituals were the life-cycle rituals, from twelve to sixteen rites of passage, including the marriage ritual, the ritual for conceiving a male child, a birth ritual, a name-giving ritual, and so forth. Whereas most of the Indo-Aryan families were able to maintain the home-based rituals, only the rich could afford the great public rituals.

As the rituals became more complex and expensive, the Brahmin priests became more specialized in one or another aspect of the ritual process. Long commentaries were composed (first orally but eventually written down) explaining the rituals, called *Brahmanas* ("pertaining to the priestly function"). Specialized schools developed in centers of learning just outside the towns in various parts of north India. The products of these schools were called *Aranyakas*, or "forest-books." Finally, the priests began to speculate on the deeper meaning of the ritual process and even began a kind of elementary philosophizing about the relation of the ritual to the cosmos and to the human community (mainly to the priestly community, but to the ruling Kshatriya or warrior community as well). These early speculative and protophilosophical reflections came to be collected in a group of compositions called *Upanishads* (meaning literally "to sit down near" the teacher or guru and to learn the special, secret teaching). Upanishads were being composed already in the ninth and eighth centuries B.C.E. and continued to be composed well into the first centuries of the Common Era. The Brahmanas and Aranyakas are somewhat older, reaching back to the eleventh and even the twelfth century B.C.E. The Vedic verse-collections, the Brahmanas, the Aranyakas, and the Upanishads are referred to collectively as the Veda or *shruti* ("scripture"—literally "that which has been heard"). These Vedas are considered to be eternal and to have been intuited or "seen" by the ancient Rishis ("seers") and thus not to have a human origin ("not derived from men," or *apaurusheya*).

The Buddhist and Shramana Period
(ca. 600 B.C.E.–300 C.E.)

With the Buddhist and Shramana Period, we begin to see some reactions against the all-powerful priestly religion of the Brahmins, as well as the first manifestations of two other kinds of spirituality that will prove to be as important in later Hinduism as ritual sacrifice, namely, ascetic or disciplined meditation (*yoga*) and focused or single-minded devotion (*bhakti*) to a personal god. We also see some important new literature taking shape toward the end of this period: the *Dharmashastras* (law books) of the Hindus and the two great epics of India, the *Ramayana* and the *Mahabharata*, the latter of which contains the most important religious text of classical Hinduism, the *Bhagavad Gita* ("Song of the Lord").

The term *Shramana* is from the root *shram*, meaning "to exert oneself" or "to practice austerities." The search for inner truth, the turn toward meditation and self-searching, and the pursuit of yoga were found not only among some of the Brahmin priests, but also among all of the non-Brahmanical mendicant groups that began to appear in north India sometime around the sixth century B.C.E. These groups did not accept the authority of the Brahmin priests, nor did they accept the validity of the Brahmanical sacrificial system. Rejecting also the sacred literature of the Brahmins, they formed their own separate communities and represent the first examples of the monastic life in ancient India.

There were many such Shramana groups, but two in particular eventually developed into independent religions in ancient India: the Jains and the Buddhists. The founder of the Jain tradition was Vardhamana, also known by the honorific epithet Mahavira ("Great Hero"). He was born into a warrior (Kshatriya) family and lived in the sixth century B.C.E. (ca. 549–477 B.C.E.) in northeastern India, in the region of the Gangetic plain in what is now the state of Bihar. He practiced rigorous asceticism and organized a Jain monastic community. "Jain" comes from the word *jina*, meaning "conqueror." Both monastic and lay Jain communities have existed in India throughout the centuries. As we noted earlier, there are about four million Jains in contemporary India and probably a few thousand who live in the United States today.

The founder of the Buddhist tradition was Gautama the Buddha (the "awakened" or "enlightened" one). Also from a warrior (Kshatriya) family, Gautama (ca. 563–483 B.C.E.) was an older contemporary of Mahavira and lived in the same region of the Gangetic plain. Since there is a separate chapter of this book on Buddhism, suffice it to say here that the Buddhist tradition was also a mendicant tradition with a focus on meditation that enables a monk to attain enlightenment and eventually release (*nirvana*) from the frustrations of ordinary life. Unlike the Jains, however, the Buddhists followed a much more moderate regimen of yogic meditation, which they called the Middle Path—a middle way between sensuous indulgence, on the one hand, and extreme asceticism, on the other.

The new traditions of the period shared a profound dissatisfaction with the older sacrificial cult of the Brahmins and represented a new spirituality focusing on the interior life and the practice of yoga. They were probably also profoundly dissatisfied, or at least frustrated, with certain social changes occurring at this time: the development of cities, the development of a monied economy, and the rise of an imperial state that would become the first to rule all of India (the Mauryan Dynasty, which ruled from 322 to 183 B.C.E.).

The other development of importance in this period is the first appearance of devotional cults, specifically the Shaiva (devotees of Lord Shiva) and Vaishnava (devotees of Lord Vishnu) traditions. Although both Shiva and Vishnu were known in the older Vedic religion and are sometimes mentioned in the Upanishads, they were clearly not dominant figures. It is in the Buddhist and Shramana Period that we first see the emergence of devotion, or bhakti, to a personal god, and it appears that these devotional cults were originally outside the Brahmanical sacrificial framework, as were the Shramana groups themselves. Shiva, Vasudeva-Krishna, Narayana, Rama, and many other later Hindu deities probably all began as local heroes of local deities outside of the Brahmanical tradition, their origins in some instances possibly even predating Indo-Aryan times. They begin now, however, to become major cults. The making of images and image worship (*puja*), the appearance of temples (possibly influenced by the Buddhist building of *stupas*, or burial mounds, for relics of the Buddha), the practice of pilgrimage (again probably due largely to the Buddhist custom of making pilgrimages to certain sacred places), singing devotional songs, observing certain religious festivals, and so forth, all now emerge as important religious practices that go considerably beyond and to a large extent supplant the old Brahmanical sacrificial cult.

The Classical Hindu Period
(ca. 300–1200 C.E.)

The Brahmanical reaction to all the developments of the Buddhist and Shramana Period was not rejection or condemnation but rather, to whatever extent possible, assimilation and accommodation. This can be seen in the new literature shaped in Brahmanical circles toward the end of that period, from about 200 B.C.E. to about 300 C.E. This new literature attains its final shape or redaction in the first centuries of the Common Era.

This new literature as a whole is referred to as literature "worthy to be remembered" (*smriti*) in order to distinguish it from the literature that is considered to be authentic "scripture" (*shruti*), that is, the Vedas (including the Upanishads) that we have already discussed. Interestingly enough, however, even though Hindus only accept the Vedas as authentic scripture, in fact, most of the basic ideas and practices of classical Hinduism derive from the new *smriti* literature. In other words, Hindus for the most part pay little more than lip service to the Vedic scripture. The most important dimensions of being Hindu derive, instead, from the *smriti* texts. The point can also be made in terms of the emerging social reality. Whereas the *shruti* is taken seriously by a small subset of Brahmins, the *smriti* are taken seriously by the overwhelming majority of Hindus, regardless of class or caste identity.

This new *smriti* literature includes the following:

1. The great epic of India known as the *Mahabharata*, the story of a great war between two branches of a family (the Kurus and the Pandus) that establishes the ancient kingdom of India. The *Mahabharata* includes within it the most popular and beloved text of the Hindu tradition, the *Bhagavad Gita* ("Song of the Lord"), which features the teachings of the famous Lord Krishna, an incarnation or "descent" (*avatara*) of the mighty god Vishnu, who fights on the side of the victorious Pandus against the evil Kurus;

2. A second epic known as the *Ramayana*, a story of another great war, this time between Lord Rama, another incarnation of the mighty Vishnu, and the great demon, Ravana, who had kidnapped Rama's beloved wife, Sita, and carried her off to his fortress in the far south (present-day Sri Lanka), from which captivity Lord Rama rescues her with the help of a mighty army of monkeys led by the beloved monkey god, Hanuman;

3. A group of texts called *Puranas* ("Old Tales"), repositories of the great myths and legends of classical Hinduism, dealing with how the world came to be, and with the beloved stories and tales about the three high gods of classical Hinduism, Brahma, Vishnu, and Shiva; and

4. A group of law books called *Dharmashastras*, the most famous of which is the "Law-Book of Manu," which provide detailed discussions of such matters as the proper purposes of life, the stages of life, the caste system, and the manner in which the community is to be governed.

All of these texts receive their final form and general acceptance by the larger Hindu population in this Classical Hindu Period, the period of the full flowering of classical Indian civilization. In this period one can properly begin to use the terms "Hindu" and "Hinduism." Classical Hinduism now shows itself as an artful synthesis of ritual action, disciplined meditation, and devotional piety, shaped on one level by the old Brahmanical religion of ritual sacrifice, and on another level by the Shramanical and non-Brahmanical religious traditions of meditation and devotion deriving from the Buddhist and Shramana Period, but resonating as well as the spiritual rhythms of the old Indus Valley civilization and the archaic village spirituality of the fourth and fifth millennia B.C.E. Clearly "Hinduism" is not simply one entity or tradition. It is a synthesis of many traditions.

Gods and Goddesses

There are, of course, many gods and goddesses in classical Hinduism, but most Hindus think of the various gods and goddesses as manifestations of one ultimate truth. Classical Hinduism combines the old Vedic notion of the Brahman, the Ultimate or Absolute, with the notion of a plurality of forms that the Ultimate or Absolute assumes, three of which are central in the everyday beliefs and practices of Hindus: Brahma, the creator god; Vishnu, the preserving god; and Shiva, the destroying god. Brahma, Vishnu, and Shiva taken together are referred to as the "three basic forms" of the Ultimate or Absolute.

The Absolute or Ultimate also assumes female forms. Shri or Lakshmi is the goddess of abundance, often linked with Vishnu. Durga or Kali is the awesome power of the Great Goddess, able to devour the demonic and evil forces in the world. She is often linked with Shiva. Sometimes the Absolute or the Ultimate assumes an androgynous form, a composite of male and female, known as the "Lord whose half is woman" (Ardhanarishvara).

The Ultimate is boundlessly various, and so too are the cultic forms that everyday puja, or worship, takes. The devotees of Lord Vishnu, together with his many "incarnations" or "descents" (*avataras*)—the two most important of which are Lord Krishna (the divine hero of the *Mahabharata*) and Lord Rama (the divine hero of the *Ramayana*)—are called *Vaishnavas* ("followers of Vishnu") and have numerous temples and shrines through the subcontinent for their puja. Well over half of all Hindus are followers of one or another form of Vaishnavism (including devotees of Lord Krishna and Lord Rama). Devotees of Shiva, whose mythology and ritual prescriptions are set forth primarily in the Puranas, are called *Shaivas* ("followers of Shiva") and have numerous temples and shrines for their puja throughout India, especially in Tamilnad in the south, West Bengal in the north, and Kashmir in the far northwest. About one-third of all Hindus are Shaivites. Devotees of the goddess, whether Kali or Devi or Durga, are called *Shaktas*, a term which means something like "followers of power," referring to the power (*shakti*) of the goddess to create and sustain the world, to destroy the demonic, or to bring an end to all things.

Karma, Rebirth, and Strategies for Release

The endless cycles of unfolding time and the boundless variety of living forms are controlled not by the gods and goddesses, as one might anticipate, but by a process of principle known as *karma*. Indeed, even the gods and goddesses are governed by karma. The term *karma* means "action" and refers to the simple principle that one's life is governed by one's own continuing behavior or practice. In other words, what one does governs what one will become, not only from the perspective of human life but from the perspective of the entire hierarchy of living forms.

Moreover, just as one passes through various stages of life, so too death is only one more stage. After death, in other words, there will be rebirth, to be followed in due time by another death, to be followed by another rebirth, and so forth. Through endless cycles of recurring time, depending upon one's karmic heritage or trajectory, one might come to be embodied in any number of life forms. There is a beginningless cycle of continuing transmigration or rebirth (called *samsara*) that parallels the seemingly endless cycles of unfolding time. These endless cycles of our karmic trajectories are frustrating and painful, and there is a deep urge within all living things to be free or to be released from these endless cycles of recurring rebirth.

The human life form, though painful like all other life forms, is nevertheless potentially liberating, since it can exercise a good deal of control over an unfolding karmic trajectory, whereas nonhuman life forms are largely victims of a mechanical unfolding of effects. By disciplined meditation that leads to correct insight or wisdom (known as the "discipline of knowledge," or *jñana-yoga*), or by disciplined meditation that allows one to become engaged in ordinary life but not to be attached to the fruits of one's actions (known as the "discipline of action," or *karma-yoga*), or, finally, by disciplined devotion to a chosen deity who will aid the devotee in the quest for release (known as the "discipline of devotion," or *bhakti-yoga*), the human being can begin to control his or her own karma and to move toward "release" (*moksha*) from the endless cycles of recurring transmigration and rebirth. These three types of yoga are discussed at great length in the *Bhagavad Gita*. The *Bhagavad Gita* is known and beloved by all Hindus, and the process of karma and rebirth together with the various strategies of yoga have been widely accepted by all Hindus down to the present time. If there is any one text that comes near to embodying the totality of what it is to be a Hindu, it would be the *Bhagavad Gita*.

The Four Purposes of Life, the Four Stages of Life, and the Four Castes

Classical Hinduism also involves a complex variety of rules and regulations regarding social life. These are set forth in the group of *smriti* texts called "law books," or *Dharmashastras*. Certain general principles or categories were devised that provide an overview of Indian social life as a whole.

The "four proper purposes of human life" refer to certain basic activities that all people can or ought to pursue: (1) Dharma ("law," "duty," "custom"), the pursuit of one's duty, including all of the general and specific social obligations related to one's place in the family and community; (2) Artha ("wealth," "work," "business"), the pursuit of worldly advantage—in other words, making a living, pursuing an occupation, including not only everyday life in the family and local community but also the proper political functioning of the kingdom or state; (3) Kama ("desire," "pleasure"), the pursuit of one's legitimate erotic and aesthetic activities, including sexuality, play, recreation, the arts, and literature; and (4) Moksha ("release," "salvation"), the pursuit of spiritual practices, such as ritual meditation (yoga), and devotion (bhakti), in order to attain release from the continuing round of rebirth and transmigration.

The "four proper purposes of life" are correlated with the "four stages of life," or *ashramas:* (1) Brahmacarin ("pursuing sacred knowledge"), the stage of being a student, when a young person lives in the home of the guru and learns about the tradition; (2) Grihastha ("householder"), the stage of becoming married, raising a family, and fulfilling one's basic social responsibilities in the community; (3) Vanaprastha ("forest-dweller"), the stage of retirement from ordinary family life and social obligations, when one begins to think about the ultimate goal of Moksha; and (4) Sannyasin ("abandoning," "renunciation"), the final stage, when one renounces all worldly attachments and becomes a naked, wandering ascetic in pursuit of Moksha. The stages are a matter of personal choice, and most Hindus go only as far as the first two.

Finally, the "four proper purposes of life" and the "four stages of life" are correlated with the four groups of "castes," or *varnas* or *jatis.* The word *caste* is from the Portuguese word *casta,* meaning "breed," "race," or "kind." The word was first used by the Portuguese, when they came to India in the sixteenth century, in order to describe the peculiar social groupings that they noted among the people of India. There were groups of families (1) having the same name; (2) intermarrying with one another; (3) following the same occupations; (4) following certain elaborate rules and restrictions about eating, drinking, and exchanging with other groups; and (5) arranging themselves in each area in certain hierarchical orderings.

The division of castes is fourfold: (1) Brahmins ("priests"), the highest castes, made up of those collections of families considered the purest and most learned among the people of India; (2) Kshatriyas ("warriors"), the next highest castes, made up of those collections of families with primary responsibilities in the areas of governance and maintenance of social order, especially the function of kingship; (3) Vaishya ("belonging to the people"), those collections of families involved in commerce, business, and ordinary economic productivity; and (4) Shudra ("servile"), the lowest castes of servants or those collections of families who serve the higher castes. The highest three castes are referred to as "twice-born" (dvija), since they are eligible for initiation into sacred learning; in other words, they are permitted to learn about the Vedas. The lowest castes of Shudras are not permitted to study the scriptures. In addition to this hierarchical fourfold grouping, there is yet another grouping that is even lower than the Shudras, namely, the "Untouchables" (asprishya or candala). These are collections of families considered to be polluted because they are involved in such activities as cleaning human waste areas, removing dead animals, tanning, and so forth. The Untouchables usually live in segregated areas outside of a main village or town.

What is distinctive about the caste system, in contrast to a class system, is that for the most part there is almost no mobility. While there has been more flexibility and mobility among caste groupings in various parts of India than was originally thought, the more rigid, modern system of caste probably developed during the long centuries (ca. 1200–1750) of Muslim dominance in India.

The Muslim Period
(ca. 1200–1757 C.E.)

Contact with Islamic culture occurred as early as the middle of the seventh century, largely through Arab traders coming to the west coast of India across the Arabian Sea. Some military forays into India by Muslim armies began as early as the eighth century. By the beginning of the thirteenth century the Turko-Afghan Muslim descendants of Mahmud established the Delhi Sultanate that ruled north India for the next three centuries (1206–1526). The Delhi Sultanate was succeeded by the famous Mughal dynasty, which lasted from 1526 to 1858 and reached its highest point under the famous Emperor Akbar (1556–1605).

Islamic rule was sometimes harsh and uncompromising. For the most part, however, the Muslim rulers accommodated themselves to the larger Hindu culture, if only because they were greatly outnumbered overall and very much in need of Hindu support. Particularly under the Emperor Akbar, an open-minded and tolerant attitude toward other religious traditions, including Hinduism, prevailed, at least among the court elite. Among the elite there emerged an interesting blend of Perso-Islamic and Rajput-Hindu traditions and styles. Discussions about religion were regularly held in the Hall of Worship with the emperor himself presiding.

Akbar's great-grandson, Dara Shikoh (1615–1659), a follower of one of the Sufi mystical orders, was also a student of Hindu philosophy and mystical practices. His brother Aurangzeb, however, who was emperor from 1658 to 1707, had Dara Shikoh executed in 1659, mainly for political reasons but with the "religious" excuse that Dara Shikoh had become too influenced by heretical Hindu ideas. In any case, with the coming of Aurangzeb's leadership, the period of accommodation between Islam, Hinduism, and other religious traditions came to an abrupt halt, and thereafter Islamic orthodoxy was enforced in court circles.

It must be said overall, however, that any compromise or accommodation between Islam and Hinduism during the centuries of Muslim domination hardly went beyond a very small elite in court circles. Generally speaking, Islam and Hinduism have barely coexisted in India over the centuries. The mutual hostility and suspicion that the two communities have for each other eventually brought about the partition of the subcontinent at the time of independence in 1947 (into India and Pakistan), and even now, nearly half a century after independence, deep distrust continues between the communities in India as well as throughout the South Asian area.

In the Muslim Period, Hindus put great emphasis on preexisting traditions such as vegetarianism, nonviolence (*ahimsa*), and the veneration of the cow as a symbol of divine benevolence, all notions of ritual purity that clearly differentiate the Hindu from the Muslim. Throughout the Muslim period the various Hindu monastic orders also continued to consolidate their traditions and practices. They even developed "militant" orders, groups of Yogis equipped with weapons and trained in martial arts to defend the monastic institutions against the encroachment of Muslim bands or hostile Hindu groups.

Of much greater significance for the development of Hinduism in the Muslim Period is the remarkable increase in bhakti, or devotional Hinduism. This growth is undoubtedly related in important respects to the growing presence of Islamic traditions, especially the Sufi devotional mysticism that was spreading rapidly across north India through the medium of the various regional languages. It is difficult to determine whether Sufi devotional mysticism influenced Hindu bhakti or vice versa. It could well be that Sufi devotionalism and Hindu bhakti have a natural affinity for one another and that, therefore, there was simply a broad-based mutual interaction between these traditions in the sixteenth century and after. The devotional focus of the Sikh religion, founded by Guru Nanak (1469–1539), on one transcendent God and its rejection of the caste system owe much to Islamic Sufi ideas, while its incorporation of Hindu devotional songs in its sacred scripture (called the *Adi Granth* or *Granth Sahib*, the "Book of the Lord") shows clear influence from the Hindu bhakti side. In the final analysis, however, Sikhism is itself a distinct religious tradition that differs from both Islamic Sufism and Hinduism.

The Modern Period
(ca. 1757–present)

Although the Mughal Dynasty survived until 1858, by the mid–eighteenth century it was a dynasty in name only and proved an easy mark for European traders and adventurers (Portuguese, Dutch, French, and British) who came to the subcontinent in the sixteenth and seventeenth centuries. Already in the early decades of the eighteenth century the Mughal empire was breaking up, with local *nawabs*, or "provincial governors," becoming de facto rulers in their areas. The 1757 defeat of Nawab Siraj-ud-daula of Bengal and his army of fifty thousand troops at the hands of Sir Robert Clive of the British East India Company with only eight hundred British troops and some two thousand *sepoys* (native recruits) is usually cited as the beginning of the modern period in the history of the subcontinent.

At first, the British controlled little more than what is now Calcutta and some surrounding regions of Bengal and Bihar, and their interest in India was almost totally commercial. Within a century, however, as a result of certain strategic military victories together with carefully crafted diplomatic alliances with local rulers, the British controlled almost the whole of the subcontinent with only small numbers of troops. With the British, of course, came all of the forces of modernization, including the involvement of the subcontinent in the world economy; new patterns of education (at least in the main urban areas with the introduction of English education after 1813); new bureaucratic and legal structures; new philosophical ideas such as humanism, liberal democracy, and Enlightenment rationalism; and new religious ideas through the aggressive work of all sorts of Christian missionaries.

Reactions among Hindus to the encounters with modernity were complex and multidimensional. On one level, there was a rapid and positive response, especially in urban centers such as Calcutta, Bombay, and Madras, to English education, government service, and new economic opportunities. A new Indian elite began to emerge, made up largely of English-speaking members of the upper castes, in such fields as modern trade, manufacturing, civil service, commercial agriculture, and the newly emerging professions of law, journalism, and education. Indeed, the present-day descendants of this new elite are the very Asian Indians that one is likely to find in today's America. On another level, there was widespread dislike, even revulsion, against evangelical Christian missionizing. On still another level, many English-educated Indians opted not only for the new language and the resulting benefits to career and personal wealth, but also for Western ideas such as liberalism, representative democracy, and social reform.

Likewise on the level of religion, Hindus responded to modernity in complex and multidimensional ways. By the beginning of the nineteenth century and thereafter, some significant innovations began to appear on at least two distinct levels. First, a reformist and nationalist recasting of Hindu values and traditions culminated in the emergence of India as a modern, secular nation-state. Second, a revisionist and internationalist recasting of Hindu values and traditions culminated in the export of a variety of Hindu guru-cults to the West, especially to the United States. Both levels can be characterized as "Neo-Hindu" in the sense that they reflect distinctly new elements being introduced into what we have called the classical Hindu synthesis as a result of the impact of modernity and the encounter with Western civilization.

Neo-Hindu Reformist
and Nationalist Movements

A variety of reform movements emerged both before independence (1947) and after, representing political strategies ranging from radical extremism to moderate reformism. Perhaps the most famous reformist and nationalist movement in the Modern Period is the Ramakrishna Mission, established by Swami Vivekananda (birth-name Narendranath Datta, 1862–1902) in Bengal, and named after the Bengali spiritual teacher or "holy man" Ramakrishna (birth-name Gadadhar Chatterjee, 1836–1886), who was Vivekananda's guru. Ramakrishna spent his entire adult life as a priest in a temple devoted to the goddess Kali in the distinct of Dakshineshwar near Calcutta. He had a number of extraordinary mystical experiences and over the years attracted a small band of followers, one of whom was Narendranath Datta, later to be given the spiritual name Vivekananda (meaning "whose bliss is discrimination"). After Ramakrishna's death, Vivekananda made a pilgrimage around India and determined, finally, to propagate the spiritual message of his guru. Vivekananda developed and taught a simplified version of monistic Vedanta philosophy and combined those ideas with a program for social action and social reform for modern India. He attended the World Parliament of Religions in 1893 in Chicago as a representative of Hinduism, and his considerable oratorical skills made a deep impression in the popular press and in certain liberal religious intellectual circles. He traveled widely in the United States and made a number of American converts. In 1897, after his return to India, he established the Ramakrishna Mission in India, along with a series of Vedanta Societies in the United States, Europe, and Latin America.

Mohandas Karamchand Gandhi (1869–1948) was born in the western region of Gujarat, studied law in England (1888–1891), practiced law for twenty-one years in South Africa (1893–1914), and then returned to India to lead the nationalist struggle for independence from the British. He was primarily a political leader, but his political work was inextricably linked to his reformed and nationalist Neo-Hindu vision that stressed (1) the oneness of all religions; (2) the pursuit of nonviolent noncooperation against the British as a political strategy, or what he called "truth-force" or "grasping truth" (*satyagraha*); and (3) the cultivation of nonviolence (*ahimsa*) in all conflict situations. He detested the inequities of the caste system, especially "untouchability," and he thought that the spiritual life was essential to political life. Although he never founded a religious group as such, it can be said that he rallied an entire nation to his Neo-Hindu vision of reform and nationalism.

Despite their varying political orientations and strategies, these Neo-Hindu reformist and nationalist movements had in common (1) a primary focus on developing among the people of India a self-confident national awareness that would provide a solid foundation for India as a modern nation-state; (2) the reform of outdated, parochial, and superstitious Hindu practices; (3) the rejection of the caste system; (4) female emancipation; (5) the improvement of social conditions for the poor; and (6) economic progress for the entire nation. These groups contributed incalculably to the identity of the modern Indian nation-state.

Neo-Hindu Revisionist and Internationalist Movements

There also emerged among other Neo-Hindu groups what can be called a revisionist and internationalist impulse. "Revisionist" and "internationalist" imply ideas and practices that have clear antecedents in older patterns of Hindu spirituality but are designed to appeal not only to Asian Indians, but also to a broad-based international audience as well. Common features of these "export" brands of Neo-Hinduism include (1) devotion to a deified guru; (2) total obedience to the will of the guru; (3) the practice of one or another type of Yoga; (4) the claim that all religions are basically valid; (5) the claim that one's national or ethnic identity has no bearing on the practice of the particular Neo-Hindu tradition; and (6) a tendency to de-emphasize social work or political activity of any kind.

Some of the better known of these "export" brands of Neo-Hinduism include:

1. The Self-Realization Fellowship in Los Angeles, founded by Paramahamsa Yogananda (birth-name, Mukunda Lal Ghosh, 1893–1952), a Bengali *sadhu,* or "holy man," who first came to the United States to attend a conference in Boston in 1920 and then remained to establish his Self-Realization Fellowship in the same year. Today the Self-Realization Fellowship maintains eight temples throughout the western United States and has its international headquarters in Los Angeles.

2. The Center of Satya Sai Baba (birth-name, Satya Narayan, b. 1926), a non-Brahmin from Puttaparthi in the state of Andhra Pradesh in South India, who at the age of fourteen declared himself to be a reincarnation of the Shirdi Sai Baba, a holy man from Maharashtra who died in 1918. Alleged to be a great healer, he has a purported following in India of two to three million. Currently Satya Sai Baba maintains three major centers in the United States (Los Angeles, San Francisco, and Phoenix).

3. The Spiritual Regeneration Movement or Transcendental Meditation (TM), founded by Maharishi Mahesh Yogi (birth-name, Mahesh Prasad Varma, b. 1911) in the 1960s. TM centers are found throughout the United States and Europe. The international headquarters of the movement is in Switzerland. The Maharishi teaches a simple technique of sound-meditation. The devotee is given a sacred *mantra,* or sound, and then told to meditate one-half hour to an hour every day.

4. The International Society for Krishna Consciousness (ISKCON), founded in the 1960s by A. C. Bhaktivedanta Prabhupada (birth-name, Abhay Charan De, 1896–1977), a Bengali businessman from Calcutta who became a Vaishnava monk. Also known as the Hare Krishna movement, the Society's followers can be seen on street corners in many American cities, chanting "Hare Krishna, Hare Rama," the basic mantra of the group.

5. The Siddha Yoga ("Discipline of Spiritual Fulfillment") Movement, founded by Swami (Baba) Muktananda (1908–1982), is currently based at an Ashrama in South Fallsburg, New York, and an Ashrama in India at Ganeshpuri, Maharashtra (near Bombay). Since the death of its founder in 1982, the movement has been led mainly by a young woman, Guru-

mayi Cidvilasananda. The movement is a blend of classical and Tantric Yoga practices, emphasizing the importance of *shakti* ("power" or "divine energy"). Followers believe that shakti can descend suddenly (a process called *shaktipat*) into a devotee by the mere presence or touch of the guru.

Although all of these and other Neo-Hindu revisionist and internationalist movements have some connection with traditional Hindu spirituality, all have clearly moved away from a specifically Indian identity. They are all international movements with sizable followings throughout the world.

HINDUISM IN TODAY'S AMERICA

Currently there are well over 150 Hindu temples in the United States, divided evenly between the eastern and western regions of the country. Many of these are quite small centers, some being little more than converted private homes. Others, however, are major temple complexes. For example, the Lord Venkateshwara Balaji Temple in Malibu Canyon near Los Angeles is an authentic South Indian (primarily Vaishnava) temple. Artisans and priests were brought from India for the actual planning and construction of the temple, and priests from India continue to assist in the temple's ritual operations.

Basic Types of Hinduism in America

A broad, general perspective would suggest five basic types of Hinduism in America: Secular Hinduism, Non-sectarian Hinduism, Bhakti or Devotional Hinduism, Reformist-Nationalist Neo-Hinduism, and Guru-Internationalist-Missionizing Neo-Hinduism. Most Asian Indians that you meet in the United States will probably fit into one of these broad, general types. By "Secular Hinduism" is meant those Asian Indian Hindus who do not identify with any particular beliefs or practices of traditional Hinduism, but who at the same time have never chosen to be in any other religious grouping. Among Asian Indian Hindus in today's America many would be of this secular variety (especially highly educated, professional Asian Indian adult males). By "Non-sectarian Hinduism" is meant those Asian Indian Hindus who do not identify with any particular branch of Hinduism, but who practice a broad, eclectic form of Hinduism that relates to the regions and castes of India from which they come. Most of these Hindus would come from the high or "forward" castes, mainly Brahmin. By "Bhakti or Devotional

Hinduism" is meant those Asian Indian Hindus who would identify themselves with a particular sectarian tradition, Vaishnava, Shaiva, or Shakta, all of which have been described earlier in the chapter. By "Reformist-Nationalist Neo-Hinduism" is meant those Asian Indian Hindus who are followers of groups such as the Ramakrishna Mission. Finally, by "Guru-Internationalist-Missionizing Neo-Hinduism" is meant those Asian Indian Hindus who are followers of groups such as the Transcendental Meditation movement or the Hare Krishna movement. What distinguishes the two types of Neo-Hinduism is that the Reformist-Nationalist type maintains a primary interest in the native homeland of India and is not especially mission-minded, while the Guru-Internationalist-Missionizing type has a broadly internationalist perspective and actively seeks converts from outside the Asian Indian population.

Basic Beliefs of Hindus in America

As we have stressed throughout this chapter, there is no specific, required set of beliefs for a Hindu. An American Hindu organization, however, known as the Himalayan Academy, has set forth what it calls "Nine Beliefs of Hinduism," as a general summary of Hindu views largely accepted by all of the types of Hinduism in America (with the exception, of course, of Secular Hinduism).[3] The nine beliefs are as follows:

1. That there is "one, all-pervasive Supreme Being";
2. That there are "endless cycles of creation, preservation and dissolution" (that is, a cyclical view of time and history);
3. That "all souls are evolving" toward or seeking "Moksha" or "liberation";
4. That there is a "law of cause and effect" known as Karma;
5. That there is "reincarnation";
6. That there are "divine beings and forces" that require "temple worship" and "personal worship," or Puja, in the home;
7. That there is a need for "an awakened Master of Sat Guru" (that is, a reliable, personal teacher) for one's personal and ethical life;
8. That "all life is sacred" and that one should pursue "*ahimsa* or non-violence"; and
9. That "no particular religion teaches the only way to salvation above all others, but that all genuine religious paths are . . . deserving (of) tolerance and understanding."

Basic Practices of Hindus in America

Generally speaking, Asian Indian Hindus, with the exception of the followers of Secular Hinduism, center their religious life around three kinds of practices: personal or family worship or Puja in the home; determining crucial times or seasons for important activities (astrology or horoscopy); and celebration of important festivals or holidays.

Personal or Family Worship in the Home

Almost every Asian Indian Hindu home will have a special room or at least a shelf or special place for daily worship and meditation (puja). Usually the puja room will have statues or color pictures of various deities (gods and goddesses) and gurus (teachers). The deities and teachers will usually be from the region in India from which the family comes (West Bengal, Maharashtra, and so forth), but also frequently include such universal Hindu figures as Vishnu, Lord Krishna, Lord Rama, Shiva, and Ganesh, for example. Candles and incense will be burned, usually at set times (dawn, evening, and so forth), and prayers will be uttered, interspersed with periods of quiet meditation and sometimes even one or another kind of yoga practice. In most Asian Hindu families, the mother is in charge of the puja room and the daily and seasonal devotional practices in the life of the family.

Astrology and Horoscopy

For many traditional Hindus and Neo-Hindus, all important events in the unfolding life of the family and community—family planning, a major journey, the marriage of a child, the building and dedication of temples, and so on—will only be undertaken after having determined the appropriate time by consulting a professional astrologer or casting horoscopes. Most Asian Indian Hindu families in America use Western traditions of astrology, but some also follow traditional South Asian horoscopy. Astrology is an important component in the family's planning, especially in determining marriage. Most Asian Indian Hindu marriages, even among the followers of Secular Hinduism, are arranged marriages, and many Hindu families will have horoscopes cast for the proposed bride and groom and for determining the day and specific time of the wedding. This is an important legacy of the traditional caste system, and even Neo-Hindus who reject the traditional caste system continue to practice the tradition of arranged marriages and the casting of horoscopes.

Celebration of Important Festivals and Holidays

Important festivals or holidays that many Hindus in America observe include:

1. "Worship of the Goddess Sarasvati," a special festival for scholars, teachers, and students celebrating the great goddess of learning;
2. "Shiva's Night," a special festival day for Shaivas but celebrated by many other non-Shaiva Hindus as well;
3. Holi, named after the demon-goddess Holika, a raucous fertility festival in which Hindus pour colored water or paint on one another and exchange humorous erotic obscenities and jokes;
4. "The Ninth Day for Rama," celebrating the birth of Lord Rama;
5. "The Guru's Full-Moon Day," a festival that honors the particular guru of the Hindu devotee;
6. "The Bracelet-Tying for Protection," a festival when brothers commit themselves to protecting their sisters symbolized by having their sisters tie a special bracelet around their brothers' wrists;
7. "The Eighth Day for Krishna," the festival celebrating the birth of Lord Krishna;
8. "The Fourth Day for Ganesh," a celebration in which businesspeople, students, artisans, and others implore Lord Ganesh (the elephant god) for blessings on their work;
9. "The Nine Nights," celebration (mainly for Bengalis) Durga Puja, or the "worship of the goddess Durga," who overcomes the buffalo-demon (the symbol of evil), or celebrating (for Vaishnavas devoted to Lord Rama) the great struggle between Lord Rama and the demon Ravana;
10. "The Tenth Day," celebrating the final victory of Lord Rama over the demon Ravana;
11. "The Festival of Lamps," involving the lighting of candles or colored lights or lamps signifying the reappearance of the sun and prosperity after the long rainy season.

CONCLUSION

This, then, brings to a conclusion our telling of the story of Hinduism, an incredible story that contains some of the oldest forms of religion known to humankind, as well as some of the newest. Hinduism is boundlessly various in its myriad forms and yet bears an unmistakable coherence in patterns of ritual performance, the pursuit of quiet mediation (yoga), and the exuberant expression of passionate devotion (bhakti).

NOTES

1. Amulya Ratna Nanda, ed., *Census of India 1991, Paper-1 of 1991, Provisional Population Totals* (Delhi: Government of India, Samrat Press, 1991), 19 and passim.

2. Ibid.

3. "Nine Beliefs of Hinduism," published by the Himalayan Academy, 3575 Sacramento Street, San Francisco, CA 94118.

STUDY QUESTIONS

1. What does "being religious" mean for the Hindu? How does Hinduism's emphasis on correct action differ from other religious traditions you have studied?
2. What are the six fundamental periods for the development of Hinduism? What are the defining characteristics of each of these periods? How is the historical development of Hinduism different from that of other religious traditions?
3. What do most Hindus think of the concepts of gods and goddesses? What are the names of three or four well-known Hindu deities? What roles do they play in the Hindu religion?
4. What are the "four purposes of life" in the Hindu religion? How do these purposes function to describe the Hindu's understanding of living in the world?
5. What are the "four stages of life"? How do these stages function to describe the Hindu's understanding of living in the world?
6. What are the four divisions of castes in Hinduism? How do they function to describe the Hindu's understanding of living in the world?
7. What were the reactions, particularly among Hindus coming to America, of their encounter with the modern world? Socially? Religiously?
8. Who is the most famous reformist of the Hindu Modern Period? What were his contributions to Hindu social and religious development?
9. What are the five basic types of Hinduism in America? Give a brief description of each. What are the nine basic beliefs that serve to define American Hinduism?
10. Name and describe some of the important festivals or holidays observed by Hindus in America. Are these festivals similar in function to other religious festivals you have studied? In what way?

ESSAY TOPICS

Hinduism and Modernity: Conflict and Assimilation
The *Bhagavad Gita:* Sacred Text of Hinduism
The Gods and Goddesses of Hinduism
Karma and Rebirth: Two Fundamental Principles of Hinduism
The Hindu Pilgrimages: Four Purposes, Four States, Four Castes
Hinduism in America: Beginnings and Growth

WORD EXPLORATION

The following words play significant roles in any discussion of Hinduism in America and are worth careful reflection and discussion.

Hindu	Vaishya	Shiva
Ritual	Shudra	Samsara
Sanskrit	Brahmin	Moksha
Upanishads	*Bhagavad Gita*	Temple
Veda	Yoga	Vishnu
Kshatriyas	*Mahabharata*	

9

MALCOLM DAVID ECKEL

Buddhism in the World and in America

If you have never thought of religion without thinking of God, or if you think that a religion has to have clear boundaries that separate insiders from outsiders, then you will be intrigued and challenged by your encounter with Buddhism. For over two thousand years in Asia, and more recently in Europe and North America, the Buddhist tradition has brought joy, consolation, and meaning to human life without affirming the existence of a personal God, and it has found ways to exist side by side with other religious traditions without many of the great conflicts that have plagued religious life in the West.

Buddhism arose in India, and the largest concentrations of Buddhists in the world can still be found in Asia. In some places, as in Tibet, Sri Lanka, and Thailand, Buddhism is clearly the dominant tradition; in others, such as China, Korea, and Japan, Buddhism has not necessarily dominated the culture but has had a deep impact on the way people think through religious questions and deal with the religious crises in their lives.

As the Buddhist tradition spread across Asia, it spawned many different varieties, and a surprising number of these varieties have made their way to North America. The most visible Buddhist community in some parts of the United States is a group known as the Buddhist Churches of America (BCA). The BCA brings together a venerable Japanese tradition of devotion to the Buddha Amida (the Buddha of Infinite Light) with many of the trappings of modern American religious life, from a Buddhist Sunday school to the Young Buddhist Association. In many communities in America you can find, for example, centers for the practice of Zen, the Japanese version of an ancient discipline of seated meditation; centers of the Nichiren Shoshu of America (NSA), devoted to meditation on a Buddhist text known as the Lotus Sutra; Insight (Vipassana) Centers for meditation that is derived from the Buddhist practice of Southeast Asia; and centers for the study of the different varieties of Tibetan Buddhism. The list seems almost endless.

Even if we could name all the centers of Buddhism in America, we still would not begin to exhaust its influence on American cultural life. For a hundred years or more, Buddhist values have left their mark on the American cultural landscape. Japanese attitudes toward nature significantly affected the way American painters and architects visualized the landscape as early as the nineteenth century. The countercultures of the 1950s and 1960s echoed the strains of Jack Kerouac's *Dharma Bums*. Bruce Lee brought the meditative tradition of the martial arts into American living rooms. Now you can hear echoes of Buddhist values almost everywhere you look. The rock group Nirvana takes its name from the Buddhist ideal of release from the cycle of transmigration, and the title of their album "Nevermind" is a direct reflection of the important Buddhist concept of "no-mind." Whether Americans have really understood Buddhist values is a question you may want to ask yourself when you have finished this chapter, but there is no doubt that Buddhism has crept into our culture in surprising and delightful ways.

If Buddhism is so varied and has influenced American culture so widely, what makes it "Buddhist"? It would be wonderful to point to a single doctrine or practice that we could identify as the "essence" of Buddhism. But Buddhists have been uncomfortable with any language suggesting that things have "essences." They insist that everything changes and nothing has any permanent identity, least of all a movement as complex and as varied as the one we call "Buddhism." It is better not to look for a single essence, but rather for a center of gravity or for lines of force around which Buddhist people have oriented themselves as they struggle to give meaning, depth, and texture to their lives. For centuries the most basic point of orientation has been the story of Siddhartha Gautama, the founder of the Buddhist tradition.

THE BUDDHA

From a modern Western perspective, the history of Buddhism begins with the story of a man named Siddhartha Gautama who lived about five hundred years before the Common Era in a small kingdom in the foothills of what is now southern Nepal. Buddhist tradition tells us that this man was born into a princely family and raised in a palace. He married, had a child, and then, in his early thirties, saw four sights that burned into his consciousness an image of the decay and death that stalks human life. He saw a sick person, an old person, a corpse, and finally an ascetic who was attempting to leave this suffering behind by renouncing the pleasures of ordinary life. Siddhartha decided to follow the example of the ascetic and abandon the princely life. He left the palace, gave away his princely ornaments, cut off his hair, and took up the life of a wandering holy man on the roads of northern India. Legends tell us that he studied with a series of teachers and starved himself until he was reduced almost to skin and bones. Siddhartha found, however, that strict denial of the pleasures of the body did not produce the insight he was seeking. He decided instead to take up a balanced discipline known as the Middle Path, where he would seek neither pleasure nor pain. On the Middle Path, he began finally to make progress. He sat down under a tree called the Bodhi Tree and, after a series of temptations, broke through to the realization that he no longer was subject to the suffering of human life. He became, in other words, a Buddha—someone who has been "enlightened" or, more accurately, someone who has "woken up" from the sleep of ignorance that binds people in the suffering of this world.

Most of the details of the Buddha's story come from traditions and legends that are now very difficult to confirm, but there is little doubt among scholars of Buddhism that something like this actually happened: there was a man who was raised in a princely setting, left it behind, and achieved a breakthrough that became the basis of a great world religion. But if you ask Buddhists where the story of the Buddha really begins, it is not just with the birth of Siddhartha Gautama. It has to be traced back many lifetimes to his career as a future Buddha, or *bodhisattva* (a Buddha-to-be), when he laid the groundwork for his eventual awakening by performing acts of generosity, moral courage, and self-sacrifice.

Buddhists tell a story, for example, about a time when the bodhisattva was born as the leader of a herd of deer. The herd was being hunted mercilessly by the king of a neighboring kingdom. To limit the king's cruelty, the deer agreed that they would make a regular sacrifice of one of the herd. When the time came to give up a particular doe who was about to give birth to a fawn, the bodhisattva, as the leader of the herd, offered to present himself to the king in the doe's place. The king was so impressed by the deer's willingness to sacrifice himself that he agreed to stop hunting and guarantee the herd's safety. The story is simple and is meant to appeal to ordinary people who do not have the chance to imitate the example of the Buddha's renunciation, but the themes of self-sacrifice are very similar. Not everyone has the chance to become a monk and formally renounce attachment to this world, but even the simplest and most worldly people can be called on to make great sacrifices to help others. To become a Buddha, Siddhartha Gautama had to leave the palace—to give up what he once was and become something new—but he also had to prepare for that final renunciation with acts of generosity and self-sacrifice in previous lives. These images of generosity and renunciation, both great and small, have colored Buddhist life throughout its history.

The stories of the Buddha's previous lives bring us face to face with an aspect of Indian religion that is difficult to fathom, but is crucial for anyone who wants to understand the ideal of renunciation that motivates so much of Indian religious life. Buddhism is rooted in the Indian doctrine of *samsara*, a word that we translate as "reincarnation" or "transmigration," but it literally means a "wandering" from one life to the next. Sometime in the centuries that preceded the life of the Buddha, Indian thinkers began to imagine that human existence involved not just a single life followed by a possible reward in heaven, but a series of lives stretching into the past without beginning and potentially into the future without end. The fate of a soul as it wanders through the forest or over the stormy sea of *samsara* is determined by its *karma*, its actions. People who perform good actions are rewarded in future lives, perhaps even by being reborn in the heaven of one of the myriad Indian gods, and people who perform bad actions are punished with birth as an animal, an insect, or an inhabitant of one of the Indian hells. But all the results of action, both good and bad, slip away, so that the gods eventually fall back down into the human realm, and the animals eventually rise to take birth as human beings.

To understand the impact of the doctrine of reincarnation it is important to grasp two points. First, the doctrine is *fundamental*. In the West ideas of reincarnation hover on the fringes of established religious traditions: they are options that people feel free to take or leave. But in India the doctrine of reincarnation has the status of a basic assumption. It poses a problem that generations of Indian religious thinkers have attempted to solve. What makes the doctrine of reincarnation so problematic? As thoughtful religious figures pondered the implications of reincarnation in the centuries that preceded the life of the Buddha, they came to feel not only that that reincarnation was fundamental but that it was enormously *burdensome*. As they looked back into the past and forward into the future, not for just one or two lives but for many, many millions of lives, they saw reincarnation as the frustration of all human hopes and desires. No matter how delightful pleasures might be, they were doomed eventually to slip away.

This sense of disillusionment with the endless cycle of death and rebirth was what gave the story of the Buddha's career its urgency and power. Siddhartha Gautama set out to find the solution to the problem of reincarnation, and the teaching that grew out of the experience of his awakening mapped a way for others to follow as they struggled to find their own passage through the forest and across the ocean of death and rebirth. Buddhists have elaborated the teaching, or the Dharma, of the Buddha with great eloquence and doctrinal sophistication. But the Buddha's Dharma is not meant to satisfy idle curiosity or serve as an intellectual game. It is meant to chart a path out of suffering and into an experience of freedom from the endless cycle of rebirth.

DHARMA: THE BUDDHA'S TEACHING

After the Buddha experienced his awakening, Buddhist tradition tells us, he rose from his seat under the Bodhi Tree and walked to a Deer Park in Varanasi (the same park that was associated with his earlier life as the king of the herd of deer). In the Deer Park he met some friends, and he sat down and told them of his awakening. This act of teaching is called the first "turning of the wheel of Dharma" and has come to represent the moment when the Buddha set the Buddhist tradition in motion. The Dharma is symbolized by a wheel, and the wheel has become the symbol of Buddhism. The words spoken by the Buddha on this occasion, as tradition has preserved them, are surprisingly simple, but they contain many of the insights that set the Buddhist tradition apart from other great religions of the world.

The content of the Buddha's first sermon is divided into *Four Noble Truths:* the truth of *suffering,* the truth of the *origin* of suffering, the truth of the *cessation* of suffering, and the truth of the *path* that leads to the cessation of suffering. The first of these truths is expressed by saying "all is suffering," a claim that has given the Buddhist tradition an unjustified reputation for being the most pessimistic of the world's religions. As one commentator said, if Buddhists mean what they say, they should go around with the world's longest faces. Like many important religious claims, however, the truth of suffering needs to be interpreted.

Buddhist tradition says that the claim "all is suffering" can be understood three ways. First, there is an obvious sense in which some things are simply painful. To be run over by a bus or crushed by a raging elephant is painful, and that pain is a form of suffering. There is a second form of suffering that comes when you become too attached to something that brings pleasure. If you try to hold on to things that bring great satisfaction, they eventually bring pain. Even the most satisfying things begin to change and slip away, and, if you cannot let them go, they cause pain. This kind of pain is the suffering that comes from change. The third kind of suffering is more difficult to grasp. Buddhists say that "pleasurable" things can cause suffering even while they bring us pleasure, because the idea of "pleasure" is based on a misconception about the nature of reality. The objects that we consider pleasurable or painful are no more than a series of "conditioned states," and the idea of "pleasure" or "pain" is something that we in our ignorance and desire impose upon them.

Buddhist texts often use the example of a vehicle or a cart to reflect on the doctrine of suffering and the vision of reality that lies behind it. To bring the example up to date, we could say that the experience of suffering is like the American experience of an automobile. If you drive a new car into a telephone pole, the feeling you have in your bones is the first kind of suffering. If you take the car home, live with it for a while, and watch rust creep slowly up the door panels, the sensation of satisfaction turning slowly to disappointment is the second kind of suffering. The third kind of suffering lurks within the experience of satisfaction itself. When you drive the car out of the showroom door and imagine that it is an object that brings you great pleasure, the pleasure itself is a subtle form of pain. It clouds the mind and prevents you from seeing reality as it truly is.

Is the truth of suffering pessimistic? Not necessarily. There is still plenty of room to smile and take quiet delight in something like a new car as you watch it change. You can still put the top down on a sunny day, drive it through the landscape, and feel the wind blowing in your hair. But the Buddhist analysis of suffering contains a clear warning against attachment—against the desire to freeze these moments of satisfaction and not let them go—and it forces a person to look carefully at the moments of satisfaction and cut through the illusions that make many objects of desire seem more satisfying than they really are.

According to the *Second Noble Truth*, suffering comes from desire, and desire comes, through a complicated mental process, from *ignorance*. Like suffering, the concept of ignorance has more than one meaning. To see the world without ignorance you have to be able to recognize things that are palpably painful. You have to see the car when it is bearing down on you and step out of the way. You also have to realize that the satisfaction you feel when you see it glistening in the sunlight is constantly changing. You have to enjoy it while you can and then let it go. You also have to realize that, while it glistens, it is nothing but a combination of plastic, steel, chrome, and glass. There really is nothing to call "car" apart from this combination of constituents, and the constituents themselves are constantly decaying and evolving into other things.

The idea that there is no car apart from an evolving combination of parts is an example of the famous Buddhist doctrine of *no-self*. From the time of the Buddha, it seems Buddhists have claimed that nothing has any permanent identity. What we imagine to be its "self" is nothing more than an illusion we impose on an arbitrary and changing flow of events. This illusion is just as true of the driver as it is of the car. What we think of as being our "selves" is nothing more than a combination of thoughts, feelings, memories, and conscious states, all of which are in a continuous state of change. We can speak in a practical way about ourselves being the "same" personality from one moment to the next, just as we can say that the fire burning in the fireplace is the "same" fire from one moment to the next, but the truth is that we are changing, just as the fire is burning, and the "sameness" we attribute to ourselves is nothing more than a convenient fiction that helps us get on with the process of living.

Sometimes people ask why Buddhists seem to pay so much attention to abstract questions of identity or selfhood, when the Buddha was concerned with the practical issue of relief from suffering. The answer is that *wisdom*, a deep understanding of no-self, starts the process of unraveling the chain of suffering. It begins to put out the fire of the personality and leads to the peace that Buddhists associate with the *Third Noble Truth*, the truth of *cessation* or *nirvana*. Nirvana is the definitive end of the cycle of reincarnation. It is difficult for people who pride themselves on being active and busy to sympathize with the traditional Buddhist concept of nirvana. Instead of busyness, it speaks of quiet and cessation. Instead of a constant drive to create and succeed, it speaks of an impulse to take a bit of what we think of as existence and let it slip away. The word nirvana refers literally to a "blowing out," as if the fire of the personality could be allowed to flicker out like the dying flame of a candle.

To understand Buddhist approaches to the concept of nirvana, it is important not to wish away the negative aspect of the concept but to confront it directly. If you assume, as Buddhists have, that life in the cycle of reincarnation has been going on from a time that had no beginning, and that the job of each individual ultimately is to bring the cycle to an end, then cessation, extinction, and stopping are positive images. They convey a sense of peace and serenity that cuts through the constant frustration of life. To touch the spirit of nirvana in your own experience you might simply imagine what goes through your mind when you crawl out of bed in the morning and begin to face the day. Is your job to do what God is pictured as doing in the Jewish or Christian scriptures—to look into the primordial chaos of the day and make something new come into being— or is it to look closely at the fire of existence that has been burning from time without beginning and allow some of it to burn away? If you choose the second option, you will find yourself become more meditative, more focused on the quiet moments of experience—the silent spaces between heartbeats—and you will feel some of the distractions of ordinary experience begin to slip away. This is not nirvana, but it is a step in that direction, and it introduces you to the basic Buddhist practice of meditation.

The practice that we call meditation is part of the *Fourth Noble Truth*, the *path* to the cessation of suffering. Standard outlines of the path speak of it as having eight parts (the "noble eightfold path"), beginning with "right understanding" and proceeding through "right action" and "right livelihood" to "right mindfulness" and "right concentration." But the easiest way to get a sense of how Buddhists have put the insights of the noble truths into practice is to divide the practice of the path into three categories: moral conduct, concentration, and wisdom. Traditionally, Buddhists have observed five moral precepts: no killing, no stealing, no lying, no abusing sex, and no taking of intoxicants. Concentration has to do with the practices of mental discipline that we usually associate with meditation. A very common type of concentration is to sit down in a stable posture and concentrate on the movement of the breath. As thoughts and distractions rise in the mind, you observe them, let them gently pass away, and bring your concentration back to the movement of your breath. The practice of the moral precepts and the practice of concentration both allow the negative tendencies that afflict the mind and body to pass gently away so that the mind can begin to see clearly the flow of phenomena that make up ordinary experience. Finally, you infuse this clear mind with the wisdom, or the awareness of no-self, that unravels the chain of reincarnation.

SAMGHA: THE BUDDHIST COMMUNITY

When the Buddha taught the four noble truths to the small band of friends who gathered around him in the Deer Park in Varanasi, he set in motion a historical movement that eventually carried his teaching through much of

Asia. The Buddha himself spent about forty years wandering the roads of northern India, preaching his Dharma and gathering followers into the community that constituted his *Samgha,* a word that sometimes is translated as "church." The community split naturally into two categories. There were *monks* and *nuns* who followed the Buddha's example by giving up their possessions and their normal social responsibilities to seek nirvana, and there were *laypeople* who followed the Buddha's basic precepts, but who did not engage in the acts of renunciation that would bring them directly to nirvana.

In time, this two-part division of the community produced a pattern of life that is duplicated in different ways throughout the Buddhist world. There are monasteries where monks study and teach the Dharma, and there are laypeople who support the monks and gain "merit" that will help them in future lives. In the countries of Southeast Asia, such as Thailand, Sri Lanka, and Burma, this relationship between the monks and the laypeople is expressed most vividly in the morning begging rounds, when the monks in a monastery go out into the surrounding villages with their begging bowls and beg food at the homes of their lay supporters. Monks are not allowed to eat after noon and cannot keep food from one day to the next, so each day begins with this basic ritual. The monk begs and the layperson gives, each one demonstrating a sense that people have to let go of the things of this world to achieve the goals they seek.

Another pattern of action associated with the life of the Buddha is a practice of worship, although Buddhist worship has a shape that makes it different from the worship you find in most other religious communities. Stories about the end of the Buddha's life tell us that the Buddha's supporters asked him how they should treat the remains of his body after his death. He made it clear that he expected monks to concentrate on following his example: to venerate him, as Buddhists say, through his Dharma Body rather than through his physical form. But he advised his lay supporters to cremate his body as they would the body of a great sage or a king, and erect a shrine to hold his ashes. This shrine, known traditionally as a *stupa,* could then be the focus of the actions that constitute worship (*puja*), the offering of flowers, water, or fragrant ointments and the lighting of lamps. The Buddha's possessions and the relics of his cremation were divided into several parts shortly after his death, and they have subsequently been subdivided and fought over in so many different ways that it is difficult any longer to trace their history, but they still serve as the focus for some of the most important shrines in the Buddhist world. In northwest India there used to be a famous shrine that housed the Buddha's begging bowl, but the shrine succumbed to one of the many barbarian invasions of India. In the town of Kandy in Sri Lanka there still is a famous temple dedicated to the Buddha's tooth. The tooth relic is paid daily homage and brought out once a year to serve as the focus of an elaborate festival.

For someone who looks at religion through Western eyes, the most intriguing aspect of Buddhist worship is that it does not need to involve anything like a belief in God. To venerate the Buddha as the Dharma Body requires only that you follow the Buddha's example. To worship the Buddha's relics requires only the belief that they have been infused with a certain power. The Buddha himself may long since have disappeared. There has been ambiguity in the Buddhist tradition about whether the Buddha lingers in some undefinable state after his death. But it is clear that the Buddha should not be considered a substitute for God. For centuries Buddhists have resisted the idea that the universe is governed by a creator god. There is nothing but a cycle of reincarnation and a man whose example made it possible for his followers to find their way out. In this respect Buddhism is genuinely an atheistic religion, a religion that does not presuppose the existence of God.

This does not mean, however, that Buddhists do not worry about the "gods" and spirits. In India and Southeast Asia different kinds of supernatural beings play as much a part in the cycle of reincarnation as human beings. They are not the God of Christianity, Judaism, or Islam: they are not the creators of the world and they do not occupy their positions forever. They rise and fall in the scale of reincarnation just as human beings do. But they do have extraordinary powers to cause illness or to bring good luck, and they need to be treated with care. In Thailand many families have special "spirit houses" in their family compounds to serve as homes for the spirits. There also are ritual specialists who control access to the spirits and preside over the rituals of spirit possession and exorcism.

Many people ask whether the "spirit cults" in Buddhist countries are genuinely Buddhist. The question is difficult to answer without raising some hard questions about what we mean by religion. The gods and spirits do not know the way to nirvana, so they play no role in the Buddha's quest for nirvana. But they are an essential part of the religious life of the people in countries that consider themselves Buddhist. Is the worship of gods and spirits Buddhist or not? Some would say no. But there is a strong tendency these days to look for religion in the things people actually do—to look for American religion, for instance, not just in the pages of the Bible but in the celebration of Halloween and the Fourth of July. By this measure, the worship of the spirits and gods in Buddhist countries is just as much a part of "Buddhism" as the quest for nirvana. It is one of the religious actions that Buddhist people perform to deal with uncertainty and give meaning to aspects of their lives that otherwise might seem out of control.

MAHAYANA: THE GREAT VEHICLE

After the Buddha's death, his teaching gradually spread across the countries of Asia. Wandering monks brought the Dharma to regions that had never heard of the Buddha. Within a few centuries, the teaching spread from its birthplace in northern India up into the northwest and down into the south. Buddhist missionaries also began to carry the Dharma beyond India to the countries of Southeast Asia, so that the tradition was well established outside the Indian subcontinent before the beginning of the Common Era. By the second century C.E. Buddhist teaching had made its way through Afghanistan and across the Silk Road, and had begun its long and productive relationship with the religious traditions of China and the rest of East Asia. As the teaching spread it also began to change. There were many small sectarian movements within the community in the first few hundred years after the Buddha's death, but none was more important or changed the face of Buddhism more dramatically than the movement that is called *Mahayana*, the "Great Vehicle."

The best way to understand the depth of Mahayana's impact on Buddhist life is to see it as a radical reinterpretation of the story of the Buddha. The texts that refer to themselves as Mahayana began to appear about four centuries after the Buddha's death and spoke of a "second turning of the wheel of the Dharma," a second major event when the Buddha initiated a new teaching. This new teaching shifted attention back from the final life of the Buddha toward the previous lives that prepared for the Buddha's nirvana—the lives, in other words, when the being who was to become the Buddha was a bodhisattva. The texts of the Mahayana spoke of the bodhisattva as an ideal that Buddhists should follow in order to imitate the example of the Buddha. This may not seem like an important change. After all, the tradition had always spoken of bodhisattvas as beings who were on the way to becoming Buddhas. But it made an enormous difference for people to begin thinking of the bodhisattva as the model of what a Buddhist should be. For one thing, it meant that a person did not have to become a monk to be an ideal practitioner of the Dharma. Laypeople could be just as good bodhisattvas as monks, and in some situations they could even be better. It also meant that Buddhist practice could no longer focus exclusively on the virtue of wisdom. The Mahayana still thought that it was important to see reality clearly, but it also was important to put that insight into practice—to act, as the deer king did, for the welfare of others. The bodhisattva ideal was a marriage of two virtues, wisdom and compassion. It combined the reflective virtues of the monastic life with the active virtues of a layperson.

The changes in the Mahayana did not stop here. The new movement also had a profound effect on the devotional relationship Buddhists had with the Buddha. Buddhists had always been able to "worship" the Buddha in one form or another, but the Mahayana opened up a whole new range of possibilities for worship and devotion. People began to think of bodhisattvas not just as human beings who struggled along in this world to follow the Buddha's example, but as celestial beings who, from many lifetimes of dedicated discipline, had developed the power to help others in extraordinary ways. Among the greatest of these celestial bodhisattvas was Avalokitesvara ("The Lord Who Looks Down"), the bodhisattva of compassion, who vowed to help creatures when they fell into danger. Avalokitesvara's compassion was crystallized in the *mantra* (a sacred phrase) *om mani padme hum.* Tibetans have understood the words of this mantra as meaning "O, the jewel in the lotus," but the meaning of the mantra (like the meaning of many religious phrases) lies less in the reference of the words themselves than in the function of the phrase as a whole. Mahayana Buddhists speak the mantra to invoke the power of Avalokitesvara's compassion. In Tibet, a country that is particularly devoted to Avalokitesvara, the mantra is carved on rocks, written on flags, and inscribed in prayer wheels so that with every spin of the wheel the country is filled with the limbs of Avalokitesvara's compassion. In China Avalokitesvara took female form as Kuan-yin, the mother of compassion, who functioned in many ways like the Virgin Mary in Roman Catholic countries. Pilgrimage sites grew up in places where people had visions of Kuan-yin, and temples were dedicated to her worship.

Mahayana texts also began to speak of a multitude of celestial Buddhas who had completed the long and arduous discipline of the bodhisattva path and achieved their awakening, not in this world (as Siddhartha Gautama had), but in the realms of the heavens. As part of their practice of the bodhisattva path, they had vowed to transport believers to their heavens if the believers had faith in the power of the Buddha's compassion. One of the most important of these celestial Buddhas was Amitabha ("Infinite Light"), known in Japan as Amida. Amida is associated with a heaven known as the Pure Land and, like Avalokitesvara, has crystallized his compassion in a powerful phrase. In Amida's case, however, it is simply his name. To touch the power of Amida, you can chant the phrase *namu Amida Butsu* ("homage to Amida Buddha") with faith and, by some accounts, Amida will appear at your deathbed surrounded by thousands of bodhisattvas to transport you to the Pure Land. I once asked a priest in the San Jose temple of the Buddhist Churches of America, the organization that represents Pure Land Buddhism in this country, what he thought was the most important thing for a young Buddhist to take with him when he went off to college. He said that it was this phrase, called the *nembutsu,* the chant of Amida's name. These words contained the essence of Amida's compassion.

The new emphasis on compassion changed the mood of the Buddhist tradition in remarkable ways. No aspect of ordinary life was so humble that it could not somehow be affirmed as part of a person's gradual pursuit of the bodhisattva path. But no change was more remarkable than the change that took place in the Mahayana vision of reality. In the earlier tradition, reality was viewed as a stream of momentary phenomena. Everything from the gods in their heavens to a blade of grass was undergoing a process of change, and nothing had a "self" that endured from one moment to the next. The philosophers of the Mahayana took a close look at the so-called "moments" that made up this process and asked whether they were any more real than the continuous "selves" they seemed to make up. The answer was no. The Mahayana philosophers claimed that nothing was ultimately real, including the moments that seemed to make up the stream of reality. The Greek philosopher Heraclitus once argued that, because everything changed, you could not step into the same river twice. Without being aware of him, of course, the Mahayana philosophers took Heraclitus a step further: they argued that you could not step into the same river once. The result was the *doctrine of emptiness,* which states that everything is illusion or is "empty" of any identity.

The doctrine of emptiness has struck many people as carrying the negative approach of the doctrine of no-self to a logical extreme and shattering all the distinctions that give life its meaning, from the distinction between you and me to the distinction between the world of reincarnation and nirvana. But the doctrine's effect on life in the Mahayana, paradoxically, was exactly the opposite. If there ultimately is no distinction between you and me, then it makes just as much sense for me to act like a bodhisattva and work for your welfare as it does for me to work for my own. And if there is no difference between the world of reincarnation and nirvana, then I can realize freedom from suffering right in the midst of suffering itself. All I have to do is see suffering for what it really is (and for what it is not). Emptiness is the glue that holds the bodhisattva practice together, and it is the realization that makes each moment of experience a possible mirror of the Buddha's awakening.

The doctrine of emptiness is beautifully reflected in the tradition of meditation that, in its Japanese form, goes by the name of *Zen*. This style of meditation is now so popular in America that you can find books to teach yourself everything from Zen in the traditional art of flower arrangement or the martial arts to the art of motorcycle maintenance or tennis. But Zen arose historically in China (under the Chinese name of *Ch'an*) as a combination of Indian monastic meditation and a form of Chinese contemplation associated with Taoism. It was simple, down to earth, and focused on the emptiness that can be revealed in a single moment of experience. Zen practice often involved long periods of study, with meditation sessions extending from early morning long into the night. It also involved intense intellectual struggle with the cryptic questions, called *koans*, that Zen teachers posed to stop the mind in its tracks and push students through to moments of awakening—questions like "Does a dog have Buddha nature?" or "What is the sound of one hand clapping?" But the most attractive and accessible expressions of Zen ideals often appear in the arts, when an artist or a poet seems to capture, in a single moment of experience, the sense of stillness in motion that lies at the heart of Zen awakening. The Japanese poet Basho crystallized this sense in a single three-line poem that is justly famous as an expression of the spirit of Zen.

Old pond
Frog jumps in—
Sound of water!

The values of the Mahayana had little enduring impact in the countries of Southeast Asia, such as Sri Lanka, Burma, Thailand, and Cambodia. There the people seemed quite content to pass on, under the name *Theravada* ("Teaching of the Elders"), the values of an earlier time in the development of the Buddhist tradition. But the more northerly countries of Asia—China, Japan, Korea, and Tibet—were deeply influenced by the Mahayana.

In India itself, the Buddhist impulse eventually ran its course and died out for reasons that are difficult fully to explain. The great monasteries that dominated Indian Buddhist life came under intense pressure from two directions between 900 and 1200 C.E.: they were threatened from the outside by Muslim armies and from within by a lively movement of popular Hindu devotion that seemed to steal Buddhism's vitality and diminish its importance in Indian religious life. But Buddhism has not ceased to be a vital force worldwide. With about 350 million people identified as Buddhists in the countries of Asia, it continues to have a crucial role in shaping the religious life of the world, and it has grown constantly in importance in modern America. Approximately half a million people in the United States identify themselves formally as Buddhist, and echoes of Buddhist values can be heard in many areas of American cultural life.

Behind all of the modern variations in the Buddhist tradition, behind the processions of monks that wind through the fields of Southeast Asia to beg their daily food, behind the parry and thrust of a Japanese swordsman, behind the lines of children in a California temple who chant to invoke the compassion of Amida, sits the figure of the Buddha, a man whose serenity and quiet smile have for centuries symbolized the human aspiration for peace in the midst of suffering and the wisdom to see through the illusions of this world.

STUDY QUESTIONS

1. How does Buddhism's understanding of a personal god distinguish it from many other religious traditions?
2. In what ways has the Buddhist tradition influenced American cultural life over the years?
3. Why is it difficult to point to any one religious practice or doctrine to decide what it means to be Buddhist?
4. Who is the Buddha? Give a brief biographical sketch of his life. What role does he play in the development of Buddhism?
5. Define karma. How does the Buddhist understand karma and the religious life? What is karma's relationship to reincarnation?
6. What is Dharma? Why is it symbolized by the wheel?
7. What are the Four Noble Truths of Buddhism? What is the importance of each in the religious life of the Buddhist?
8. Describe the doctrine of emptiness. How does it relate to the meditative practices of other religious traditions you have studied?
9. What role do gods play in the Buddhist tradition? How does this differ from other traditions you have studied?

ESSAY TOPICS

The Life and Thought of Gautama, the Buddha
The Four Noble Truths and the Buddhist Spiritual Journey
Buddhism and Suffering
Zen and the Doctrine of Emptiness

WORD EXPLORATION

The following words play significant roles in any discussion of Buddhism in America and are worth careful reflection and discussion.

Gautama	Reincarnation	Nirvana
Buddha	Dharma	Mahayana
Bodhisattva	Karma	Zen
Suffering		

10

ROBERT S. ELLWOOD

East Asian Religions in Today's America

In a suburb east of Los Angeles, amid shopping malls and upscale homes with pools and gardens, a spectacular bit of old China rests atop a scenic hill. The Hsi Lai ("Coming to the West") Buddhist Temple, built by a Buddhist organization in Taiwan and staffed by priests and nuns from that energetic island, is a dramatic token of the presence of East Asian religion in America today. Its ornate eaves turn upward, and its high steps are worn by the continual coming and going of worshipers. The worshipers, largely in family groups, come to bow and light sticks of incense placed in huge pots as they pay respects and offer prayers, perhaps on behalf of a deceased relative.

These practices are different from those of many other American religious groups, in which spiritual life tends to be more focused on public ceremonies. Although there are rites at Hsi Lai that center around chanting sutras or Buddhist scriptures and formal offerings of flowers and fruit, the conspicuous "life" of the temple, as in traditional China, is the continual coming and going of small groups of worshipers with their own purposes. That this is a distinctive style of religious life is also indicated by the coming and going of students and sightseers who, unless they have journeyed to East Asia, have never seen anything quite like this unforgettable temple.

The Hsi Lai Temple has two great halls. The outer hall is the hall of *bodhisattvas*, individuals once human but now virtually godlike who, after tremendous effort, have attained perfect wisdom. With wisdom they have perfect compassion as well, for anyone truly wise will understand that, in a universe in which all beings are interrelated, what you do to another you do to yourself as well; therefore, compassion or sympathetic love is the only absolute ethical value.

Along with wisdom and compassion, bodhisattvas have "skill in means," or in knowing how to put compassion into practice effectively. Their unlimited wisdom shows them how things work down to the subtlest levels. They can do things—come in various guises, make things appear out of nowhere—that look to the ordinary eye like miracles. Technically, however, these things are not magic but the manipulation of subtle laws of causation known only to holders of supreme wisdom.

In the outer hall are huge gilded images of five different bodhisattvas, all human but godlike, waiting to receive prayers. They stand on the borderline, so to speak, between this ordinary world—"the world of red dust," the Chinese call it—and the golden world of Buddhas and bo-dhisattvas, with their marvelous powers and winning compassion. The central one is Maitreya (Sanskrit; Mi-lo in Chinese), the popular and familiar portly, smiling lord of the coming paradisal Buddhist world.

Across an enclosed courtyard is the Buddha-hall, higher up and deeper in that golden realm. Present on the vast main altar are three large Buddhas, or enlightened beings. In Mahayana Buddhism—the form of Buddhism practiced in China, Japan, Korea, and Vietnam—a Buddha is not just the historical person who began the religion. There are countless Buddhas known and unknown throughout the depths of space and time, awesome minds able to comprehend the cosmos and whose meditations sustain worlds and galaxies. The Buddha-hall contains statues of three of the known Buddhas: the historical Buddha in the center; to the left Amitabha, a compassionate Buddha best known as the giver of salvation after death in his "Pure Land" to all who call upon him in faith; and on the right the healing Buddha.

The walls of this Buddha-hall are covered with a striking display of tiny Buddha images, like reflections of the cosmic Buddhas in the Buddhas of every world—and in the Buddha-nature in every person, for Mahayana says that we are all Buddhas, all enlightened, but that many of us don't realize it.

The majority of the neatly dressed men and women and the lively children coming to this temple and this hall, like the majority of worship-ers in any holy place, perhaps do not consciously reflect on the deeper points of their faith. They are content to sense here the presence of something sacred, something that lifts them for a moment out of the everyday grind, and at the same time links them to family, community, and roots in a faraway land. Here they can hear language, see smiling

Buddha-faces, smell incense, and on certain occasions even taste foods that bring back other days and other vistas in a country of rivers, mountains, rice paddies, and numberless temples like this one. For some, it may have been grandparents or great-grandparents who knew that country, but it still helps them feel a connection with their past.

Several miles away, in a modern American city, is a church of Tenrikyo, the "Religion of Heavenly Wisdom," one of the so-called new religions of modern Japan. The arrangement of its altar is similar to that of Shinto, the ancient Japanese religion of many local gods and shrines that goes back to prehistoric times, even before the coming of Buddhism to the island nation around the sixth century C.E. But whereas Shinto worships many deities, Tenrikyo has but one, the Creator of the world, Oyagami, "God the Parent." This Father/Mother God was revealed to Nakayama Miki,[1] a peasant woman, in the nineteenth century. She composed a scripture under God's inspiration describing the making of the world, and taught her followers beautiful dances that pantomime that creation story; they are still performed as major acts of the religion's worship in order to call humankind back to its true origins.

This altar contains no image, for divinity in the Tenrikyo and Shinto tradition generally does not take human form. Instead there are three simple cabinetlike shrines. When they stand open for worship, they reveal the gleaming mirrors that in Japan betoken the presence of *kami* (gods). On tables in front of these four shrines are stacked attractive piles of fruits and vegetables and bottles of rice wine as offerings. The shrine to the right, always open, is dedicated to the founder of the faith; in front of it are two red lanterns because Nakayama Miki always wore red to indicate her difference from other human beings. The shrine to the left is dedicated to the ancestors of Tenrikyo faithful—this faith, like most in Japan, has found a way to incorporate the veneration of ancestors, an important constituent of the East Asian spiritual mentality. The largest shrine, in the center, is dedicated to Oyagami.

In Japan an entire town of some fifty thousand people, Tenri-shi, is dedicated to this faith. It contains Tenrikyo schools from kindergarten through college, the religious headquarters, and extensive hostels for pilgrims. The main feature is a vast temple complex centered around an upright pillar, the Kanrodai, located at the spot where, it was revealed to Nakayama Miki, the creation of the world commenced. Once a month, around the base of this pillar, the leaders of the faith perform Tenrikyo's most solemn rite, the sacred dance commemorating this event. In Tenrikyo churches across the world, similar rites are held on the same day.

They begin with music from the gongs and reedy flutes of classical Japan, and with prayers and offerings by richly robed priests. The rite concludes with a portion of the sacred dance, showing God's search for lost humankind, and the symbolic wiping away of the spiritual dust or pollution that causes human error and suffering.

These vignettes should give something of the flavor of East Asian religion. It is colorful, with ornate temples and worship involving prayer, offerings, and often incense and dance. It is strongly linked to family, both living and departed, and to community. It includes both ancient religions, such as Buddhism, and religious movements started in modern times by charismatic figures, often women like Nakayama Miki.

THE MAJOR RELIGIONS OF
EAST ASIA

The major religious traditions of East Asia are Buddhism and Confucianism, both of which have profoundly influenced all East Asian societies; Daoism (the following of the Dao or "Way," the all-embracing course of the universe, which has philosophical, mystical, and magical dimensions, sometimes spelled "Taoism") in China; and Shinto, the ancient polytheistic "Way of the Gods" in Japan. These are joined by many new religions such as Tenrikyo. Because most East Asians who are religious (many today in the People's Republic of China and other parts of East Asia are not) have relationships with two or more traditions—being both Shinto and Buddhist in Japan, or embracing Confucianism, Daoism, and Buddhism in China—religious membership figures for this third of humanity are virtually impossible to obtain or assess.

Many manifestations of East Asian religion, to be sure, have arrived on our shores. The personal spiritual quest for one's own Buddha-like enlightenment is important to many. It may be typified by the rows of monks in seated meditation in a Zen[2] Buddhist monastery, seeking to still the activity of the ordinary "monkey mind" in order that the enlightened mind may arise. There are Zen temples of Chinese, Japanese, Korean, and Vietnamese background in the United States.

In Hawaii I once visited a family ceremony celebrated by a Daoist priest, who stood dramatically robed before an altar, calling up higher and higher celestial beings until he stood before the Great Dao, the universal Path or Way, itself. Many American cities and towns today have centers where one of the East Asian "martial arts," such as Japanese karate, Chinese kungfu, or Korean tae kwon do, are taught. These are not in themselves, religions, but they are influenced by values borrowed from Daoism and Zen.

All East Asian society has been profoundly influenced by Confucianism, the tradition of ethical teachings combined with rituals started by the great ancient philosopher Confucius. In traditional China there were Confucian temples and rituals, particularly in connection with centers of government, and these rites are still performed in Korea and Taiwan. But by far the most important influence of Confucian values has been in the arena of family life and society. Confucianism, with its high regard for education, tradition, hard work, loyalty to one's family and benefactors, and its emphasis on cooperation rather than individualism, has made East Asia what it is. Both communism as it is practiced in the People's Republic of China and the ethos of the highly successful corporations of Japan and South Korea largely reflect various applications of Confucian values under other names. East Asian American families are also frequently noted for the same emphasis on education, family cohesiveness and cooperation, and traditional values—sometimes to the point of tension with their younger, more "individualized" members over issues such as marriage or going into the family business versus striking out on one's own.

Confucianism has indeed been repressive, especially toward women and girls. Yet it has shaped societies that have run smoothly and achieved much, and the same can be said of many, many American families of East Asian background. Confucianism today is not so much a separate religion as a set of values and a way of life that speaks through the ethical ideals of virtually all East Asian religions, and through East Asian educational and family systems as well.

Who are these followers of Asian religions in the United States? According to the 1990 U.S. Census, there were 2,794,130 Americans of East Asian descent: 1,645,472 Chinese, 849,809 Japanese (including 2,247 Okinawans), and 298,849 Koreans. The figures would be larger if they included persons of partial or unacknowledged East Asian ancestry.

Not all of these persons practice a traditional East Asian religion. Some, especially Koreans, have become Christians. Reliable figures for the religious affiliations of East Asians are impossible to obtain, since the U.S. Census does not ask religious questions, the religious groups involved are very disparate and keep very different kinds of records, and many East Asians observe traditional religious practices only in a family, not an institutional, context. A very rough guess might be that half of Americans of East Asian descent maintain some kind of significant link to the traditional religions of their homelands.

On the other hand, more than a few Americans of occidental background have also become involved with an East Asian religion. Sometimes it has been through a personal spiritual quest, sometimes through marriage, sometimes as a by-product of an interest in, say, meditation or one of the martial arts. Commitments range from entering a Zen monastery to taking class or doing practices on a level that does not preclude primary adherence to another faith. Presbyterians have stilled and focused the mind like the wise men of the East as they have striven for budo[3] black belts, and Roman Catholic monks and nuns have meditated with Zen masters. Again figures are elusive—fifty thousand might be a conservative guess—and are less significant than the general cultural and even political impact these East Asian religions have had in America. On that score one need only mention the influence of Zen on the "Beat" writers of the 1950s, especially Jack Kerouac and Gary Synder. Daoism, through the martial arts mystique, has made a diffuse but discernible impression on popular culture through such vehicles as the Star Wars and Ninja Turtles movies. Confucianism, believed by many in Europe and America in the eighteenth century to have molded a virtually ideal rational, nonsectarian society in China, helped inspire both the U.S. Constitution and, later, the civil service examination system. As early as 1771, Benjamin Franklin called for closer study of China in the preface to the first volume of the American Philosophical Society's *Transactions*.

CHINA—DAOISM AND CONFUCIANISM

We should now look at the history and teaching of the major East Asian religions that have influenced Asian American life. Let's begin with China around 500 B.C.E. by the Western calendar. This was the time known as the period of the Warring States, for it was a time of recurrent conflict among various feudal lords, accompanied by great cruelty. As is usual in such situations, the suffering was greatest of all for the common people, as armies campaigned and looted back and forth through their villages.

Not surprisingly, perhaps, the Warring States period was closely followed by the period of the Hundred Philosophers. For people began asking, What went wrong? How can we get society back on the right course again? Or if we cannot, how can a person nonetheless live a personally meaningful and worthwhile life in such times? Many answers were given, but two are of particular interest to the study of East Asian religion. One is that of Confucius (551–479 B.C.E.), the other that of the more legendary Laozi, the "Old Man," whose book, the *Dao de jing*, "The

Book of the Way and Its Power," is the fountainhead of the tradition known as Daoism.

Both traditions had one thing in common. They were both concerned with the Dao (Tao in older transliterations), the Way or Path down which the universe is moving, and how human life can best get in harmony with it. But they held differing ideas about where it can be found. For Confucius and the Confucians, we human beings are social creatures. For us, therefore—however it may be with sharks or trees or other entities— the Dao is found in society. The supreme human good is a good society, and it is through the interrelationships on which good societies depend that true virtue is expressed.

Thus Confucianism taught that the family, the bedrock of the social order, and above all "filial piety," the relationship of parents and children, is where virtue is first learned, and is its most important locus. By being filial children and benevolent parents, people acquire those virtues that will also make the larger society humane and the state benign. All right relationships, whether parent and child or sovereign and subject, entail "mutuality," recognition that there are obligations on both sides. *Li*, or ritual, such as the rituals of mourning for deceased relatives, is very important to Confucian society because it gives persons an opportunity to "become what they are," that is, to act out the part society has given them, whether ruler or servant, parent or child.

Confucianism, in other words, depended on the formal promulgation and enactment of ethical principles. It tended to hold that although persons were good and inclined by nature to do the right, they were unformed and needed the benefit of education and example to become effective members of a well-running social order. The way to get the corrupt society back on track was to follow the example of the ancient sage-emperors whom Confucius, as a deeply principled conservative, always exalted. One should be a scholar-statesman who embodies virtue in teaching and action, whether it is immediately rewarded or not, by promoting both rites and justice, and if necessary remonstrating against those in power if they fail to set a like example.

The *Dao de jing* and Daoism took an opposition tack. To them, as to many romantics in the West, society was fundamentally artificial and corrupt. The way to get in touch with the Dao was not with other people amid social convention. It was in rapport with nature and, especially for the poets and artists who tended to find their spiritual path in Daoism, through contact with their inner being, the place from which dreams and visions stream.

The *Dao de jing* did not forget the state and the social order. But it idealized a small and simple society, and it held up as its model the leader who leads by indirection, hardly even letting his name be known, so that when the society achieves something the people will say, "We did this ourselves."

As Daoism matured, it became a religion as well as a natural philosophy. As religion, it emphasized the immortal power of the Dao, made up of yang and yin (male and female energies) and of the five elements (earth, water, wood, fire, and metal). Immortality, on earth or in heaven, could be achieved by balancing all these constituents so that the person had no place for death to intrude; power could be attained by aligning oneself with the force of any one of the entities, particularly when it was at a time of prominence.

For the great majority of Chinese, both in China and in America, the Confucian and Daoist strands of their spiritual culture are not mutually exclusive. In fact, it is said that the traditional Chinese gentleman was a Confucian at work and a Daoist on vacation. The sober Confucian principles of diligence, rectitude, and loyalty upheld him on the job, while away from it he could permit himself the pleasures of nature, art, fantasy, perhaps the spiritual luxury of a retreat in a well-situated Daoist monastery, and even of assessing the prospects of his own immortality. Chinese American communities also reveal both sides. The Confucian quality of Chinese attitudes toward family, business, and education are well known. Yet a glimpse at the art in Chinese homes and shops, or a glance into a Chinese temple, reveals the magical world of Daoism, with its wizardlike hermits and immortals, its mysterious martial-arts powers, and its gentle poetry of love and nature.

In some places in the United States, such as Hawaii and parts of California, there are old, traditional Chinese temples which, like many in China itself, feature both Buddhist and Daoist elements. On the Daoist side, there may be such godlike immortals as the Jade Emperor, Ruler of the Heavens, and Ma-zi, "Queen of the Sea" and protector of sailors. In traditional homes one may find the Kitchen-God, to whom offerings are made at the end of the year, when this familiar deity is said to present his report to the Jade Emperor on the family with which he resides.

The annual offering to the Kitchen-God is one aspect of the Chinese New Year, which in traditional China was the most important annual holiday. Another prominent New Year's custom is the dragon procession. A great paper dragon is paraded through the streets mobilized by numerous human feet. The dragon represents yang, the force associated with maleness, the sun, day, growth, and expansion—and therefore the first half of the year, when the crops are growing and days are getting longer. According to Daoism, humans desire to harmonize with what the Dao is doing, which at this time of year is accentuating the yang force. (At midsummer, when the Dao is shifting to yin, the energy associated with femaleness, night, moon, gathering-in, harvest, and shortening days, the famous Chinese lion-dances are held, for that animal is the patron of yin.)

JAPAN: TRADITION AND MODERNITY

In Japan, the primordial religious stratum is Shinto. No one can visit Japan and fail to see, in mountain strongholds, in traditional villages, and in the heart of modern industrial cities, the graceful gates called *torii* that span the entrance to a Shinto shrine. The path going through the gates will lead to a simple but well-proportioned building with a mirror and *gohei* (zigzag strips of paper) in front to mark the presence of deity, an eight-legged offering table, and massive doors sealing off the chamber where the kami-presence dwells. The kami venerated in these shrines are limited deities, for the most part patrons of particular families, communities, and areas, but they are deeply interfused in lives of those who worship them.

The Shinto shrine has a tranquil, natural atmosphere. But Shinto is also noted for its colorful *matsuri,* or festivals. Every shrine of any size has an annual matsuri, full of traditional festivities, like carnival or mardi gras in Latin societies. Some matsuri draw visitors from all over Japan and around the world.

There are no regular Shinto shrines in the United States except in Hawaii, which has a large population of Japanese descent, though modest shrines in homes and businesses may sometimes be seen elsewhere. However, as we have noted, some of the new religions of Japan have altars and worship with marked Shinto overtones.

One of the more interesting of contemporary religious phenomena, the Japanese new religions have emerged more or less parallel to the emergence of Japan as a modern nation. As many as one-fifth of all Japanese now belong to one of the new religions. Most began as special revelations to their founders, often women and persons of humble background, such as Nakayama Miki of Tenrikyo. They have characteristically emphasized healing, belief in the coming of a new paradisal world, and a simple practice that transmits the faith's power; they also usually have simple but definite processes for entry, modern organization, and (like Tenrikyo in Tenri City) imposing centers for pilgrimage.[4]

Besides Tenrikyo, several other Japanese new religions have established themselves in America. One of these is Konkokyo, which was founded in 1859 when a farmer, Kawate Bunjiro, received what he believed to be a commission from God to initiate a ministry of mediation between the divine and the human. Although this religion draws substantially from Shinto, it is monotheistic, worshiping one God. A distinctive practice is *toritsugi*, in which a minister gives formal counseling through a mediation rite that has been compared to confession in the Catholic Church.

The Omoto ("Great Source") movement began officially in 1892 with revelations given to a peasant woman, Deguchi Nao, who had undergone extremes of deprivation and suffering in her life, and who was told that God was now bringing in a new and better age. Her son-in-law, Deguchi Onisaburo, a man of great religious creativity, subsequently developed the religion much more fully with new teachings about the spirit world, healing, the sacred importance of art, and the power of the mind. He also took on the role of social critic, even challenging the position of the emperor in a time of rising nationalism in Japan, and thus brought persecution and considerable reduction of numbers to Omoto in the 1920s and 1930s. However, other movements carried on various aspects of the Omoto tradition, and these are represented in the United States.

Sekai Kyusei Kyo, often translated "Church of World Messianity," was founded by Okada Mokichi, a follower of Omoto, on the basis of revelations he had beginning in 1926. It emphasizes belief in a coming paradise, and also a healing practice called *jorei*, which involves channeling light through a cupped hand. There are several World Messianity churches in the United States with both Asian American and occidental members. A daughter religion of World Messianity, Mahikari ("True Light"), founded in Japan in 1960, has a similar practice involving the channeling of light and has been relatively successful in both Europe and North America.

Seicho no Ie, the "House of Growth," was founded in 1930 by another one-time follower of Omoto, Tasniguchi Masaharu. Influenced substantially by an American "New Thought" or "Positive Thinking" faith, the Church of Religious Science, Seicho no Ie stresses the power of mind, affirming that good thoughts can bring one health, happiness, and success. It has an American church headquarters in California and publishes a widely circulated inspirational magazine.

The PL Kyodan ("Perfect Liberty Order") was organized by Miki Tokuchika in 1946, on the basis of a series of prewar movements. It is not a direct offshoot of Omoto, but was undoubtedly influenced by Deguchi Onisaburo's stress on the importance of art. One of its basic precepts is that "Life is Art," meaning that one should express oneself through one's life as an artist does through art. PL churches, which teach the importance of balance to works of art, sponsor sports and educational centers and perform beautiful rituals. They also have a formal practice for receiving spiritual guidance in writing from a leading teacher. PL has several churches in the United States predominantly but not entirely Japanese American in membership.

Several of the new religions are based in Nichiren Buddhism and are discussed later.

BUDDHISM

How can we understand Buddhism in a way that helps us understand what it is in East Asia and among East Asians in America? In its heart Buddhism can be seen as a spiritual path that has to do with the mind, with consciousness, and with the relation of the individual mind to the infinite universe. It says that by stilling the mind in meditation we can cut through all the attachments and barriers that hobble the mind and make us unhappy. One can transcend all of the mind's limitations and join it to the universal. Then we have all the compassion, wisdom, and power of the universal, like the Buddhas and bodhisattvas at the Hsi Lai Temple.

The Mahayana Buddhism of East Asia puts particular emphasis on the Buddhas and bodhisattvas. It points out that even in our own imperfection, even given our own inexperienced efforts at meditation or the bodhisattva path, we can receive the help of those much further ahead of us and in a deep sense become one with them. What they have attained through immensely profound meditations over countless aeons, we can share in by their grace. So it is that Mahayana temples present their rows of such transcendent Buddhist figures and teach the worth of simple prayer and faith.

The Enryakuji temple complex on Mount Hiei, just outside Kyoto, Japan, is an example. Its many different temples, set amid deep, meditative woods, all represent varied angles on the Buddhist mystery. There is a temple to Dainichi, the "Great Sun Buddha,"[5] the personified essence of the universe whose unfathomable meditations sustain all things, a Buddha perhaps especially attuned to the perspective of mystics and philosophers. There is one to Kannon,[6] the so-called "Goddess of Mercy," actually a bodhisattva who expresses wisdom and compassion by answering simple prayers like a deity in heaven, appealing to the religious needs of more ordinary folk.

Down the road looms a shrine to Amida,[7] the Buddha of faith. Amida is the central personality of "Pure Land" Buddhism who has vowed to bring all who call upon his name in pure faith to that paradisal realm, from which entry into ultimate Nirvana is easy, after death. Everywhere in East Asia Pure Land Buddhism is popular among the laity because it makes salvation accessible to everyone through the help of another who has realized ultimate wisdom, compassion, and power, not just to those priests and monks who have leisure to do it "on their own."

Finally, in a woodsy nook is nestled a little temple to Fudo,[8] his black figure as fierce as other Buddhas are serene. Fudo's countenance is wrathful, he holds a sword and lasso, and he is poised against a backdrop of flames. But this fearsome warrior is entirely on the side of righteousness, for his rage is directed against error and the enemies of the Buddha's good teaching. Fudo's style of Buddhist commitment may call out especially to those of activist, samurai-like temperament.

Buddhism in China

This Indian faith first appeared in China around the first century C.E., apparently brought by traders and teachers from Buddhist kingdoms in central Asia, visitors who had traveled along the fabled Silk Road to the teeming cities of Han China. (It may also have reached South China by ships from India and Southeast Asia about the same time.) It did not become an important presence, however, until after the fall of the Confucianist Han Dynasty in 220 C.E. For more than three centuries thereafter, China was disunited and old ways were to some degree discredited. It was a good time for a new faith from outside to present itself as a serious alternative, and Buddhism did. Its ideals of universal compassion, monasticism, other-worldly salvation, and karma all challenged Confucianism's family-centered values. Many persons of means embraced Buddhism, endowing temples, monasteries, and works of mercy such as orphanages and hostels for travelers.

Buddhism was criticized for allegedly undermining loyalty to family and the state by putting religious celibacy and personal enlightenment first, and for being an imported, non-Chinese religion. It was sometimes persecuted. But by the Middle Ages a general pattern was worked out by which Buddhism accommodated itself to the Chinese system. Monks maintained filial piety by taking their teachers as surrogate parents, and by praying for their family's departed. Confucianism reasserted itself as the ideology of the state and the elite, while Buddhism and Daoism—often, as we have seen, intermixed—were tolerated as the religions of the masses.

Buddhism in traditional China took both monastic and lay forms.. Monasteries were generally run along Chan (Zen) lines, except in those extreme northern and western areas where Buddhism of the esoteric Vajrayana (Tibetan and Mongolian) type was to be found. In Chan cloisters monks devoted themselves to a quiet round of labor, as in the gardens and kitchens, of some study, and of long hours of seated meditation together with sutra-chanting and other rituals. A similar pattern can be found in various Zen centers in the United States today. The priests of old China's many thousands of local temples were usually trained in monasteries, then released and assigned to local temples, which they maintained and where they provided religious services.

Popular or lay Buddhism, on the other hand, generally centered around Pure Land, the honoring of O-mi-to (Amitabha) Buddha, along with worship of Guan-yin, the bodhisattva that expressed the compassion of O-mi-to. It also gave much attention to funerals and memorial services for the dead; these family obligations consumed much of the priests' time, as well as the money of the bereaved families. From this cult also stemmed admonitory teachings, graphically illustrated in temples and popular prints, about reincarnation, judgment, and Buddhist hells and purgatories for various sins. Whether portraying the horrors facing the damned or the wonders of the Pure Land, Buddhism was the religion especially concerned with the afterlife and its mysteries.

Buddhism in Japan

Buddhism spread from China to Korea, and then from Korea to Japan. The traditional date of its arrival in Japan is 532 or 552, and the traditional story of its coming is rather interesting. According to an ancient Japanese chronicle, the king of one of the small states into which Korea was divided at that time wanted to make an alliance with the emperor of Japan. As part of his approach, the Korean ruler, full of Buddhist enthusiasm, sent his Japanese colleague an image and scripture of the new faith, together with a letter stating that all the other nations of the region worshiped the Buddha and asking why Japan alone did not.

The Japanese sovereign, intrigued but unsure what to make of the unusual gifts, turned to his council. The prime minister, of the ambitious

Soga clan, urged acceptance of Buddhism, saying this would make Japan as up-to-date as the other nations. But two other ministers, of the Nakatomi and Mononobe families, both houses with traditional Shinto priestly responsibilities, advised caution instead, saying that the ancient kami of Japan would be angered if this foreign god were honored.

The ruler, with a certain wisdom, resolved the matter in this way. He told the Soga that, since they had recommended the new cult, they should venerate the Buddha-image experimentally and see what happened. Not long afterward a pestilence broke out, and the Shinto loyalists were quick to put the blame on kami anger at the intruding deity. As a consequence, the image was thrown into a river. But then fire destroyed a part of the palace, and now reproach went the other way. In time the controversy degenerated into civil war. The Soga eventually emerged victorious in the 590s and established Buddhism as a national religion.

But the test between Shinto and Buddhism did not result in the complete suppression of one religion by the other. Then, as so often right down to the present, the Japanese psyche was divided between an eagerness to learn and accept all it could from the outside world, and a no less compelling need to preserve something ancient and highly distinctive in its own soul, something often represented by Shinto and its native gods.

It is interesting to observe that Buddhism came in force to Japan at just about the same time Christianity was doing the same in Britain and other parts of northern Europe, and that Shinto was, broadly speaking, much the same kind of religion as the polytheistic faiths of pre-Christian Europe, the worship of Zeus or Minerva, Wotan or Thor. But whereas Christianity effectively abolished or drove underground the older gods, the Shinto kami instead achieved a kind of harmonization with the Buddhas and bodhisattvas. Shinto shrines shared the same precincts with Buddhist temples, and various theories proposed that the kami were there as students or guardians of the Buddha's dharma. Some even said the kami were the same as the Buddhas or bodhisattvas, but in native Japanese dress, so to speak. The two faiths coexisted in this way until the nineteenth century, when, for nationalistic reasons, Shinto and Buddhism were again separated.

In the seventh and eighth centuries Buddhism was a great vehicle for cultural development in Japan. The government sent promising young priests to China to study in various leading monasteries, and these priests brought back not only sacred texts and mystic practices, but also practical arts, such as printing, and fresh perspectives on government and education, including those of Confucianism.

In 794, when the government was established in the new city of Heian (modern Kyoto, still the center of traditional Japanese culture), new forms of Buddhism emerged that not only combined Shinto and Buddhism more effectively than before, but also combined the popular and aristocratic forms of Buddhism. The principal schools were Shingon and Tendai Buddhism, denominations that still number their followers in Japan in the millions, and both of which have churches in the United States. Tendai and Shingon both represent the complex Mahayana Buddhism we have already discussed; the Mount Hiei monastery is in fact the headquarters of Tendai. Shingon, more in the tradition of Vajrayana Buddhism with its use of powerful meditations on particular Buddhas and bodhisattvas, and its use of chants and hand-gestures (mantras and mudras), also has a many-templed headquarters, on Mount Koya.

The pattern of Japanese Buddhism changed significantly in the Kamakura period (1185–1333), which followed the Heian period. Most Japanese Buddhists today belong to Buddhist denominations that arose in this era. The Kamakura era commenced when the samurai, or warrior class, based in the north seized effective control of the country from the old imperial court and the Fujiwara family, which had dominated Heian politics and society. Regarding the old capital in Heian (Kyoto) as effete, under the leadership of the Minamoto house they established a new center of government in Kamakura, on Sagami Bay not too far from modern Tokyo. Although they did not dare depose the emperor, who was regarded as sacred, the Minamoto had him designate their leader as shogun—a sort of military dictator—who ruled in the sovereign's name from Kamakura.

The new order had important religious as well as political consequences. Indeed, what happened next has sometimes been called the Kamakura Buddhism Reformation, and in some ways it paralleled the Protestant Reformation in Europe three centuries later.

The new samurai class—and with them a rising merchant class, as well as the peasants, who in these troubled times had at least relatively more influence—wanted a simpler, more clear-cut religion than that offered by Shingon and Tendai. Like Martin Luther in Europe, they were preoccupied by the question, How can I be sure that I am saved? They wanted an assurance of salvation that was just as accessible to the warrior on the field of battle, the merchant in his shop, or the farmer in his rice paddies as it was to the priest or monk with time and expertise to undertake the deep but complex meditations of the older schools. Again like Luther, they found the answer in forms of simple faith that undercut the ideological and institutional underpinnings of the existing forms of Buddhism.

The new forms tended to be easy but exclusive, teaching that all that one needed was a single, simple, sure key. They can be thought of as simplifications and popularizations of Buddhism. Although these new denominations had earlier roots, they came into their own as separate religious movements in the Kamakura era.

Pure Land Buddhism

The first was Pure Land or Amidist Buddhism, founded as a separate movement by Honen (1133–1212) and his disciple Shinran (1173–1262). Their respective denominations, Jodo-shu (Pure Land School) and Jodo Shinshu (True Pure Land School), are both found in the United States, and the latter, as the Buddhist Churches of America, has been the largest and best-established form of Buddhism among Japanese Americans.

Pure Land centers on the Mahayana cosmic Buddha Amitabha (Amida in Japanese), whom we met as one of the three Buddhas in the Hsi Lai Temple and in Chinese Pure Land. Pure Land in Japan, as in China, is based on simple faith in the original vow (*Hongan* in Japanese; hence many temples have this expression in their names) of Amida to bring all those who call upon his name to the Pure Land or Western Paradise after death. But Honen and above all Shinran, with a radical thrust typical of the Kamakura spirit, taught Pure Land as a single exclusive practice. It is expressed in the *Nembutsu* ("Remembering the Buddha"), as the chant *Namu Amida Butsu* ("Hail Amida Buddha") is called. This chant is all that is needed for salvation. Shinran, like Luther, gave up his monastic garb and married, realizing that if the simple faith of the Nembutsu is sufficient, celibacy, monasticism, meditations, elaborate rites, and the rest of traditional Buddhism are superfluous. He further denied that any particular number of recitations of the Nembutsu is required—once may be enough—because we are not saved by anything we do, but by the grace of Amida received through simple faith.

Pure Land Buddhism was a popular movement in medieval Japan, spread not only by the two founders, but also by wandering evangelists who preached faith and taught spectacular Nembutsu dances. In the end the two schools became large and established denominations boasting fine temples with married, and often hereditary, clergy. (Although Jodo Shinshu paved the way, now clergy in virtually all forms of Japanese Buddhism can be married.)

Nichiren Buddhism

Nichiren Buddhism follows the teachings of Nichiren (1222–1282), a fiery prophet who insisted that the Lotus Sutra, one of the great Mahayana texts, is the supreme expression of the Buddha's teaching and the one and only version of Buddhism for our day. His disciples are divided into two denominations, Nichiren-shu and Nichiren Shoshu. The former sees him as a bodhisattva or priest mentioned in the Lotus text, and as such a radical new teacher for the era beginning with his life. Nichiren Shoshu sees Nichiren even more radically as a Buddha for the new age (said to have begun in 1052), presenting a new dispensation based on the Lotus Sutra.

Nichiren Buddhism has two central focuses in practice. First is the *Daimoku*, the chant *Namu Myoho Rengi Kyo*, "Hail the Marvelous Teaching of the Lotus Sutra." Repeated constantly by Nichiren believers, it is thought to have extraordinary power. For them it is the single, simple, sure key characteristic of Kamakura Buddhism. Second is the *Gohonzon*, a diagram calligraphed on white paper containing the names of leading bodhisattvas and Buddhas in the Lotus Sutra, with the Daimoku in large characters down the center; it is the major object of worship on Nichiren altars both in temples and in homes.

Nichiren Buddhism displays both dynamism and exclusivism. Nichrien himself promoted his truth enthusiastically, and he denounced other forms of religion with no less vigor. His movement has presented itself as the one and only true form of Buddhism for our day, promoting the Daimoku in good times and in bad. This has been particularly true of the movement known as Soka Gakkai, a lay organization within Nichiren Shoshu. Begun in the 1930s, its founders were harshly treated by the militaristic Japanese regime of those days, but it came into the postwar era with a good reputation for its refusal to compromise with militarism. It advanced the Nichiren faith by promoting the healing, this-worldly benefits of chanting, by forming highly organized block and precinct cell-groups, by means of popular music concerts and energetic youth work, and even by establishing its own political party. By such means Soka Gakkai spread so phenomenally in the 1950s that it was sometimes called "the fastest growing religion in the world." Its aggressive tactics, though often criticized, have made Nichiren Shoshu the largest single religious denomination in postwar Japan.

Soka Gakkai also brought Nichiren to America. The first chapter of Soka Gakkai in America was established in 1960 in California. It quickly became Nichiren Shoshu of America (NSA), later Nichiren Shoshu Academy, and grew at a remarkable rate in the fertile spiritual climate of the 1960s. NSA claimed some 200,000 American followers by 1970, predominantly non-Asian Americans. While the number of active members is probably much lower, it has undoubtedly made an impact, especially among young people and in the entertainment industry, with its colorful rallies and its claims for the power of chanting.

NSA meetings I have attended in California have suggested anything but the ethereal meditative image Buddhism holds for many people. Here were energetic, personable youths chanting the Daimoku together over and over at a rapid clip, then doing cheerleader-type yells and jingles on behalf of the cause, and finally giving testimonials on behalf of how chanting had brought them better grades or better jobs. The feeling was overwhelmingly of a modern, streamlined Buddhism for the rock 'n' roll era—but one which produced in its own way an inner confidence and joy corresponding to the inner peace of older meditative varieties.

Two other modern Nichiren movements that have come to America are Rissho Kosei Kai and Reiyukai. Both emphasize Buddhism for the laity and group counseling activities and are predominantly Asian American in constituency.

Zen Buddhism

The third form of Kamakura Buddhism, Zen, is probably the best known in the West. It was supported in the Kamakura and several subsequent eras primarily by the samurai class, including some shoguns. The best Zen masters taught, and themselves exemplified, a stern monastic and meditative discipline that favorably impressed the warriors as matching their own ideals of rigorous self-control. In addition, the famous Zen-related arts—the tea ceremony, flower arrangement, gardens, and of course the "martial arts"—enabled the new upper class to exercise its own pretensions to gentility.

These two "wings" of Zen are not as far separated as it might appear on the surface. Zen emphasizes that we all have the Buddha nature within us, as do all things. Ordinarily it is woefully obscured by our out-of-control passions, attachments, and lack of mental concentration. But long hours of *zazen*, seated Zen meditation, can bring the "monkey mind"—as Zen people sometimes call it—under control. Further, the skillful tactics employed by a seasoned Zen master can lead to a radical breakthrough, sometimes called *satori* ("surprise"), into enlightenment. Stories of such breakthroughs focus on the famous one-on-one interviews between masters and disciples, and may include use of the *koan,* the Zen riddles ("What is the sound of one hand?" "What was your face before you were born?") intended to bring the ordinary rational mind up against its limits, and even the "shock therapy" of shouts and slaps celebrated in Zen lore.

With the realization of the unstained mind comes freedom—freedom of expression; freedom to see the same Buddha nature everywhere; freedom to "be here now," to live in the fullness of the present. So it is that a Zen adept makes and serves tea with the simple grace of one who is fully at home with himself and what he is doing. The Zen artist sees a bird on a branch and captures it in a few seemingly spontaneous strokes of the brush that find the eternal Buddhahood within that frail creature. With a shout and a single sure lunge, the Zen swordsman hits his mark. This discipline and freedom can be illustrated by a music student's hard, disciplined practice of a piece on the piano over and over, until the day comes when it just flows out; she does not need to think "put this finger here, put that one there," but it "plays itself" masterfully without thought, and no doubt sounds far better than ever before.

In the two dozen or so Zen centers in America, one can see Zen meditation practiced by persons of diverse backgrounds. The posture is properly the cross-legged lotus, or some approximation of it; this gives one a sense of balance and stability. As one sits, a proctor walks back and forth with a stick, ready to tap anyone who nods back into mindfulness. Zazen meditators may focus their minds inwardly on counting breaths, on pure awareness, or on one of the koans that bring one to the limits of the rational mind and beyond it into cosmic freedom. From time to time, they may go in for an interview with the *roshi,* or Zen master, who will give advice and perhaps ask them to demonstrate the meaning of the koan on which they are working. A satisfactory answer would be less a verbal analysis of it than a spontaneous gesture that showed, in a leap or a shout, the freedom of a breakthrough to satori.

Tibetan Buddhism

Other Americans, both Tibetans and others, follow the demanding but rewarding practices of Vajrayana, the school of Buddhism for which the Himalayan nation of Tibet is famous. Its leader, the Nobel prize–winning Dalai Lama, has brought world attention to his land and his faith. Vajrayana puts particular emphasis on the importance of serious practitioners receiving initiations from lamas (teachers/priests) in well-qualified lineages. To prepare for initiation, disciples are taught to do numerous prostrations and chants; further practice includes deep and powerful visualizations of Buddhas and deities and complex but colorful ceremonies. Tibetan centers of several schools can be found in most major American cities.

CONCLUSION

East Asian religions are today a part of American life, and are followed by Americans of virtually every background. They have also had an influence on American life through many media—such as poetry, architecture, cinema—that extends far beyond their number of official adherents.

In the twentieth century, the United States and the very different societies of East Asia have found themselves in increasing interaction. Whether through the tragedy of war or the more benign means of economic interaction, tourism, and cultural exchange, Americans and East Asians have found their lives and nations more and more intertwined. In this situation the religions of East Asia located in the United States have a very special role. By familiarizing themselves with these outposts of East Asia, Americans of all backgrounds, whether or not they are personally drawn to these religions, can learn about East Asia on levels inaccessible by most other means, make East Asian friends, and prepare themselves and their country for the pluralistic world of the twenty-first century.

NOTES

1. In Japanese and most other East Asian languages, the surname—Nakayama in this case—comes first.

2. This tradition, emphasizing meditation and enlightenment in the midst of everyday life, is called *Chan* in China, *Son* in Korea, and *Thien* in Vietnam.

3. Budo is Japanese for "the way of the warrior" (i.e., the "martial arts"), including such traditional forms as karate ("empty hands"), kendo ("way of the sword"), kyudo ("way of archery"), aikido ("way of harmonious energy"), and others. All these have developed a strongly spiritual dimension, emphasizing the cultivation of a quiet and clear consciousness for the sake of full concentration on the immediate present, direct intuitive action, and balancing one's breath and vitality. Acting in profound unity with the energies of the universe is stressed. Especially in aikido, nonaggressive practices are accentuated. Many in both East and West study budo primarily as spiritual/physical exercise with little intent of making warlike use of these skills. (Ninjutsu, the "art of invisibility," that is, of the ninja, "invisible or

secret person," much popularized in America recently through films and other means, is not regarded as a spiritual path by followers of other martial arts because of its stress on violence rather than on harmony with the way of the universe. Perhaps the Ninja Turtles will lead to changes here!)

4. New religious movements have also appeared in China and Korea. A Korean movement that has attained quite a bit of publicity is the Unification Church, popularly known as the "Moonies," founded by the Rev. Sun Myung Moon, a Korean minister. Although it has incorporated some elements of Korean shamanism, it is essentially a Christian movement presenting unconventional views of the role of Christ and suggesting that a new coming of Christ, perhaps in the person of Moon, may be imminent. It is an example of new forms that Christianity is taking in "non-Western" parts of the world where it was brought by missionaries; this is one such movement returning to the country from which many of those missionaries came.

5. Dainichi is the same figure called Vairocana in Sanskrit.

6. Kannon is Guan-yin in Chinese, Avalokitesvara in Sanskrit.

7. Amida is O-mi-to in Chinese, Amitabha in Sanskrit.

8. Fudo is Pu-tung in Chinese, Acala in Sanskrit; these names all mean "The Immovable One." Fudo is technically not a Buddha or bodhisattva but one of five Myo-o or Maha-devas, "Wondrous Kings," who are manifestations of Dainichi, or Vairocana. Their mission is to protect truth and combat evil.

STUDY QUESTIONS

1. How has Confucianism influenced East Asian thought, particularly regarding family life and society? Give specific examples.
2. What are examples of East Asian religion's influence on American Christianity? Be specific.
3. How would you define the Dao? How did Confucius and the Confucians differ from Laozi in their understanding of the Dao?
4. How do you understand the East Asian religious idea of yin and yang? What are some examples you see, perhaps from your own religious tradition, in which opposites work to create a balanced life?
5. What are the several Buddhist movements that have come to and established themselves in America? By what practices and rituals do they distinguish themselves?
6. Why do you think Zen Buddhism has had such a popular appeal in America?

ESSAY TOPICS

Exploring the Lives of Confucius and Laozi
Popularizing Zen in America: *Zen and the Art of Motorcycle Maintenance* by Robert Pirsig
The NSA and Its Development in America
Women and the Religions of East Asia
Japanese Gods

WORD EXPLORATION

The following words play significant roles in any discussion of East Asian religions in America and are worth careful reflection and discussion.

Confucius	Zen	Yin
Laozi	Omoto	Yang
Dao	Confucianism	Kami
Daoism	*Dao de jing*	Shrine
Chinese New Year	Shinto	

FOR FURTHER READING

Buddhism

Ch'en, Kenneth K. S. *Buddhism: The Light of Asia.* Woodbury, N.Y.: Barron's Educational Series, 1968.

Robinson, Richard H., and Willard L. Johnson. *The Buddhist Religion.* Belmont, Calif.: Wadsworth, 1982.

Buddhism in America

Fields, Rick. *How the Swans Came to the Lake: A Narrative History of Buddhism in America.* Boulder, Colo.: Shambhala, 1981.

Prebish, Charles S. *American Buddhism.* North Scituate, Mass: Duxbury, 1979.

Chinese Religion

Ch'en, Kenneth K. S. *Buddhism in China: A Historical Survey.* Princeton, N.J.: Princeton University Press, 1964.

Thompson, Laurence G. *Chinese Religion: An Introduction.* Belmont, Calif.: Wadsworth, 1969.

Japanese Religion

Earhart, H. Byron. *Japanese Religion: Unity and Diversity.* Belmont, Calif.: Wadsworth, 1982.

Ellwood, Robert S., and Richard Pilgrim. *Japanese Religion: A Cultural Perspective.* Englewood Cliffs, N.J.: Prentice-Hall, 1985.

11

JOHN L. ESPOSITO

Islam in the World and in America

A basic knowledge of Islam is becoming essential for every American today. There are five million Muslims now living in America. In fact, Islam is the third largest U.S. religion, and by the year 2010 it is expected to be second largest. Therefore, it is no longer appropriate to think of Muslims as those people in the Middle East or Africa or Asia. Islam, like Judaism and Christianity, is an American religion.

Islam suffers from a number of misconceptions. Many are surprised to discover that it is not some strange, remote religion in the Middle East but the second largest religion in the world. In addition, although many Arabs are Muslims, most Muslims are not Arab. The majority of the world's one billion Muslims are Asian and African. The largest Muslim communities are found in Indonesia, Bangladesh, Pakistan, India, Central Asia, and Nigeria rather than Saudi Arabia, Egypt, or Iran. Islam is also a major religion in Europe.

Muslims worship the same God who is revered by Christians and Jews.[1] Muslims also recognize the biblical prophets. They especially consider Moses and Jesus to be great prophets who received revelations from God. Like Judaism and Christianity, Islam began in the Middle East. Moses, Jesus, and Muhammad were all born there. Like Judaism and Christianity, Islam also spread throughout much of the world. Islam is truly a world religion that embraces people of many races and languages.

The word *Islam* means "peace" and "submission" to God. Just as Jews use the greeting "Shalom" (peace), Muslims say "Assalam wa alaykum" (peace be upon you) whenever they meet a friend or say goodbye. Many Muslims say "In the name of God the Merciful and Compassionate" each time they begin to speak, read, write, or do just about anything. Muslims, like most religious people, believe in peace and compassion and indeed are raised from an early age to associate these qualities with God and their religion.

However, at the same time, the Muslim community from its beginnings had to defend itself against its enemies as well as to spread the message of Islam. The word *Muslim* means one who submits to God's will. The term *Islam* really reflects not only a religion, but also a way of life and a community. Islam puts heavy emphasis on one's community. To be a Muslim is not just an individual activity; it is a community identity and responsibility. Every Muslim, regardless of his or her race, sex, and tribal, ethnic, or national background, is also considered to be a member of a worldwide community of believers, called the *ummah*. They are bound together by a common faith in God and God's prophets.

Like Judaism and Christianity, Islam includes a number of communities or branches. The two major groups are Sunni Muslims, who comprise about 85 percent of Muslims, and Shii (or Shiite) Muslims, who account for 15 percent of the world's Muslim population. Despite their differences, all Muslims share a common faith in Allah (God) and follow the teachings of their prophet, Muhammad. In addition to their shared belief in God and his prophets, Muslims share the practice of daily prayer, concern and responsibility for the poor, and an emphasis on community and family.

GOD AND GOD'S MESSENGER

Just as Moses in Judaism and Jesus in Christianity hold a special place as messengers and models for their communities, Muslims believe that Muhammad is the revealer of God's will for two reasons. First, he received God's message, which was later written down. This message is the Quran, which is Islam's scripture, like Christianity's Bible and Judaism's Torah. Second, the way Muhammad lived his life is used as an example for believing Muslims today. As you can see, there are many links between Judaism, Christianity, and Islam. In fact, from a Muslim's point of view it is more correct to speak of the Judeo-Christian-Islamic tradition.

Muslims, like Jews and Christians, believe that there is one God, the Creator, Sustainer, and Judge of the universe. Although one can come to know God through the wonders of creation, Muslims believe that God's will was revealed to a long series of prophets or messengers, first to Adam, Abraham, Noah, and Moses, then to Jesus, and then to Muhammad, the final prophet. Muhammad is of key importance to Muslims as a living example of the "ideal Muslim," the model for all to learn from and copy. Many Muslims are named after the Prophet; in some countries all males have the name Muhammad as one of their names. Not surprisingly, Muhammad's birthday is celebrated as a great feast.

Muhammad (570–632 C.E.) was born in Mecca, a commercial, cultural, and religious center in Arabia. An orphan raised by his uncle, he worked as a caravan manager, traveled extensively, and eventually married Khadija, the woman who owned the caravan company. Muslim tradition tells us that he was very happily married and was a well-respected businessman, known for such honesty and trustworthiness that he was often called upon to mediate disputes. He was a pious man who often spent time in meditation and reflection. At the age of forty, Muhammad had an experience that would change his life. In fact, Muhammad's experience would affect the lives of hundreds of millions of people across the world and throughout history.

Muhammad liked to withdraw from time to time to be alone and reflect. One day he heard a voice which commanded him, "Recite!" Muhammad was stunned and confused. Was he hearing voices? Was there something wrong with him? Frightened and bewildered, he responded that he had nothing to recite. The angel Gabriel again commanded him to recite. Finally, the words came to him: "Recite in the name of your Lord who has created, created man out of a germ-cell. Recite for your Lord is the Most Gracious One Who has taught by the pen, Taught man what he did not know!"

Muhammad began to receive a series of revelations from God through the angel Gabriel. Like the biblical prophets, Muhammad spent many years communicating the message he received from God, calling upon the people to repent their sinful ways and to return to the worship of the one true God. These revelations continued for approximately twenty-two years until shortly before Muhammad's death at the age of sixty-two. Muhammad served as a moral conscience for his community, warning that God would judge people for their pagan practices and social injustices. Like the biblical prophets, he was rejected by many who saw him as a threat to their beliefs and lives of privilege. He was a reformer who seemed like a revolutionary to them.

The leaders of Mecca persecuted Muhammad and his followers. As a result, in 622 an event occurred that proved pivotal in Muslim history. Muhammad and a group of his followers moved to a nearby city, Medina, where he established and governed the first Muslim community. Muslims date their calendar from the year that the Muslim community was established in Medina rather than the year that Muhammad was born or the year that he received the first revelation of the Quran.

Muhammad was both a religious and a political leader, a prophet and a statesman. His charismatic authority was so strong and overpowering that much of Muslim practice came to be identified with him. After Muhammad's death, narrative stories (called "traditions," or *hadith*) preserved accounts about the Prophet's example, what he said and did, which is called his *Sunnah*. These stories or traditions covered everything from Muhammad's advice about prayer, fasting, marriage and divorce, diplomacy, and holy war, to his teachings and example. During the early centuries of Islam, collections of these traditions (which mushroomed into the thousands) and biographies of the Prophet became sources of guidance for Muslims as they struggled after his death to better understand what it meant to be a good Muslim.

ISLAM: A WAY OF LIFE

Islam is considered a total way of life for the religious community. For many in America who are raised with the idea of the separation of church and state and the sense that religion is a private affair, Islam can seem confusing, especially since Islam does not have a "church" to preserve and promote its beliefs. Islam, like Judaism, responds to this challenge through Islamic law and the activity of its religious scholars, or *ulama*. When Muhammad died and the community no longer had the Prophet to guide it and resolve its problem, many Muslims felt the need to define more clearly what it meant to be a Muslim and how Muslims should live. If being a Muslim meant submission to God's will, and if eternal reward in heaven or punishment in hell was dependent upon following God's law, then it was important to know what that law required. This became even more of an issue as Islam spread across the world, absorbing peoples in different regions who had different laws and customs and encountering new situations, problems, and questions.

Unlike Christianity, Islam does not have a pope or group of bishops to determine what people are to do or believe. Answering the question, "What should a good Muslim be doing?" became the job of the ulama, scholars who devoted their lives to study, debate, and spelling out as fully as possible God's law (known as the *Shariah*). The ulama were like the great theologians of Christianity and rabbis of Judaism in this regard, and they became the teachers and guardians of Islam.

Of course, the starting point for developing Islamic law was to look at the teachings of scripture, the Quran, and the life or example of the Prophet. Since these sources did not offer specific answers for every situation, Muslim scholars relied upon their personal interpretation and opinion to determine God's will in a given situation. For example, the ulama have prohibited the use of drugs by pointing out their similarity to alcohol, which the Quran explicitly bans.

Depending on where a Muslim is born, he or she follows the regulations or guidelines of a specific Sunni or Shii school of law. Islamic law covers all aspects of religious life, including prayer, fasting, and pilgrimage, but also all aspects of social life, ranging from marriage, divorce, and inheritance to self-defense and warfare.

THE FIVE PILLARS OF ISLAM

Profession of Faith (*Shahada*)

No matter what country they live in, all Muslims share certain basic beliefs and practices. These are called the five pillars of Islam. The first and foremost pillar is the profession of faith, which is called the *shahada*. Muslims proclaim: "There is no God but God and Muhammad is the Prophet (or messenger) of God." This statement expresses the essence of Muslim faith: faith in the one true God and recognition that Muhammad is the last in a long line of prophets, all sent to communicate God's message to the world. When a Muslim pronounces these words of belief, he or she formally becomes a member of the Muslim community.

Like Jews and Christians, Muslims believe that God communicates to the human community through prophets. Professing that Muhammad is the final messenger of God implies acceptance of the Quran as the literal and final revelation from God. For Muslims, the Quran represents the very words of God that were sent down through Muhammad to guide humankind. Although Muslims believe that God also sent revelations to the Jews through their scripture or Torah, and to the Christians in Jesus' *Message* or New Testament, they believe that over time foreign ideas and beliefs corrupted the original revelations to Jews and Christians. Thus, the Quran was revealed to Muhammad and contains the final, uncorrupted, and complete message from God.

Prayer or Worship (*Salat*)

The second pillar of Islam is prayer or worship (*salat*). Muslims worship God five times each day. At designated times throughout the day and night, in whatever country they are in, whether they are at home, in the office, or on the road, Muslims stop to face Mecca and to worship God. Their prayer is preceded by a ritual ablution, which includes the washing of the hands and face. Both physical and spiritual cleanliness, purity of body and spirit, are required for approaching God and reciting God's holy word in prayer. When performing the salat and reciting God's revelation, Muslims believe that they are in the presence of their Lord.

Muslims may pray alone or in a group. If in a group, since there is no priesthood in Islam one of the worshipers serves as the prayer leader (*imam*), guiding the movements and recitation. Prayer consists of a series of prostrations before God. Muslims stand, then kneel and touch their foreheads to the ground, and then stand again. Throughout, they recite verses from the Quran.

On Friday, Muslims are expected to perform the noon prayer in a congregation. Like the Sabbath (Saturday for Jews and Sunday for Christians), this is a special time when the community comes together at a mosque. In American communities most Muslims are not able to pray at their mosque on Friday because they have to work. Many will gather on Sunday to worship and socialize as a community. During the congregational prayer, the imam is especially important because the imam supervises the rows of worshipers and coordinates the recitation and prostrations. People tend to dress up to go to their local mosque, and a preacher delivers a sermon. The sermon usually begins with the recitation of a passage from the Quran which provides the subject for the sermon. Depending on the personality and style of the preacher, the sermon is often presented in a dramatic style. At other times, it may sound more like a scholarly lecture, exhorting the faithful to obey and follow God's commands. The imam relates relevant Quranic passages and traditions of the Prophet to issues in Muslim life.

Almsgiving (*Zakat*)

Just as the obligation to pray has an individual and a community dimension, so too almsgiving (*zakat*), the third pillar of Islam, is an individual obligation that instills and reinforces a sense of community identity and responsibility.

Islam teaches that because God is the creator of the world, all wealth ultimately belongs to God. Human beings are caretakers who are given an opportunity to share in and use that wealth. The pursuit and accumulation of wealth by Muslims has always been recognized as an acceptable and indeed noble endeavor. After all, Muhammad was himself a businessperson, as was his wife, Khadija, who owned the caravan business for which he worked. Throughout history, merchants and traders have been a respected class among the leaders in the Muslim community, providing support for religious institutions and activities. Thus, for example, they were effective missionaries, bringing the message of Islam along with their business interests to India, Southeast Asia, and Africa. Often, Muslim religious leaders have had close family ties with the merchant class and have themselves, like Muhammad, been engaged in business or land ownership.

Although wealth is a legitimate reward for one's labors, it also brings responsibility. From earliest times, charity has been recognized and strongly encouraged in Islam. Individuals may perform such actions as often as they wish. However, in addition to voluntary concern and care for others, Muslims also came to recognize a corporate responsibility; it is the duty of all who are financially capable to pay an annual 2.5-percent wealth tax to address the needs of less fortunate members of the community.

Integral to the mission and message of Muhammad and one of the major concerns of the Quran is the welfare of the poor and oppressed. This passage emphasizes his message: "Who denies religion? It is the person who repulses the orphan and does not promote feeding the poor. Woe to those who worship but who are neglectful, those who want to be noticed but who withhold assistance from those in need" (Quran 107:1–7). Payment of the zakat is an act of worship; it is a way that Muslims thank God for their material success and well-being. Many passages in the Quran and in the teachings of the Prophet Muhammad emphasize socioeconomic justice. Exploitation of the poor, weak, women, widows, orphans, and slaves and the hoarding of wealth are condemned. All Muslims belong to a broader community, so it is not surprising that Islam emphasizes the obligation of the more successful and prosperous members of the community to share their wealth with those who are less fortunate.

Fasting (*Sawm* or *Siyam*)

Once a year, all adult Muslims who are physically able fast during the month of Ramadan. Fasting (*sawm* or *siyam*), the fourth pillar of Islam, is a special time for reflection and discipline. It is a time to thank God for his blessings, repent and atone for one's sins, discipline the body and strengthen moral character, remember one's ultimate dependence upon God, and respond to the needs of the poor and hungry. For one month, each day from dawn to dusk Muslims abstain from eating or drinking anything, even water. The Islamic calendar is a lunar calendar, so over the years Ramadan falls during different seasons. When it occurs in the summer months, fasting can be especially difficult for those who live in very hot climates and must fast while they work. In such countries, it is often common to start work very early in the morning in order to finish by early afternoon.

The rigors of daytime fasting are offset at dusk when families come together for a quick, light meal to break the fast. This meal is popularly called "breakfast." Breakfast is then followed by a round of visiting and a full late-night meal with family, friends, or neighbors. Muslims will retire quite late in the evening only to rise early enough before sunrise to have a full meal before they face another day of fasting. In some parts of the Muslim world, special foods and desserts are served only at this time of the year. Similarly, many go to the mosque for evening worship, followed by a special prayer recited only during Ramadan. Ramadan is a time for many other special acts of piety, ranging from reciting and reflecting on the entire Quran over the course of the month to looking after the needs of the poor.

Near the end of Ramadan (on the twenty-seventh day), Muslims commemorate the "Night of Power and Excellence," the night when Muhammad first received God's revelation. Finally, the month of Ramadan comes to a close with a grand celebration, the Feast of Breaking of the Fast (*Id al-Fitr*). This joyful celebration is similar to Christmas or Hanukkah, as families come from near and far to celebrate together, wear their finest clothing, feast, and exchange gifts in a three-day affair that sometimes stretches into a week or more.

Pilgrimage to Mecca (*Hajj*)

The last pillar of Islam is the pilgrimage, or *hajj*, to Mecca. Every Muslim who has the health and financial ability is obliged to make the pilgrimage once in his or her lifetime. In many faiths, devout believers travel to the sacred cities of their faith—Jews and Christians to Jerusalem; Catholics to Rome, Fatima, and Lourdes; Hindus to Benares; and Sikhs to Amritsar—where they commemorate and often ritually reenact important moments from their sacred history. So too in Islam, once each year almost two million Muslims journey to Saudi Arabia, to the cities of Mecca and Medina, to perform the hajj. They come by plane, boat, car, and on foot. Men and women, rich and poor, black and white, from America, Asia, Africa, Europe, and the Middle East, descend upon Saudi Arabia during the last month of the Muslim calendar. Pilgrims come with awe and great excitement as many fulfill the dream of a lifetime. They return to their spiritual roots, the very land and sites where much of the early Muslim community's history unfolded. It was here that Abraham, regarded as the first prophet or purer monotheism, and his son Ismail are reported in the Quran to have built the *Kaba*, the "House of God." This cube-shaped structure houses the black stone that tradition says was given by the angel Gabriel to Ismail as a sign of God's covenant with Abraham and, by extension, with the Muslim community. This is also where Muhammad was born, received God's revelation, proclaimed his message, established and guided the Muslim community, and died.

As pilgrims from all over the world near Mecca their excitement erupts into joyous shouts of "I am here, O Lord, I am here!" Whatever their backgrounds and social class, all are equal before God. Fine clothes, jewelry, and perfume are set aside. All don the simple garments of the pilgrim; men and many women wear two seamless white sheets, a sign of their purification as well as a symbol of the unity and equality of the Muslim community. During the pilgrimage, participants visit sacred sites associated with Abraham, Ismail, and Muhammad and ritually reenact and commemorate sacred events.

The pilgrimage ends with one of the great feasts or holy days of Islam, the Feast of Sacrifice (*Id al-Adha*), also known as the Great Feast. The feast commemorates God's command to Abraham to sacrifice his son, Ismail. In the Bible, Abraham is commanded to sacrifice Isaac. Just as God in the Bible ultimately permitted Abraham to sacrifice a ram instead of his son, so too Muslims at the conclusion of the hajj sacrifice animals (sheep, goats, camels) in memory of Abraham's willingness to sacrifice his son at God's command. The animal sacrifice serves as a symbolic reminder to the faithful of their declaration that they too are willing to sacrifice what is most important and precious to them. Whatever meat is not consumed is distributed to the poor. The Feast of Sacrifice is celebrated across the Muslim world.

At the end of the pilgrimage, many pilgrims visit the mosque and the tomb of Muhammad in Medina before returning home. For many Muslims the special character of this moment is remembered by sharing their pilgrimage experience with family and friends and by preserving it through some memento. Many commemorate this milestone in their lives with a picture of the Kaba in their home or office. In some parts of the Muslim world, people paint a picture of the Kaba on the front wall of their house. Other pilgrims symbolize the significance of this event in their lives by placing the noun designating one who has made the hajj, *hajji*, before their given name, as in Hajji Muhammad Ali.

THE WORLDWIDE COMMUNITY
OF MUSLIMS

Wherever Muslims may live, however devout or nonobservant they may be, most are acutely aware of their common bond with other Muslims throughout the world. They share a common faith and a common sense of a rich and vibrant early religious history: the spread of Islam in its first centuries and the creation of Islamic empires that extended from North Africa, across the Middle East, to Southeast Asia. Islamic empires brought with them the development of a rich Islamic civilization that made major contributions to the arts and sciences. Muslim scholars contributed to the development of algebra (which comes from the Arabic *al-jabr*), as well as to medicine, astronomy, philosophy, and literature. This brilliant legacy is part of the history and identity of all Muslims wherever they may live and however diverse their national origins.

Because Muslims belong to the *ummah*, a worldwide faith community, they are concerned about what is happening to their Muslim brothers and sisters in other parts of the world. Thus, events as widespread as the invasion and occupation of Afghanistan by the Soviet Union in 1979, the Iranian Revolution of 1978–1979, the plight of Muslims in Palestine and Kashmir, or the condition of Muslims in Europe and America capture the attention of many Muslims worldwide.

THE ISLAMIC REVIVAL

Perhaps the most visible sign of the vitality of contemporary Islam is the Islamic revival or resurgence. Too often, it is mislabeled "Islamic fundamentalism" and simply equated with radicalism and violence. In fact, in many parts of the world in recent years, many Muslims have become more conscious of their Islamic faith and identity, and this religious reawakening has expressed itself in a variety of ways in Muslim life. The contemporary revival of Islam may be seen both in personal and in public life. Many Muslims have become more religiously observant, expressing their faith through prayer, fasting, and Islamic dress and values. This is reflected in an increase in the number of mosques, religious schools, and organizations. Not only has mosque attendance increased, but also a growing number of Muslim women, both overseas and in the United States, choose to wear Islamic dress, in particular a headscarf, or *hijab*, as a sign of modesty.

The belief that Islam is a total way of life has led some to want to create and live in a more Islamically oriented society and state. This phenomenon is often referred to as Islamic revivalism or "Islamic fundamentalism."[2] Islam has reemerged in politics both in highly visible and in more subtle ways. While many in the West are familiar with some of the more explosive examples, from the Iranian revolution to Saddam Hussein's call for a holy war in the Persian Gulf crisis of 1990–1991, these are headline events that often obscure or ignore a far more pervasive change in Muslim societies.

There is a great diversity of opinion and activity among the world's Muslims. While some leaders and movements have turned to violence to achieve their goals, the majority of Islamic activists wish to live peacefully in societies that are more firmly grounded in their faith and that are socially just. Their organizations call upon those who were born Muslim to become better or more observant Muslims and to work to transform their societies. They emphasize education in order to produce a sector of society that is well-educated but oriented toward Islamic, rather than secular, values. Many are graduates of the best universities in their countries or in the West, professionals in law, medicine, teaching, business, or engineering. The social dimension of this movement can be seen in the growth of Islamic schools, banks, student groups, publishing and media, and social welfare agencies (hospitals, clinics, legal aid societies).

Islam today is a vibrant faith in which Muslims, like all religious peoples, seek in diverse and sometimes conflicting ways to adapt their lives and religious tradition to the changing realities of modern life. This vitality and diversity may be seen not only in the traditional countries of the Muslim world, but also in America.

MUSLIMS IN AMERICA/AMERICAN MUSLIMS

Muslim Immigration

Although Islam is a world religion, for many years the presence of Muslims in the West was small enough to go unnoticed. They often existed in Western societies that consisted predominantly of Christians as well as small Jewish communities. However, today that situation has changed remarkably. In France, Islam is the second largest religion; in England and the United States, Islam is the third largest religious community. It is estimated that by the year 2020 the number of American Muslims will surpass that of American Jews. These changes raise many questions for non-Muslims and Muslims alike. Who are these Muslims? How did they get here? What does it mean to be an American Muslim?

As we have said, there are approximately five million Muslims in the United States, and more than a thousand mosques are spread across the country. We have often been unaware of the Muslim presence because many Muslims have kept a low profile, preferring, like many immigrants before them, to "blend in" and be accepted. Others have sought to avoid special notice and harassment in an America that has often portrayed Islam as a violent religion, thus forgetting that like any other religion or ethnic group, Islam and Muslims represent great diversity.

About two-thirds of the American Muslim population consist of immigrants or descendants of Muslims who came to America from overseas. (The remaining one-third are African American converts to Islam plus a smaller number of white American converts.) Waves of Muslim immigrants began to come to America in the late nineteenth century and have continued to do so in the twentieth century. At first, they were primarily laborers from Syria, Jordan, and Lebanon; then came Palestinian refugees who fled or were homeless after the creation of Israel in 1948. In recent decades, Muslim immigration has included well-educated Muslims who fled oppressive regimes in Egypt, Iraq, and Syria, or who came from South Asia seeking a better life. Like most immigrants from Italy, Ireland, Poland, the former Soviet Union, and other countries, many Muslims were concerned with economic survival. Many lived among other Muslims and attempted to assimilate rather than to stand out in society. Others came with the intention of striking it rich and returning home. Few were anxious to emphasize their differences by preaching Islam, seeking converts, or building mosques.

Large numbers of Muslim students have come to America during the past two decades from countries extending from Sudan to Indonesia—for example, from Egypt, Tunisia, Algeria, Saudi Arabia, Kuwait, Iran, Iraq, Pakistan, Bangladesh, and Malaysia. Muslim students now can be found at universities across the country. America provides an environment in which these students can share their faith and ideas. The freedom in America enables them to explore political ideas that would be impossible in their own countries, as well as to come to know about the teachings of Muslim leaders from other parts of the Islamic world.

African American Muslims

During the first half of the twentieth century a number of American blacks converted to Islam and established communities or movements. The most prominent of these was Elijah Muhammad (formerly Elijah Poole) and his Nation of Islam. Combining an emphasis on hard work and a strict moral code with an insistence on black separatism, the Nation of Islam promoted its ideas by opening temples and mosques in many poor urban neighborhoods and recruiting its members especially from the younger generation.

Elijah Muhammad's message of black separatism, with its denunciation of "white devils," created suspicion and fear among many white Americans, as well as Muslim immigrants, all of whom regarded it as a radical organization. However, in the black community the message proved extremely effective and had a significant impact not only among the poor, but among a growing number of students and professionals. Cassius Clay (born 1942), the heavyweight boxing champion of the world (1964–1967, 1974–1978, 1978–1979), drew headlines across the world when he joined the Nation of Islam, taking the name Muhammad Ali.

Another prominent convert was Malcolm X (1925–1965), who learned about the Nation of Islam in prison and subsequently became one of its most prominent ministers. In the mid-1960s Malcolm X made the pilgrimage to Mecca, where he saw and experienced Islam as a universal community of believers that was blind to differences of color and race. He returned from that experience rejecting the notion that the white race was inherently evil. He sought to preach an Islam that was more consistent with mainstream Muslim belief and practice, and therefore broke with Elijah Muhammad. In 1965, Malcolm X was assassinated at a religious rally. Two members of the Nation of Islam were subsequently charged and convicted of his murder.[3]

After the death of Elijah Muhammad in 1975, his son, Warith D. Muhammad, succeeded him. Warith subsequently rejected the separatist teachings of his father and brought many of his other teachings into line more closely with Islamic belief and practice. By 1985, he had integrated his organization into the worldwide Muslim community. However, a minority of African American Muslims, under the leadership of Louis Farrakhan, still retain the name Nation of Islam along with its separatist outlook.

Challenges Facing Muslims
in America

As our discussion demonstrates, there is as great a diversity among Muslims as there is among other religious communities in America. Not only do Americans come from different countries and races, but we relate to and practice our faith in differing ways. For some Muslims, like members of other faiths, being a Muslim is part of their social and cultural background. However, they may not practice their faith regularly. Some pray or go to a mosque only on religious holidays, in the same way that some Christians celebrate only Christmas or Jews commemorate only Passover. Other are quite observant, praying regularly and living according to their faith. Still others, emphasizing that Islam is a total way of life, struggle to implement their faith in their public as well as private lives, in state and society.

Like all peoples and communities who have come to the United States as a minority, Muslims face special problems. Because America is predominantly Judeo-Christian in its origins and population, it is sometimes easier for Christians and Jews to practice their faith. For example, schools do not recognize Muslim religious holidays. Attending Friday congregational prayer and taking a break to perform the salat during working hours are often difficult. Because Muslims should not drink alcohol, eat pork, or eat meat that has not been slaughtered in a properly Islamic way (similar to Judaism's strict preparation of kosher foods), attending social functions or eating at restaurants can sometimes be awkward. However, things are changing. Recently, Muslim chaplains were permitted in the armed services and in the prison system. Similarly, in 1991 a Muslim religious leader joined Christian and Jewish chaplains for the first time to recite an opening prayer for sessions of the U.S. Congress.

Life in America also brings with it new situations and challenges. For those who come from Muslim societies that emphasize strong religious and family values and modesty in dress, life in a more secular and pluralistic American society can contribute to tensions and changes in values and outlook. American coed schools, dances, beaches, and social events may challenge traditional values. The greater sexual freedom in the West can bring out the tension and contradictions between living in a new society and abiding by the values of the past. Although socializing with non-Muslims is not a problem for Muslims, dating and intermarriage can be.

In the face of adversity, Islam in America has proven to be a dynamic faith. As a result of their experience, Muslims are constantly demonstrating the flexibility of their faith. Incorporating American customs, Islamic centers often include not only the mosque, but also a Sunday school where children study their religion, and a social hall for community events that range from bake sales to feature speakers. Those mosques that can afford it often have a professional religious leader (imam). In contrast to his role in the Muslim world, where he would look after the mosque and lead the prayers, an imam in the United States often performs such duties as counseling, social work, and public relations.

For more than fourteen centuries, Islam has been a dynamic and expansive faith, providing inspiration and meaning to the lives of many. Today, that dynamism is seen not only abroad, but also by the growing presence of Islam in America. Like Jews and Christians before them, and indeed all religious peoples, Muslims struggle to preserve their faith while adapting it to the realities of American life. The increased visibility of Muslims adds to the tapestry of nationalities and faiths that have come to constitute the richness and diversity of America.

NOTES

1. Throughout this chapter, I have drawn on my previous work, especially *Islam: The Straight Path*, expanded edition (New York: Oxford University Press, 1992).

2. See, for example, John L. Esposito, *Islam and Politics*, 3d ed. (Syracuse, N.Y.: Syracuse University Press, 1991); and Esposito, *The Islamic Threat: Myth or Reality?* (New York: Oxford University Press, 1992).

3. For more about Islam in America, see Yvonne Y. Haddad, *A Century of Islam in America* (Washington, D.C.: Middle East Institute, 1986); Yvonne Yazbeck Haddad and Adair T. Lumis, *Islamic Values in the United States* (New York: Oxford University Press, 1987); and *The Muslims of America*, ed. Yvonne Yazbeck Haddad (New York: Oxford University Press, 1991).

STUDY QUESTIONS

1. Why is it important for Americans to have an understanding of Islam?
2. How is Islam similar to Judaism and Christianity? Name several major differences between these religious communities.
3. Who is Muhammad? Give a brief biographical description. What role does he play in the development of the Islamic religion? Name a figure in Judaism and in Christianity to whom Muhammad is similar.
4. What are the five pillars of Islam? How do they function in a Muslim's understanding of religious life?
5. What role does the month of Ramadan play in the practice of Islam? How is fasting believed to contribute to the Islamic way of life?
6. What is the goal of the religious pilgrimage in the Islamic faith? How is it similar to "faith journeys" in other religious traditions?
7. Why did Muslims come to America? When and how did the African American Muslim community develop in the United States?
8. What is Malcolm X's relation to the Nation of Islam? Why did Malcolm X believe that Islam represented an important religious experience for the African American community?
9. What problems do Muslims face in America? How has the Muslim community grown in light of such diversity?

ESSAY TOPICS

The Life of Muhammad
The Quran: Sacred Scripture of Islam
Malcolm X and the Nation of Islam: Religious Alternatives in the African American Community
Mecca: Holy City of Islam

WORD EXPLORATION

The following words play significant roles in any discussion of Islam in America and are worth careful reflection and discussion.

Allah	Quran	Pilgrimage
Ramadan	Elijah Muhammad	Mosque
Muhammad	Mecca	Imam
Theocracy	Islam	

12

ELIZABETH FOX-GENOVESE

Religion and Women in America

Throughout American history, religion has played a central role in the lives of most women. At the funeral of my grandmother, who had been a devout Congregationalist throughout her life, the minister read from the book of Proverbs, "Who can find a virtuous woman? for her price is far above rubies." The virtuous woman of Proverbs worked willingly with her hands and brought food from far off. She wove and spun and gave generously to the poor. Never idle, she spoke in wisdom and in kindness. Her husband and children praised her for her virtues and works. "Favor is deceitful, and beauty is vain: but a woman that feareth the Lord, she shall be praised." I remember thinking at the time, and still do, that the words perfectly captured the standards my grandmother set for herself. She was human, not a saint, but she turned to religion to give meaning and purpose to a life that was frequently difficult.

Since the early seventeenth century, when European settlers arrived on the coasts of North America, religion has been important to women in America. During the seventeenth and most of the eighteenth centuries, Protestant Christianity emphasized women's subordination to men within families and households, but it also expected them to develop a personal faith and direct relationship with God. By the beginning of the nineteenth century, American culture in general was attributing a new importance to women, especially in their roles as mothers. During this period, as men became more and more concerned with the nonreligious values of business and politics, religion became increasingly associated with female values of purity and morality. This "feminization" of religion slowly granted women a new kind of moral authority, which women used as justification for founding a variety of charitable associations.

Following the Civil War, during the late nineteenth and early twentieth centuries, women's organizations grew in membership and ambition. More and more, women turned to the religious values with which they were associated to justify social reform. My grandmother was a member of the Woman's Christian Temperance Union and pioneered the development of recreation programs for the young and the elderly. For her and women like her, religion provided a thread of righteousness that ran through everything they did. Even more, religion provided them with a sense of identity and calling—the sense that their lives had meaning and served a higher purpose. Our own times are witnessing dramatic changes in women's roles and in religion, but even these changes are grounded in the history of American women's special sense of their own religious identity and vocation.

RELIGION AS A WOMAN'S CALLING

Throughout the year 1856, in Mobile, Alabama, Augusta Jane Evans, a young woman of twenty-one, wrote long letters to a Methodist minister. She feared that she had lost her faith in God and wanted to recover it. With his help she did, and three years later, in 1859, she published a novel, *Beulah*, in which her heroine suffered a similar crisis. The novel became a best-seller. Girls and women throughout the United States devoured the account of Beulah's doubts and relished her return to faith, probably because so many of them identified with her experience.

Beulah was no typical female heroine. Fiercely determined to be independent, she impatiently told one of her closest friends not to talk to her "about woman's clinging, dependent nature." Beulah wanted to become a teacher and a writer, and she succeeded. But her success satisfied neither her spiritual nor what Evans called her womanly nature. Only after Beulah regained her ability to pray did she gain the ability to recognize love and, eventually, to marry the man whom she loved and who had long loved her.

Today, the popularity of *Beulah* in its time seems surprising. In many ways, it is more like an intellectual tract than a popular romance. Yet many an American woman believed that *Beulah* was a story about her own life. Maybe not everyone who loved the novel understood all of the religious issues. Surely most did not recognize all of the references to male writers. But they were apparently willing to skip the difficult parts because of the story's relevance to their own lives. These readers were white, middle-class women from all parts of the country who deeply believed that a solid faith was as important to a woman as marriage to the right man. They were women who believed that religion and marriage should go together; who believed that women had a special responsibility to uphold and spread Christian belief and to live a model Christian life. At the end of the novel, Beulah, sitting with her husband, lays her Bible on his knee. And Evans writes, "May God aid the wife in her work of love," for it is her responsibility to bring her husband to a faith as strong as her own.

In the mid-1800s many American women, with Evans, believed that religion was women's special sphere. Religion asked a lot of women: that they be good wives and mothers, obey their husbands, learn to suppress their anger and hold their tongues. Women were expected to lead their children and their husbands to church and to convince them to lead good Christian lives. Everyone knew that men could be angry, use bad language, and not pay enough attention to religious belief and practice. By the nineteenth century, most people assumed that men would mainly be interested in business and politics. And few people believed that you could be successful in a competitive world and always follow the Sermon on the Mount. Men were not supposed to be meek. They were not expected to turn the other cheek. They were not even expected to do unto others as they would have others do unto them. Women were a different matter. They were expected to do all of those things and more. They could be expected to live a Christian life in what clearly was not a Christian world.

Today, more and more women believe that it was not fair to ask women to sacrifice themselves for the good of others. Why should women have to be "better" than men, especially when being better means having less power in the world? But in the nineteenth century many women thought differently. Many saw their religious responsibilities as a vocation or a "calling." Even when religious faith did not come easily, they saw the struggle for faith as a central part of their lives. Religion offered them a meaningful story about their own identity. It helped them to define who they were in the world. Even as religion taught them to be meek and self-sacrificing, it gave them a higher standard by which they could judge others.

IMAGES AND ROLES OF WOMEN
IN RELIGION

Christianity had not always given women this special spiritual power. The traditional religions of the Native Americans actually gave women

261

somewhat more power. These religions worshiped the spiritual powers of nature and were, therefore, likely to recognize the important place of women and to associate them with the forces of life. Since women bore children, it seemed reasonable to link them to other sources of fertility, especially the earth and agriculture. Native Americans' religious worldview thus acknowledged the spiritual importance of the female side of humanity, and their religious practices also permitted women to play significant roles. Among the first European Christian settlers, however, women generally played subordinate religious roles.

Puritan Women

The Puritan settlers of New England did attribute some religious independence to women. Puritan women, like all other Christians, in the end were responsible for their own souls. But God was worshiped as male, and men were viewed as the natural leaders of the churches. In Puritan New England, church and government largely overlapped, so that the authority of men spread over most aspects of women's lives. The Puritans viewed marriage both as the basic unit of social order and as a sign of religious grace. They strongly encouraged affectionate, compassionate marriages in which women and men were expected to delight, help, and comfort each other. But men had primary authority for maintaining this social order. Thus, for example, husbands could by law beat their wives. Although they were not allowed to beat them too severely, other men defined what constituted "too severely."

Anne Hutchinson

The Puritans were dissenters from the Church of England who left England in order to be able to worship in their own way. Like many other religious radicals, however, they placed the highest possible value on maintaining discipline within their own community and did not easily tolerate internal dissent, especially from women. In general, Puritan women accepted the position assigned to them, but their assigned roles led them to develop special bonds with one another. In particular, they developed ties with other women out of their experience of childbirth and the fear of death associated with it. In the 1630s one woman in particular, Anne Marbury Hutchinson, a midwife and the mother of fifteen children, emerged as a leader of this female piety. The ministers of the Bay Colony, notably John Winthrop, saw Hutchinson's religious radicalism and growing authority among women as a direct challenge to their authority.

In 1637, the ministers tried and convicted Hutchinson of heresy. The main charge against her was that she claimed that God spoke to her directly, as God had spoken to Abraham and Daniel. She thus claimed equal standing with the men as a minister. She told her judges that she was divinely inspired and that the Spirit assured her that "an immediate revelation" sanctioned her ministry. The male ministers were not convinced. They found her claim to independent authority illegitimate and subversive, and they banished her and her followers from the colony.

Hutchinson's case illustrates some of the main tensions women face in Christianity. In effect, her punishment warned all women that it was one thing for them to pray directly to God and to take responsibility for their own sins, but it was another thing entirely for them to claim to speak publicly in God's name. The Catholics who settled in Maryland and the Anglicans who settled in Virginia would have agreed wholeheartedly. The Quakers who settled in Pennsylvania were even more radical than the New England Puritans or Congregationalists. They placed special emphasis on the inner light that emanates from each individual soul and did not acknowledge the special authority of any minister or preacher. In their meetings, each person present could speak as the spirit moved her or him. And yet even the Quakers normally expected women to observe the conventions of society and to accept their subordination to men.

WOMEN AND
THE GREAT AWAKENINGS

During the eighteenth century, the religious life of most American women, especially members of the various Protestant sects, centered on the family and household. Wives and mothers were instructed to represent the special womanly virtues and thus to help sustain the spiritual well-being of their families. In the middle of the eighteenth century and at the beginning of the nineteenth century, American society experienced two Great Awakenings—popular religious revivals that drew many thousands to camp meetings and reinvigorated churches. The Awakenings reflected the growing influence of evangelical religion and the growth of new denominations, notably the Methodists and the Baptists.

In both Awakenings, women and men alike were urged to embrace Christ for themselves and to rededicate themselves to his service in every aspect of their lives. They were to make their lives into examples of purity and service and thus to help redeem a sinful society. The First Great Awakening helped to strengthen many individual women's sense of their own spiritual mission, but it did not produce any significant changes in women's situation relative to men. The Second Great Awakening, especially in the northeastern states, reflected clear changes in what we might call the religious division of labor by sex.

The Second Great Awakening, which began in the South in the late 1790s and lasted nationally until the 1820s, followed the American Revolution and the ratification of the Constitution. It therefore occurred in what was then a new nation. The Awakening thus reflected new attitudes about the appropriate roles of women and men that flowed from new political institutions and new economic developments.

A New View of—and
a New Role for—Women

The generation that had lived through the Revolution and the ratification of the Constitution was very much concerned with the new responsibilities of women in a new republic. They especially saw women as the mothers of new citizens and charged them with the moral and political education of the young. Men, they assumed, would devote most of their energy to government and economic occupations and, accordingly, would spend most of their time outside of the household and in the public sphere. This was an important shift from colonial society, in which the household itself had been viewed as the nucleus of government and economic life. Under these new conditions many began to see the household as a *home:* a private sphere that specialized in childrearing and sustaining the emotional life of its members.

None of these changes took place overnight. But as they gradually occurred, a new view of women took shape. The emphasis on women as potentially disorderly and dangerous began to disappear. In its place arose a new view of women as especially moral and good. This "cult of true womanhood," as it came to be called, pictured women as pious, dutiful, obedient, and nurturing. Such women, it was believed, were naturally suited to preside over the home. Clearly, there was a strong religious influence on this view of women's nature and roles. Women were to be especially Christian, and their influence was to permeate the home.

The founders of the new republic recognized that it would include people of different faiths. To be sure, the vast majority of Americans were Protestants, but even they were divided into many denominations. Hence, it seemed wise to avoid the establishment of a state church and to recognize religion as a private matter. At the same time, the founding fathers expected the nation to remain fundamentally Christian and to observe the basic precepts of Christian morality.

As a result of these possibly contradictory beliefs that (1) there must be no state church and (2) the nation must be fundamentally Christian, they arrived at a novel compromise that would make the religious mission of women even more important. First, they encouraged the disestablishment of churches in the various states. In practice, disestablishment meant that no church would have the right to be supported by public taxation, as most had been before the Revolution. Second, they encouraged the private development of moral and religious sensibilities in individual citizens.

The Second Great Awakening consisted of a long series of revivals in different parts of the country, each of which tried to light the fire of religious conversion in the hearts and souls of individuals. The revivals assumed a different character in different parts of the country, but all shared the conviction that the religious life of the country would depend upon the private conviction and behavior of individuals. In the South men continued to play important roles as religious leaders of their families and households. In the Northeast and the new settlements in places such as western New York, however, women began to emerge as an important factor in the success of the revivals.

With the growth of towns and commerce in the Northeast, many women began to fear that they would lose their children, especially their sons, to the dangerous temptations of the public sphere. Fearing even that their husbands were being caught up in decidedly non-Christian habits and interests, they began to take their responsibilities for the morality of their families very seriously indeed. Often, they would be the first member of their families to give themselves to the passion of religious revival. Then they would take their young children to a revival or to church. And finally, they would begin to work on their husbands and their adolescent sons. Even the most pious wife and mother did not always succeed in persuading the grown men of her family to attend church regularly, much less in leading them to conversion. As a result, women significantly outnumbered men in church membership.

The growing presence of women among church members led ministers, who depended upon their congregations for support, to preach more and more directly to their female parishioners. The various Protestant denominations in the Northeast increasingly emphasized the importance of individual conscience. This slowly led to the "feminization" of religion. In other words, official religion came more and more to emphasize matters of special concern to women.

Throughout the country, women were especially concerned with death. Every woman knew that every time she gave birth to a child, she risked her own death or the death of the child. Women were also especially conscious of the chance that an infant or child might die. Many women felt that the Angel of Death shadowed their lives, and they sought ways to learn to accept inevitable loss. Ministers, responding to these fears, increasingly emphasized consolation in loss and the promise of reunion in heaven, and the picture they painted of heaven increasingly resembled a middle-class home on earth.

Religious Conviction and Northern Women's Social Influence

Concerned as they were with the sinful worldliness that threatened to seduce their husbands and sons, women in the Northeast began to organize charitable associations that reflected their special concerns and especially to help the poor, in particular widows and orphans. Women's organizations began to mount a sustained crusade against vice, notably illicit sex and alcohol. Some women began to form organizations for mothers that helped women to support each other in protecting their children against worldly dangers and temptations. Today the organization MADD (Mothers Against Drunk Driving) follows this pattern, as do various organizations of mothers for peace. In the 1850s, some women even began to support the abolition of slavery in the South based on their concern with the purity of families, which slavery disrupted or destroyed.

Until the Civil War, many, but not all, of these organizations were associated with similar male organizations or had a male leader, frequently a minister. Men were especially visible in the temperance and abolitionist movements, as well as some moral reform associations such as the short-lived New York Magdalen Society. During the first half of the nineteenth century, most Americans still believed that women should remain in the private sphere, should not speak in public, and should not lead men. Most women, moreover, lacked the time or experience to devote themselves full-time to organizations outside the home. Women nonetheless persevered in their causes and organized societies to support mothers or reform morality, especially men's. The experience they gained in these movements gave many middle-class women an extraordinary apprenticeship in using their influence in the world. Their self-confidence and strength of purpose in attempting to change the world came from their conviction that they were the chosen representatives of religious values. Having gained authority in the home, women were now intent upon imposing the values of the home upon a sinful world.

Southern Women

The women of the slaveholding South were no less committed to religion, but their experience differed from that of their northern sisters. The vast majority of southern women continued to live in rural households over which men firmly presided. Since most of southern economic life remained based within households, most southerners did not experience the separation between home and work that shaped the lives of northeasterners. The presence of slaves within households made clear to everyone that the physical strength of men was necessary to maintain order. For, at the limit, an effective slaveholder needed to be able to whip a prime male field hand himself. Slavery thus prevented southern women from assuming a new role as guardians of the home. Slavery, moreover, led southerners to continue to place great value on the idea of hierarchy—the idea that some were naturally superior to others.

Religion did not lead white southerners to experience crippling guilt about slavery. As southern religious leaders regularly insisted, the Bible did not condemn slavery, so white southerners had no reason to feel guilty about holding slaves. As they also regularly insisted, however, the Bible did instruct slaveholders to be good Christian masters and mistresses. Slaveholding women and men both saw religion as central to their responsibilities. For various reasons, they were eager to encourage their slaves' conversion to Christianity. Many of them were also just as eager to live up to their own ideals of what it meant to be a Christian master or mistress.

Southern women, like northern women, enthusiastically participated in the Second Great Awakening. But like women of the rural West and unlike northern women, most of those who did participate did so together with their husbands, and in the countryside rather than in towns. Typically, a revival in a particular area would draw large crowds of people, who arrived in carriages or wagons and might stay for as much as a week. Families would come together, and slaveholding families occasionally would bring some of their slaves. The days would be spent in sermons and prayer, and the meeting would frequently culminate in a significant number of conversions to Christ.

Both slaveholding and nonslaveholding women valued revivals and tried to carry into their everyday lives the religious enthusiasm that revivals generated. Southern women, living in rural households that were frequently distant from neighbors and churches, could not always count on being able to attend church regularly. Most went whenever they had the opportunity, but if there was no man to accompany them, if the weather were especially bad, or if they or one of their household were ill, they could not. Town women, of course, found it easier to get to church and many also attended prayer meetings, Sabbath school, and (for the Methodists) fellowship meals called "love feasts." But even when they could not get to church, many strove to keep religious faith at the center of their lives.

For white southern women, like many other white women throughout the country, religious training began at their mother's knee. More often than not, they learned to read from the Bible. One slaveholding mother noted in her diary that her young daughter had finished reading the New Testament before she was five. A seventeen-year-old woman from a slaveholding family in Tennessee noted in her diary that she had just finished reading her Bible for the eighth time and was beginning again. North and South, women kept diaries in which they carefully recorded their religious progress and backsliding. These diaries suggest that many women turned to religion to set standards for themselves. Religion taught them what it meant to be a good woman.

Women's Views on Slavery

If religious faith joined women of different regions, their attitudes toward religious justification for slaveholding divided them. If slaveholding women did not feel guilty about owning slaves, most did worry about meeting their responsibilities to the slaves they owned. Surprising numbers taught some of their slaves, normally female house slaves, to read the Bible, even though teaching slaves to read at all was against the law. Many prayed with their slaves, either by including them in regular family prayers or by praying with them individually. Many worried in their diaries about whether they were doing enough to help convert their slaves, and about how they could be true Christians if they did not.

Perhaps above all, however, slaveholding women worried about their ability to manage slaves responsibly. For them, slave management was directly linked to their worries about whether they were leading a Christian life in general. In their diaries slaveholding women would pray for the patience to "govern" their children and their slaves properly. They knew full well that when they failed to do so it was because they were not accepting God's will. They knew that they were too likely to lose their tempers, to say things that they did not mean, to slap a child or a slave when they should have been more patient. These women prayed for the patience to keep their tongue, to control their temper, to observe God's commandments, and, in general, to lead a good Christian life.

Northern women also turned to religion for consolation and strength, worried about controlling their tempers and keeping their tongues, and especially worried about whether they were raising their children properly. Northern women, however, did not own slaves; most did not even employ servants, and those who did employ servants did not normally feel much personal responsibility for their religious life. Over time, a small but growing number of northern women began to believe that slavery directly violated Christianity in general and women's special domestic Christian mission in particular. According to Harriet Beecher Stowe and those who shared her views, slavery introduced disorder and sexual immorality into the heart of a woman's domestic realm.

Slave women shared northern women's opposition to slavery, but for intensely personal reasons. They knew firsthand that slavery destroyed families and threatened the most sacred bonds of motherhood. Yet some slave women also turned to Christianity for consolation and strength—even if they vehemently disagreed with their mistresses about its meaning. Slaveholding women were especially drawn to such biblical passages as "Servants, obey your masters." Slave women were much more likely to cherish the passages that proclaimed that the last shall be first. Slave and slaveholder could, in other words, share a general belief in Christianity but interpret its meaning and lessons differently. For the slaveholders, the Bible sanctioned slavery; for the slaves, the slaveholders' religion mocked the Bible, which promised the deliverance of the slaves much as Moses had delivered the Israelites from Egypt.

The Protestant Image
of Womanhood

Not all women of any social group were equally devout. Some women, especially along the frontiers, joined one of the new sects that sprang up throughout the first half of the nineteenth century—the Mormons, the Shakers, the Campbellites, and others. All of these new sects tended to be more extreme than the established churches, although often in very different ways. Many women who considered themselves Christian never joined a church, perhaps because they could not decide which to join, or perhaps because they could not experience conversion and, therefore, believed themselves unfit. During this period, there were also increasing numbers of women who were not part of the Protestant majority. Catholics, especially Irish and German, steadily increased in number. Jews, though fewer, were also becoming more numerous. In these and other ways, the religious experience of American women differed significantly by class, race, region, and ethnicity.

Mainstream Protestantism nonetheless left an indelible mark on the experience of American women. During the years before the Civil War, the Protestant view of woman as the angel and guiding spirit of a moral home in an increasingly secular and competitive world was so firmly established that it became the main view of womanhood. In other words, the Protestant image of womanhood transcended denominational boundaries to become the norm for all women, even if all women did not accept it. For those who did accept it, even if they did not always live up to its ideals, the Protestant image of womanhood offered a model of womanly excellence and an internal standard of character and virtue. It also offered women a special mission and a special form of power: It promised them that they had become the guardians of the moral fiber of the nation.

WOMEN AND CHRISTIAN VALUES IN THE POST–CIVIL WAR PERIOD

Following the Civil War and the abolition of slavery, industrial development greatly accelerated. The size and number of cities grew dramatically, as did the industrial working class. With the new flood of immigration and the ever more visible social problems that accompanied urban growth, the United States began its move toward a modern, industrial, and multicultural nation. Many saw the challenges of this new world as primarily political and economic, but to many women the challenges seemed primarily moral and social. And many women responded by claiming that the cities were nothing but the home writ large. Urban problems ranged from poor sewerage and inadequate lighting to hungry children to domestic violence. Women who had grown up in the Protestant, moral reform tradition enthusiastically claimed these and other problems as their special responsibility.

In the decade following the Civil War, a large number of new women's reform organizations sprang up, many of them with origins in women's sewing and nursing associations during the war, or moral reform associations before it. Two of the most significant, both in the numbers they attracted and in the kind of work they did, were the Woman's Christian Temperance Union (WCTU) and the Young Women's Christian Association (YWCA). Significantly, both organizations explicitly called themselves Christian, by which they really meant Protestant, and both explicitly devoted themselves to introducing women's moral values into the public sphere. The members of the WCTU firmly believed that men's abuse of alcohol directly threatened women and children and made the defense of Christian values impossible. The original members of the WCTU expressed their convictions in an uncompromising and militant fashion, notably by direct action to close saloons and retail liquor stores. But as membership rapidly grew, the WCTU adopted more compromising tactics. Their ultimate goal nonetheless remained to ban all public sale and consumption of alcohol within the United States. With the passage of the Eighteenth Amendment to the Constitution in 1919, they temporarily succeeded.

Under the rubric of "home protection," the WCTU's long campaign for prohibition gradually expanded to include efforts to improve urban conditions and, especially, to protect the wives and children of working men who drank. At its peak in the 1890s, the WCTU had some 200,000 members, making it the largest women's organization in the country. It drew countless women from small towns across the country into associations with other women. Initially, many members of the WCTU tended to accept the traditional view of women's domestic roles, but over time they came to believe that their cause required them to defend women's right to participate in politics in order to accomplish their goals.

The YWCA emerged as a strong organization during the last quarter of the nineteenth century. Although it shared many of the WCTU's goals and was affiliated with it in the struggle for temperance, it also paid special attention to the needs of single women. YWCA chapters became common on college campuses, and YWCA summer retreats brought young women together to discuss the plan for their responsibilities as Christians. The YWCA also attempted to meet some of the needs of the growing number of young women who were being drawn into the cities to work. They offered "Traveler's Aid" services, to welcome young women and give them information on neighborhoods and lodging. They also established rooming houses for single women in some of the larger cities. In these and other efforts, the YWCA tried to prepare young women to live as Christians and to defend Christian values in a complex and threatening urban world.

Both the WCTU and the YWCA recruited members nationally and exerted national influence. Well before racial integration, the YWCA included black as well as white women, although frequently in separate chapters. The YWCA nonetheless pioneered the promotion of black women to positions of leadership. Southern-born Katherine DuPre Lumpkin powerfully describes in her autobiography her shock when her all-white YWCA chapter was told that they would be addressed by a Miss Jane Arthur, who was black. When the address was over, she found that

271

"the heavens had not fallen, nor the earth parted asunder to swallow us up in this unheard of transgression." Moreover she had to admit that, as she listened to Miss Arthur, she would not have known whether she was white or black. The experience, Lumpkin wrote, was similar to the biblical story of the man in the book of Samuel who had defied the law by touching the sacred Tabernacle of Jehovah. She had, by thinking that nothing essential distinguished Miss Arthur from a white woman, touched the "tabernacle of our sacred racial beliefs" and nothing, "not the slightest thing had happened."

The WCTU and the YWCA were both explicitly concerned with how women could defend and implement religious values in an increasingly secular world. In this respect, both organizations encouraged women to think of themselves as the special representatives of Christian values in the world. They thus strengthened many women in the view that religion offered them an important mission and the best way to organize and make sense of their lives. As more women became active in defense of domestic and religious values, however, some of them became increasingly caught up in secular values. Others, like Katherine DuPre Lumpkin, began to interpret old values in new ways. Many began to see social reform as its own justification: It was important to clean up slums or to make sure that babies had pasteurized milk simply to have a fair and decent society. Others, however, continued to draw upon religious faith in order to justify the activities in which they were engaged. For such women the ultimate purpose of social reform was to ensure moral reform; in other words, social reform was the best way to practice Christian benevolence. These women were insisting that Christian morality must be a matter of public concern.

WOMEN AND RELIGIOUS CHANGE IN THE TWENTIETH CENTURY

Throughout the twentieth century, different groups of women have continued to attempt to encourage, or even to impose, moral values in the public sphere. As the century has progressed, Protestant women have found themselves increasingly drawn into alliance with Catholics, Jews, and others to defend the values they care most about. In the 1930s, Protestants and Catholics together brought so much pressure upon the motion picture industry that the major producers agreed to a code that would restrict displays of sexuality and "immorality" in films. Since the 1960s, most restrictions of this kind have collapsed, although industry ratings such as PG, R, and X warn viewers about the levels of sexuality and violence in films. Increasingly, many Americans insist that moral questions be considered as entirely private matters, that no one has any business telling others how to live or what to read or view.

What is most striking in these changes is that there is no longer a clear dividing line between women and men. Both women and men may be extremely permissive on moral questions; both women and men may be conservative. Rather than dividing the sexes, the line seems to divide different social, political, and religious groups. The public debates about pornography and abortion, in which women and men can be found on both sides, clearly demonstrate that at least in the case of sexual morality many women no longer view traditional religious values as the foundation for their identity.

As the role of religion in public life is coming under more and more attack, especially with regard to personal morality, debates about the place of women within religious denominations are becoming more intense. Throughout most of American history, the vast majority of women were devoted to religions that worshiped a male God. Although women have occasionally preached in most of the Protestant denominations, until recently they were not ordained as ministers. Women, in other words, have devoted themselves to religions that did not accept women as leaders or saviors, much less as persons created, at least literally, in the image of God. These discussions cut across all of the major faiths in the United States—Protestant, Catholic, and Jewish. Today, some Protestant denominations are beginning to accept women as ministers and pastors, and some Jewish temples are accepting women as rabbis.

To the extent that women are beginning to be accepted as religious leaders (though not in Catholicism), we may be witnessing a new stage in the "feminization" of religion. How far this feminization will go remains unclear. Ironically, it seems to be occurring in close association with the decline in older standards of morality with which women had long been especially associated.

From the beginning of American history, religion has played a central role in women's lives. Throughout the centuries, society expected women to view marriage and motherhood as their primary roles. Until very recently, society also expected women to accept their subordination to men as natural. Religion reinforced these social norms, but it also expected women to be responsible for their own souls. From the early nineteenth century on, it even encouraged them to assume special responsibilities for the morality of society itself. In this sense, there was always some tension in women's sense of themselves as religious beings: They simultaneously had to accept subordination and assume responsibility. Many women rose to the challenge and embraced religion as the best way to make sense of their lives and to justify their actions. In the name of religion, women gradually began to move beyond their traditional roles, to organize with other women, to challenge what they saw as immoral social practices, and to act independently in the world. Today, they are even challenging religious traditions and may be transforming religion itself.

STUDY QUESTIONS

1. How did the "feminization" of religion take place during the eighteenth and nineteenth centuries in America? What was women's role in organized religion at that time? How much change do you think has taken place since then?
2. What role did women play in the American Great Awakening?
3. What issues in the North were most affected by women's religious convictions? How did northern women's religious experiences differ from those of women in the South? What role does slavery play in understanding women in the South and their understanding of religion?
4. What were women's views toward slavery? Do you see a difference between the views of women in the North and women in the South? Do you see any relation between the plight of slaves and the lives of white women during the nineteenth century?
5. What was the "cult of true womanhood"? Do you believe that such an image exists today?
6. How did the role of women in American religion change during the post–Civil War period? What do you see as the most significant change? Do you believe that there is no difference between men's and women's relations to religion in America?

ESSAY TOPICS

Religion, Women, and Slavery during the Civil War
Women, Their Religion, and the American Temperance Movement
Harriet Beecher Stowe's *Uncle Tom's Cabin:* An Antislavery Novel
Women and Ordained Clergy in America
Men and Women in American Religion: Still No Equality

WORD EXPLORATION

The following words play significant roles in any discussion of religion and women in America and are worth careful reflection and discussion.

Abolitionist	Anne Hutchinson	Woman's Christian
Young Women's	Feminist	Temperance
Christian	Katherine DuPre	Union
Association	Lumpkin	

13

ANDREW M. GREELEY

Religion and Politics in America

Religion and politics don't mix in America, it is often said. Church and state are separated by a wall. Religion is a matter of private life; politics pertains to public life. In your heart and in your church on Sunday (or whatever day of the week) you can be religious if you want to, but the political life of the country ought to be purely secular. Many Americans would agree with those cliches, though fewer would agree with the logical conclusions that can be drawn from them, such as the prohibition of prayer in public schools and of Christmas decorations in public parks.

The Constitution forbids the establishment of a state religion, as well as interference in the free exercise of religion. Historically, however, these two clauses have not created an impenetrable wall between church and state. Judicial interpretations that take the metaphor of the "wall" literally are heavily influenced by secularist theory, which often seems to others to want its "anti-religion" established as the only permissible approach to religion. Religious behavior should be banned, it would seem, from every area of life where its presence might be an embarrassment to those who are not religious. Some of these controversies will be addressed later in this chapter. It should be noted, however, that balancing the "establishment" clause with the "free exercise" clause has always required a neat tightrope act by the courts.

In fact, as a description of American history and American life, the metaphor of the "wall" between religion and public life could not be more inaccurate. The Pilgrims and Puritans came to New England for religious reasons. Religion has shaped decisive turning points in American history: the abolition of slavery in the last century; the prohibition of alcohol sales and consumption in the early years of this century (remnants of which still persist in state alcohol laws); and, more recently, the black civil rights movement. Religion is also part of the personal identity of most Americans; their denominational affiliation is an essential component of the way they think about themselves. Those who think religion has no place in the public life of America only deceive themselves. Indeed, what they often mean is that other people's religions have no place in the public life of the country.

There are three aspects of the relationship between religion and public life: (1) religion and personal identity; (2) religion and party affiliation and voting; and (3) religion and public controversy.

RELIGION AND WHO YOU ARE

In most American communities, when a new family moves in people want to know "what they are." This includes a number of questions: What kind of occupation are they engaged in? Where do they come from? What is their religion? "He's Catholic and she's Jewish." "They're Protestants, Methodist I think." "They're Irish Catholics. Can't you tell by the name?" "Italian Catholics—she's devout, he doesn't go to church much." "Staunch Christians." "They're Missouri Synod Lutherans." "They're some kind of Asian religion."

None of these comments is meant to put down the new family. Rather, they locate the newcomers on a map of religious differences that most Americans carry around in the back of their heads. These maps are a kind of quick and easy way of figuring out where other Americans come from and who they really are. If the new neighbors are a certain kind of Protestant, you hardly will bring them a bottle of wine as a welcoming present or invite them to a card party or a dance. If they are Jewish you would want to be sure that bacon will not cause them a problem at brunch. If you're active in Democratic politics, you'd have reason to suspect that they might be on your side should they be Catholic.

If you know someone's religion, you have some preliminary hints about what kind of a person he or she might be. You may revise or confirm these preliminary notions as you get to know the person better, but they are tools that enable you to begin your relationship with the other in something more than total ignorance.

Moreover, when you tell someone what your religion is you're laying down for that person some preliminary notions of who you are and where you stand: "I'm Jewish, so don't tell anti-Semitic jokes in my presence," for example. Religion defines some of the boundaries that make us different from other people—not totally different, perhaps, but different enough to be important.

Even if we tell others that we have no religion, or if we think the question is irrelevant and offensive and say so, we nonetheless place ourselves on the religious map and tell them something important about who we are and how we want to be treated. Even those who think religion is a purely private matter still have a pretty good idea of the religious identification of their friends and neighbors.

Religious affiliations, then, are part of the map that enables us to navigate through the uncharted waters of human relationships. Instead of encountering a mass of people about whom we know nothing and who seem totally like one another, we sort them out on several different criteria, one of which is religion. Think of the people you know reasonably well, your friends, neighbors, and family. How many are there whose religious affiliation you don't know? Chances are you can locate them in the three-part paradigm that embraces 90 percent of all Americans: Protestant, Catholic, Jew.

The more heterogeneous the place you live or go to school, the more likely religious identification is to be important to you and to others. If you live in a neighborhood where four out of five people are Italian Catholics, then the only codes that make much difference are "Italian" and "other." But if your neighborhood is a mix of many different kinds of people, then you are more sensitively tuned to these differences, not as a matter of principle but as a matter of practical necessity. This is an important point: Consciousness about religious identity does not result from an explicit conviction that you *should* know the religion of other people. Rather, it is an implicit and unselfconscious diagram that you need to have to find your way among others.

If you give a group of American young people a list of last names and ask them to provide the religion and ethnic background of each name, some of them will be right more than 90 percent of the time; none of them will be right less than 70 percent of the time. How do they know? They just know, that's all. "I mean, Kelly is Irish Catholic, isn't it?" Usually it is, though not always. (Indeed there are more Irish Protestants in the United States than Irish Catholics. The former tend to live in the South and in rural areas and to be descended from immigrants who came before 1820.)

"Gargiulo, that's Italian Catholic for sure."

You got it.

"Lewis . . . that's hard, but maybe it's Welsh and probably Methodist."

"Washington? If she's black I bet she's Baptist."

"Greenblum? Most likely Jewish."

Then ask them what kind of behavior they would expect at a party organized by these various people.

If the name is Kelly there would be, you'll be told, a lot of drinking. If the name is Gargiulo, there'll be a lot of hand waving. If Washington is a good Methodist or Baptist, there's not likely to be much drinking. If it's a Greenblum party, there'll only be a beer or two and a lot of heavy conversation.

These predictions are not necessarily accurate, nor does anyone believe that they are a hundred percent true. They are rather presuppositions with which we operate, models to be tested against further experience. They are benign stereotypes until one holds them despite contrary evidence.

Kelly may in fact be a Lutheran. Or she may be one of those rare Irish Catholics who don't drink at all. (I never had a drop to drink, save wine at the Eucharist, till I was thirty-six years old. Then I went to Italy and fell in love with wine—but two glasses at the most.) If this happens we are mildly surprised but quickly correct our assumptions. Then we ask if Ms. Kelly's father is a lawyer and active in politics and learn that he is. Well, some of our predictions were accurate.

Religion (sometimes combined with ethnicity) provides us with a set of questions to ask (discreetly of course) about other people—and also a set of questions we expect to be asked about ourselves. No one is particularly surprised or offended by these sets of questions. They are considered "natural" questions to ask in our society.

In a country like Italy where almost everyone has the same religion, or a country like England where most people are vaguely identified with the same church, the religious question seems much less "natural" and other questions are necessary to shape our first and tentative impressions of strangers.

Why is it different in America? Mainly because we are a "nation of immigrants" (as President Kennedy said) from many different places and backgrounds (including the first Asian tribe that migrated across the Bering land bridge and settled in North America, though of course it didn't become North America for many thousands of years). In Italy the Italian style of intense family relationships is taken for granted by almost everyone. In the United States, the first time you meet a person you don't know how that person relates to his or her parents and brothers and sisters and how tight a control the family is likely to exercise on his or her behavior. Religious (and ethnic) background give you a hint of what to expect. The diversity of our origins makes religious affiliation so important (and so useful) in our country. It is a way to tell others who we are and to learn from others who they are.

These differences do not go away over times. Research shows that there is very little difference between the family patterns of those who identify as Irish in the United States today and the Irish in Ireland (a lot of conversation in both countries). And there is no difference at all on a wide variety of measures between Italians and Italian Americans (both groups are more likely than anyone else to turn to family members when they need help).

We usually are not conscious of the subtle but important role that religion plays in tentatively defining people and relationships and indeed are inclined simply to deny that role when someone begins to talk about it. It is therefore necessary to think about it for a while and to understand that in a religiously heterogeneous society, especially one with a long history of intense religious devotion, religious affiliation is a terribly important map through our society. This fact of religious pluralism and identification is the basis for the intricate and at times difficult relationship between religion and politics in America.

PARTY IDENTIFICATION AND VOTING

American electoral politics have been shaped through the years roughly by four major events: the emergence of urban–rural differences at the time of the country's formation (Federalists tended to be urban, Republicans rural); the Civil War (the North tended to be Republican, the South Democratic); industrialization (workers tended to be Democratic, business Republican); and immigration, especially the massive immigration around the turn of the century (immigrants tended to be Democratic, native-born Americans Republican). Perhaps the most significant change in this pattern occurred in the 1930s when blacks, who had been Republicans because that party was responsible for the end of slavery, turned to the Democrats, who were on their side economically.

Obviously, the components of this four-part model overlap, which is why the great political coalitions that constitute the American political parties are so fractious. Moreover, a tendency is not an absolute prediction. Some immigrants and their children vote Republican. Some businesspeople are Democrats. Many people vote one way in presidential elections and another way in congressional elections—in recent decades most notably Democratic in congressional elections and Republican in presidential elections. Party identification is not as strong an influence in voting as it used to be.

Most Americans do tend to identify, however weakly, with one political party, usually the same party as their parents. Moreover, the choice of a party identification takes place at about the same time (early adulthood) as does the choice of religious identification—and as part of the same process: for example, Catholics who identify strongly with their church also tend to identify strongly with their political party. Both party and religious choice are components in forging your identity as you mature. Not everyone, of course, has both forms of identity, but most people do.

All that need concern us in this chapter is the fact that Catholics and Jews tend to be Democrats, while Protestants—especially white Protestants who do not live in the South—tend to be Republicans. (And white Protestants in the South are shifting to Republican identification, particularly in presidential elections.) There are many reasons for these tendencies. When Catholics and Jews came to this country in large numbers, they were poor urban workers. The Republican party represented—or was perceived to represent—the native born, who did not like the immigrants, and the well-to-do who exploited them. The Democratic party, on the other hand, already the party of white urban workers, quickly organized the immigrants and persuaded them that the party supported their causes. To look at the same process from a different perspective, the urban Democratic "machines" wanted the immigrants in their party and the affluent and native-born Republicans did not. The Democrats offered immigrants political power and jobs; the Republicans were much less likely to do so.

The Democrats also supported or came to support reforms that would benefit the immigrants and were congruent with their more communal social policies, while the Republicans remained the party of "rugged individualism." Thus social security, regulation of business and banks, unemployment insurance, legalization of unions, occupational health, and, in the case of Jews, support for Israel became standard planks of the Democratic platform in the years between 1930 and 1950. These kinds of legislative programs confirmed the allegiance of Catholics and Jews to the Democratic party despite subsequent developments.

Party positions on critical issues, however, were no more important than the matter of jobs in the big cities. The "machines" (which had been Protestant in many cities before immigration) were Catholic and Jewish, and they effectively traded influence, money, favors, and jobs for votes in the cities for many years. Republican Protestants often thought this exchange was corrupt and supported "reform" movements to "clean up" the cities and end political "corruption." However, when they gained political power it was usually their allies who got the jobs and the contracts.

The old "machines" are less powerful than they used to be because the children of the immigrants are no longer poor and Democratic party organizations have less to offer the more recent immigrants (though they tend to be Democrats, too). The Irish Catholics, the first of the large immigrant groups and those with the most political skill, are reputed to have been the masters of "machine politics" and the dominant force in urban politics. There remain many big-city Irish mayors (think of Boston, San Diego, and especially Chicago in the early 1990s), and Irish Catholics still disproportionately choose political careers, in part it would seem because of their love for the political game.

It is often said that as Catholics became more affluent and moved to the suburbs they left the Democratic party and joined the Republican party because that's where their self-interest would be best served. In fact, most Catholics still identify as Democrats and almost two-thirds of them still vote for Democratic congressional candidates, as do four-fifths of Jews.

Is there a "Jewish vote" and a "Catholic vote"? If you mean, Can the leaders of either religion "deliver" the votes of their people the way a skilled precinct captain could in the old days of the urban machines? then the answer is certainly no. Catholic bishops, for example, have been notoriously ineffective in persuading their laity to vote against "pro-choice" candidates—and most major Catholic political leaders believe that in a pluralistic society the woman herself must make the choice about abortion, despite what bishops might say. Jewish voters are deeply concerned about government policy toward Israel, but they do not need the guidance of Jewish leaders to demonstrate that support by voting for pro-Israel candidates (just as the Irish did not need their clergy to tell them to vote for congressional candidates who supported Irish Independence in 1920). Voters of both religions think for themselves. Their leaders do not dictate to them and indeed are often unsuccessful when they try to do so. In that sense there is no "Jewish vote" or "Catholic vote."

How, then, does it happen that Jews and Catholics still tend to be Democrats even when their purely economic interests might put them in the other party? Why do affluent Jews and Catholics still vote Democratic? Why are Jewish and Catholic Democrats more likely to vote for Democratic presidential candidates, even when they don't like the candidate and think, as they have more often than not for the last twenty years, that the candidate is a "loser"? There are two reasons—one rational, the other non-rational (but not irrational).

The rational reason is that the religious imaginations of Jews and Catholics tend to be "communal." They picture society as organized into families, local groups, and communities, and they picture humankind as relating to God as members of such clusters of people. Therefore, they have a strong inclination to identify with a party that historically has supported human and community well-being over against rugged individualism. Neither religious tradition sees government intervention as inherently wrong or dangerous. Thus, they do not abhor an activist government and are more at ease with a party heritage that favors such government.

The "non-rational" reason is that Catholics and Jews still tend to think of Democrats as "us" and Republicans as "them." "They" didn't like "us" when "we" first came here and "they" still don't like "us" all that much. Only those who think that the history of one's religious community is unimportant will have trouble understanding this argument.

Another way of viewing the same phenomenon is to observe, as we have said, that party identification (at least a weak link to one party tradition or the other) is part of the personal identity of most Americans. Most, though not all, Americans end up choosing to identify with the party of their parents in young adulthood. Thus, party affiliation is to some extent a matter of inheritance, of choosing for "us" against "them."

By itself the inheritance of party affiliation would not be so strong if it were completely "non-rational" (as support for the Cubs or the White Sox is in Chicago, a very powerful if utterly "non-rational" choice—particularly if you have the bad taste, as this writer thinks, to identify with the White Sox). However, when it is combined with different pictures of what a "good society" is and how humans relate to God, party inheritance on religious lines remains an important factor in American political life, regardless of how the mass media (whose commentators tend to be alienated from all traditions) try to minimize it.

There is no single "Catholic" issue like the State of Israel is a "Jewish" issue, which perhaps makes Catholic affiliation with the Democratic party somewhat weaker. It also makes it more difficult for Democratic candidates on the national level to activate their potential Catholic supporters— not that any of the presidential candidates in recent decades have tried to do so. Thus, to appeal to the Catholics in their coalition, Democrats would have to stress issues of family, neighborhood, and local community that have special appeal to Catholics, though they appeal to many other Americans too.

It also should be said in passing that there is a certain kind of political style, an impression of somber self-righteousness, that may appeal to many Protestants but turns off many Catholics. (Some historians say that Catholics were virtually driven into the Democratic party by the prohibition of alcohol during the 1920s. Unfortunately for the Democrats, the style of their candidates since the 1960s has tended to rub Catholics the wrong way. The Catholic political "style" tends to emphasize loyalty and compromise, whereas one kind of Protestant political style tends to emphasize high political principle and integrity. Neither style is necessarily better than the other, but they are different and there's no point, particularly for the politician, in pretending that the difference does not exist.

Is there a Catholic vote or a Jewish vote or a Protestant vote? A directly and explicitly religious vote based on doctrine? No. An indirect vote, a correlation based on history, image, and style? Yes. And there is no sign of it going away.

RELIGION AND PUBLIC CONTROVERSY

Religion, it is often said, ought not to be involved in public controversy over political issues. That often means, however, that it's all right for religious leaders to take a stand in favor of my side, but it's wrong when they oppose my side. If I support a war and religious leaders support it, they're nothing but patriotic Americans. If I support the same war and they oppose it, they are traitors. If I oppose a war and they oppose it, they are courageous leaders. If I oppose a war and they support it, they have failed to teach religious truth. One must beware, therefore, of those who tell you that religion should not become involved in politics. What they usually mean is that religion ought not to be on the other side.

A certain Catholic bishop in a western state condemned a Catholic candidate who was running on a ticket of racial hatred, and the bishop was praised by many good "liberals" for this outstanding exercise of religious leadership. Subsequently, he denounced a "pro-choice" Catholic candidate and was roundly condemned for interfering in a political campaign by many of the same people. When I pointed out the inconsistency to a pro-choice supporter who was appalled at the bishop's action, I was told, "But racial hatred is sinful!"

Many conclusions about the relationship between politics and religion in America can be drawn from that little story, not least of which is the old dictum that it depends on whose ox is being gored. If my ox is being gored, then I want the clergy on my side. If your ox is being gored, the clergy have no right to intervene.

A second conclusion is that the typical American (indeed the typical human) tends to think that morality is on his or her side and immorality on the other side. Religion should back morality and condemn immorality. Hence, it should always be on my side.

A third conclusion is that Americans are not very good at listening to the "story" that lies behind the position that the other side is taking. Nor are they very good at admitting that those who disagree with them can do so in goodwill and good faith.

The abortion issue currently is a classic case. Pro-choice and pro-life activists do not listen to each other and do not concede to each other even the beginnings of good faith and goodwill. It is not the first time in American history that such conflict has occurred and presumably it will not be the last.

In fact, there is little difference between typical Catholics and typical Protestants in their attitudes toward the *legality* of abortion. More than nine out of ten approve of the legality of abortion when there is a threat to the mother's life or health. More than six out of ten disapprove of it when the mother simply does not want another child. (Black Protestants are more likely to disapprove of legal abortion than white Protestants, indeed more likely to disapprove of it than white Catholics.) However, such "balanced" or "inconsistent" opinions (depending on your perspective) are anathema to the activists on both sides of the debate, and the activists set the tone and terms of the public debate. Jews are more likely to support "abortion on demand" than are Christians, though not by any means all Jews, especially the Orthodox. The "secularists" (those with no religion at all) are the most likely to approve of abortion.

Both sides of the controversy are in favor of life in the sense that they think their position is the most supportive of human life. Very few people think that it would be permissible to kill a newborn baby if the mother did not want it. Almost everyone would agree that the baby is a human person. Most people would also say that a fetus that can survive outside its mother's womb is a human person. The pro-choice side (generally) denies that a human person is present until viability is achieved and hence argues that the termination of a pregnancy is not murder. The pro-life side says that the human person exists from the first moment of conception and hence abortion is murder. Moreover, most of those on both sides are convinced that their position is self-evidently true and that the other side is not only in error but in bad faith.

"Life begins at the moment of conception," a Catholic pro-life advocate will tell you. "We've always known that is true because God has revealed it to us."

One might want to argue that many Catholic theologians in ages past disagreed, believing that life did not begin for several months (though they had different biological models than we do today). However, the point is that the Catholic tendency is to think of life beginning early. (The fundamentalist pro-life advocate would probably say the same thing as the Catholic in this dialogue.)

"We don't consider a fetus to be a person," a Jewish pro-choice advocate might reply, "until it exists outside the womb."

"You're wrong," says the Catholic, "and you know you're wrong."

"No" says the Jew. "You're wrong and you're trying to impose your religious ideas on me."

"Abortion is mass murder just like the holocaust," says the Catholic.

"Don't talk to me about holocaust," says the Jew.

If a secularist were present at this shouting match, he or she might contend that both are wrong to worry about when human life begins. The issue is really the welfare of the mother. No one may tell a woman what to do with her body. She and she alone has the right to choose what is best for her own happiness. It is certainly true that society has always found it difficult to force a woman to bring a baby to term when she does not want to. However, many pro-choice advocates see no problem with accusing the mother of a baby born addicted to cocaine, or with a law that imposes punishment on a woman who ingests too much alcohol into her body and then drives a car. In fact, this response would not bother the secularist, who in all probability does not believe in God or life after death, does not accept the need for a consistent moral system, and thinks that human happiness is necessarily the basis for all moral choice.

Each of these positions is profoundly religious in the sense that it is based on a religious "story" that tells of the meaning and purpose of human life and of the way humans should live if they are to be fully human. Each story comes from a tradition that is ancient and usually unexamined. In most people the traditional story is so strong and so unselfconscious as to seem self-evident and unarguable. Therefore, the other side is wrong and proper religion has no choice but to denounce it.

The conflict, then, is less about abortion than about why humans exist at all (a profoundly religious question). Each side assumes that anyone with half an ounce of sense and a modicum of integrity *knows* that its story is correct.

A related issue, of course, is whether in a pluralistic society like the United States, in which many different stories are told, one has the right to try to impose by law on others the conclusions drawn from one's own religious story. However that question may be answered, one might still make a case that religious leadership ought to ask its members to at least listen to the story on the other side.

On issues that involve major moral questions (issues about how humans should behave, and hence what human existence means) religion will inevitably be drawn into public conflict. Northern religious leaders were among the leading advocates of the abolition of slavery. A certain kind of Protestant religious leadership, convinced that the consumption of alcohol is wrong, imposed the Prohibition amendment on the rest of the country (and still impose laws regulating the sale and consumption of alcohol). The leaders of the civil rights movement were and are for the most part black clergy. The Constitutional right of freedom of speech guarantees the right of religious leaders to take public stands on what they take to be critical moral issues. Such public intervention in the political order can be prohibited only by denying freedom of speech to religious leaders. (Whether such intervention is always wise, prudent, appropriate, or even likely to be effective is another matter.)

The suggestion of some secularists that churches ought to lose their tax-exempt status if they take such moral stands on public issues is in effect an attempt to deprive religion of freedom of speech by taking away from it a privilege that it has long enjoyed. (Secularists, following the conclusions of their own story, often feel that religion should be denied all its privileges—military chaplains, congressional chaplains, the motto "In God we trust" on U.S. coins, and all other references to God and religion in public discourse.)

Despite the secularist complaint, the tradition of religious involvement (based on religious stories) in major political issues that are also moral issues is too old and too powerful in America ever to be abolished. We must understand that this involvement becomes exceedingly controversial when the issues are based on conflicts between underlying stories about human nature and the meaning of human existence.

For example, a strong component in the traditional Protestant story is a conviction that human nature is "fallen" and is therefore fundamentally perverse. Left to its own amusements, human nature will engage in all kinds of "wicked," "unseemly," or "Godless" behavior. Therefore, to preserve social order and to protect men and women from their own wickedness, the government should intervene to forbid such evil as drinking, gambling, dancing, and smoking, especially on the Sabbath.

Dancing you can pretty much get away with these days. Smoking has become a public health rather than a religious issue. What President Hoover called the "noble experiment" of Prohibition ended sixty years ago. But you still can't buy liquor on Sunday in many states. And most states forbid gambling or regulate it closely.

The Catholic story of human nature is more benign. The human personality may be "flawed" but it is not fallen. Legal efforts to constrain humans to virtuous lives are not likely to work. There is nothing wrong with a drink, a game of cards, or a dance (though the old-fashioned Irish clergy would have disagreed on the last). They are harmless human amusements that, within proper limits, can legitimately be enjoyed.

To the strict Protestant this story sounds like a pact with the devil. To the Catholic the Protestant response sounds like Puritanism (which may be a bad word for Catholics but is not so bad for their Protestant counterparts).

Hence, when a law was being proposed in my state that would permit charitable organizations to run bingo games, a Protestant cleric said to me, "But gambling is wrong!" To him that conclusion was so self-evident that only the irredeemably corrupt or hypocritical could possibly deny it. So gambling continues to be illegal in one form or another in most states, although the laws are routinely broken in taverns, country clubs, athletic stadia, and family card parties. Similarly, teenage drinking laws are on the books in every state, laws which are no more effective in preventing consumption of alcohol by young people than gambling laws are effective in preventing football pools.

Americans are often astonished to learn that other countries, especially Catholic countries, are much more lenient on the subject of young people's drinking than our country is. Currently, arguments about the effect of teenage drunken driving are used to support these laws, but logically such arguments would lead again to total Prohibition. A twenty-two-year-old is no less likely to be drunk at the wheel of a car than a twenty-year-old. It would be more appropriate to use mechanisms in cars—such as combination locks on the ignition—that would prevent someone who was drunk, at whatever age, from starting a car. Moreover, young people might drink less if it were not forbidden.

Another current controversial issue is the matter of religion in public places. Secularists, along with many other Americans (Protestant, Catholic, and Jewish), believe that there should be no religious instruction or prayer in the public schools, no displays of religious symbols (nativity scenes, menorahs, etc.) in or near public places, no prayer at high school or state college graduations, and no prayer before athletic contests in public stadia or when the contestants are from public schools.

The courts currently are wrestling with these issues. It should be clear, however, that the legal arguments are masks for underlying "stories" about the meaning of human life. One story believes that human life will be better if religion is banned in every possible place, or at least that the "purity" of religion is contaminated if it is used at every possible secular occasion. The other story believes that religion is an essential part of human life and ought not to be excluded.

National survey data show that, despite court rulings, Americans overwhelmingly support some kind of prayer in public schools. However, that issue, like the others mentioned above, is not sufficiently important for enough people to generate massive voting blocks. Hence the conflict is waged between elite pressure groups (and their lawyers) on both sides.

The "story" still matters and matters greatly in American political life.

CONCLUSION

Most Americans are repelled by noisy religious controversy. The self-righteousness and dogmatism that often accompany such controversy somehow offend the American propensity to permit the other person the right to his or her own opinion. Many American religious leaders are also cautious about becoming too involved in political debate because they sense such involvement may be more harmful than helpful to religion. Yet, because of the different stories that underpin the different religious traditions (and the different versions of the stories within each tradition), major political disagreements over moral issues will certainly call forth some religious participation—always welcome when the leaders happen to be on your side!

Such exercise of the rights of freedom of expression and freedom of assembly are part of the American way. They seem messy and troubling only when the alternative is not seriously considered. Nonetheless, it does not seem contrary to the American tradition to hope that those who mix religion and politics will remember that it is also part of the American way to respect the opinions, integrity, and goodwill of others and at least to listen sensitively when they try to present the "stories" that support their political positions.

STUDY QUESTIONS

1. What does "separation of church and state" mean to you? Give examples of how you see such separation reflected in American society. Give examples of how church and state appear not to be separated.
2. How does your religion reflect who you are? Why do we often want to know what religious community people belong to when we first meet them? What does the author mean when he says that religious affiliation is a "map" for guiding us through human relations?
3. How does religious affiliation affect the way Americans vote? Give specific examples. Do you believe these examples are merely stereotypes? Can there really be a "Jewish vote" or a "Catholic vote"? Why? Why not?
4. Why do people believe that it is powerful to have religion on their side in arguments about public policy? Does religion always stand on the side of morality?
5. Why is it important to place positions on public policy within the context of religious story? In this context, what gives "story" its power?
6. What is the secularist position concerning religion and public policy in America? Why do secularists argue that religion should not interfere in public policy?

ESSAY TOPICS

The Separation of Church and State in America: Why It Does Not Exist
The Separation of Church and State in America: Why It Is Important
Images of Church and State in Government and Religion
Religion, State, and Abortion (feel free to choose any other issue)
Being American and Jewish (or Christian, Muslim, Buddhist, etc.)
The Seculariziation of America

WORD EXPLORATION

The following words play significant roles in any discussion of religion and politics in America and are worth careful reflection and discussion.

Secular	Nationalism	Patriotism
Public Policy	Secularist	Religion

14

WILLIAM SCOTT GREEN

Religion and Society in America

When it comes to religion, America is different. The uniquely American value of the separation of church and state makes the role of religion in American society, politics, and culture distinctive and complex. Religions from the ends of the earth converge and flourish in America. What does the presence of the world's religions in America tell us about the country's character? Conversely, how does the American experiment with religion affect religion? This chapter considers these questions.

THE CHRISTMAS CHALLENGE

Religion matters because it affects people's daily lives, so a good way to begin thinking about religion in America is to focus on a typical, real-life event. Consider the following story:

It is a cold December morning in a small rural northeastern city, and Joey's father is going to school. Joey is the only Jew in the second grade of the municipal grammar school, and his father is going there to tell his son's class about the Jewish holiday of Hanukkah.

Explaining Jewish holidays to his son's schoolmates is not something Joey's father normally does. He did not go to his son's school in the fall to explain the Jewish New Year (*Rosh Hashanah*), the Day of Atonement (*Yom Kippur*), and the Festival of Booths (*Sukkot*), and he is not planning to go again in the spring to tell them the stories of Purim and Passover (*Pesah*). Although all those holidays are more important than Hanukkah in the Jewish religious calendar, they usually do not attract much general interest. But Hanukkah falls in the winter, usually in December, and its proximity to Christmas gives it a visibility in American culture and a consequence in American Jewish life that are far out of proportion to its minor significance in Jewish religion. Many Americans, Jews and non-Jews alike, regard Hanukkah as a Jewish counterpoint to Christmas. And, in fact, it is precisely the impact of Christmas on the life of Joey's school that prompted his father to ask permission to make his visit.

Joey goes to a public school, but the Christmas holiday has been the center of the school's activities since before Thanksgiving. Christmas decorations are everywhere. Trees and ornaments blanket the corridor walls, Santas are stenciled in classroom windows, Christmas cookies are served in the cafeteria, the third and fourth grades are writing in-class letters to Santa Claus, and the fifth grade plans a Christmas pageant for the whole school.

Most of the people in this small city either are Christians or have a Christian heritage. For them the sights and sounds of Christmas are natural, uncontroversial, culturally affirming, and inviting. But for non-Christian Americans—whether Muslims, Jews, Buddhists, Hindus, secularists, or others—those same sights and sounds can be, and often are, vivid indicators of separation, exclusion, and minority status. Indeed, recent court cases about the permissibility of displaying a nativity scene on public property suggest that the symbols of Christmas may now exemplify the challenge of living with difference that religious pluralism present to American society.

The presentation about Hanukkah begins well. The students are intrigued by the special Hanukkah candelabra (*menorah*) and the prospect of lighting candles. They delight in the Hanukkah top (*dreydl*) children play with during the holiday. Most of all, they love the idea of eight nights of gifts. In the midst of this easy cheer, one student turns to Joey with a question, "Do you celebrate Christmas too?" Before the father can answer, another boy blurts out, "Oh no! Jews can't have Christmas because they think Jesus hasn't came yet." This remark makes some students uncomfortable. They look at Joey. "You don't believe in Jesus?" "Why not?" Joey stiffens, uncertain how to answer. His father, feeling awkward, begins to reply, but the teacher quickly intervenes. "There are many different religions and peoples in the world," she says, "and we should respect them all. But the important thing is that people are really the same underneath." The tension eases, and the lesson ends.

Almost every day across America—in schools, clubs, and homes; on dates; at weddings, funerals, and family reunions; in living rooms and even bedrooms—some version of this story takes place. Americans of varied religious traditions and convictions encounter one another and try

to deal with their differences. That encounter frequently—perhaps usually—creates tension and confusion. Typically, the tension and confusion
are resolved, as in our story, through an easy affirmation of pluralism
("There are many different religions and peoples in the world . . .") but a
denial of the significance and consequences of difference (". . . people are
really the same underneath"). In a down-to-earth way, our story illustrates a central feature—some might say a dilemma—of religion in
America. At the level of political principle, America has a national
commitment to religious liberty. But at the practical level of everyday
living, religious difference is a sensitive and awkward topic in American
life. The story and the problem it illustrates prompt a question: What is
unique about the American context for religion? Is there something
special about religion in America?

DISESTABLISHMENT: THE SEPARATION OF
CHURCH AND STATE

The political principles that preserve religious liberty in America illustrate
the core American values of freedom of religion and the separation of
church and state, as expressed in the First Amendment to the Constitution
of the United States. These values have shaped the way Americans
perceive, understand, and practice religion. Let us briefly review the main
features of the First Amendment and then ask about its consequences for
religion in America. The First Amendment states: "Congress shall make
no law respecting an establishment of religion, or prohibiting the free
exercise thereof; or abridging the freedom of speech, or of the press; or the
right of the people peaceably to assemble, and to petition the Government
for a redress of grievances." The First Amendment declares freedom of
religion to be a fundamental civil right of all Americans. Significantly, it
lists religious liberty together with other freedoms, particularly freedom
of speech and freedom of the press. This is an important and revealing
association that Americans often overlook. Just as free speech and a free
press shape, ground, and define American politics, society, and culture, so
too does freedom of religion. Religious liberty is a basic freedom that gives
American life its distinct character.

It is well to note that the language of the First Amendment applies only to
the federal government, not to state governments. However, in two important modern cases, *Cantwell v. Connecticut* (1940) and *Everson v. Board of
Education* (1947), the Supreme Court of the United States included the First
Amendment within the Fourteenth Amendment, which was ratified in

1868. The Fourteenth Amendment reads, in part, "No State shall make or enforce any law which shall abridge the privileges or immunities of citizens of the United States; nor shall any State deprive any person of life, liberty or property, without due process of law." By asserting that the Fourteenth Amendment applies to and includes the First Amendment, the Supreme Court holds all states to the standards of the First Amendment.[1]

American freedom of religion is based on an idea called "disestablishment," which denies to the government the power to endorse or support ("establish") religion. The disestablishment of religion—more popularly known as the separation of church and state—aims, in the words of Justice Wiley B. Rutledge, to "create a complete and permanent separation of the spheres of religious activity and civil authority."[2] The United States was the first nation in history to apply the separation of church and state as a practical political principle, the first nation to make disestablishment of religion a foundation of its national life. It is important to note that the disestablishment of religion was advocated by and largely achieved through the efforts of religious minorities—from Baptists to Quakers—in several of the original states. They did not want the denominations that constituted the majority in their states to control their religious life.

The First Amendment is composed of two clauses: the so-called Establishment Clause and the Free Exercise Clause. The meaning of the Establishment Clause ("Congress shall make no law respecting an establishment of religion") is explained in a classic statement by Justice Hugo L. Black:

> The "establishment of religion" clause of the First Amendment means at least this: Neither a state nor the Federal Government can set up a church. Neither can pass laws which aid one religion, aid all religions, or prefer one religion over another. Neither can force nor influence a person to go to or remain away from church against his will or force him to profess a belief or disbelief in any religion. No person can be punished for entertaining or professing religious beliefs or disbeliefs, for church attendance or nonattendance. No tax in any amount, large or small, can be levied to support any religious activities or institutions, whatever they may be called, or whatever form they may adopt to teach or practice religion. Neither a state nor the Federal Government can, openly or secretly, participate in the affairs of any religious organizations or groups and vice versa. In the words of [Thomas] Jefferson, the clause against establishment of religion by laws was intended to erect a "wall of separation between Church and State."[3]

The Free Exercise Clause of the First Amendment (". . . or prohibiting the free exercise thereof") inhibits the government—except in certain kinds of cases, such as child welfare—from restricting or controlling people's religious beliefs or behavior.

How are these two clauses applied in practice? For our purposes two brief examples will suffice. In interpreting and applying the Establishment Clause, the Supreme Court has ruled that a school district may not display the Ten Commandments in classrooms because that would be government advocacy of religion.[4] To protect free exercise, the Court has ruled that the state may not require the children of the Old Order Amish to attend public secondary school because the group regards such schooling as a sin.[5] The government would be forcing people to transgress their own teachings and would thereby violate their right to the free exercise of their religion.

It is useful to observe—particularly for readers of this book—that most of the legal battles over the Establishment Clause have been fought in the arena of education. The combination of a system of compulsory education and the separation of church and state has made the expression of religion in public schools—from prayers in classrooms or at assemblies or graduations, to Bible study on school property, to the content of textbooks—a thorny and difficult legal issue.

In fact, American education divides over the issue of religion. On the one hand, although studying religion—as opposed to instruction in religion or in how to be religious—has been affirmed by the Supreme Court as legitimate, concern about violating the Establishment Clause or offending local constituencies keeps religion out of the curricula of most American public school systems. On the other hand, more than 90 percent of private schools in America are religious or of religious origin. One important reason that religious difference is a delicate topic in American conversation is that, historically, too few Americans have had the opportunity to study it and learn how to think about it.

Let us now explore how the First Amendment shapes the way religion is understood and practiced in American life, and how it reveals and expresses a distinct American attitude toward religion.

RELIGION AS A NATIVE CATEGORY

The very language of the First Amendment assumes a domain of behavior and thought, a realm of experience, called "religion" that is a normal and familiar aspect of American life. By naming religion and setting it apart for special consideration, the Constitution embeds the notion of religion in American culture so that it seems a natural part of the way things are. Because of the First Amendment, American culture easily assumes that there is an aspect of life called religion that can be distinguished from other aspects, such as politics, law, psychology, or economics.

This does not mean that the First Amendment assumes or requires that all Americans are or must be religious. On the contrary, in America freedom *of* religion implies freedom *from* religion, both from religion in general and from someone else's religion in particular.

Religion is so unquestioned and uncontroversial a part of American life that it can be called a "native category." A native category is a fundamental concept, a basic classification, that people use to identify and explain to themselves what is happening to them. A classification is a native category if it is so elemental in a society that it carries cultural weight and so familiar that people use it constantly and intuitively; they know what it means without needing to define it.

Native categories usually don't travel well from one culture to another. They have connotations, nuances, and shades of meaning that are understood in one society but not in another. Sports terms are a kind of native category. Terms like "strike out" and "home run" have meaning for most Americans beyond the baseball field. But these terms, so familiar to us as categories of value ("I hit a home run on my math test," "I struck out with Laura last night"), are meaningless to Europeans, and explaining them to people from other cultures is not easy. The idea of "stress" is one of modern America's newest native categories. People use it constantly to explain their feelings or account for their actions. They know that "stress" can make you ill, or worse. They know what stress is, acknowledge its importance, but would have difficulty giving a precise definition of it.

Because of the First Amendment, religion is a native category of American culture. The Constitution assumes religion as a given. Americans use religion prominently both to distinguish our culture from others (as when elected officials once described Communist states as "godless") and to differentiate individuals within our culture. A consequence of the First Amendment is that Americans take religion for granted as a meaningful and conventional trait of being human. But because religion is a native category, we grasp it intuitively rather than spell it out. We think better *with* religion than we do *about* it.

RELIGION AS PLURALISM

By restricting government control over religion, the First Amendment guarantees that America will have more than one religion. It affirms that religion is a legitimate, legally protected form of difference in American society. Americans are supposed to differ from one another religiously. The First Amendment means that America is multireligious by design and not because of an accident of history or immigration. As we have seen, America is the first nation of history to declare itself religiously pluralistic. Religious difference was built into America from the start, and it is a hallmark of national life.

The guarantee of multiple religions undermines any claim that America has a particular or even a fundamentally national religious character. Some people commonly assert that "America is a religious nation" or "a Christian nation." Even if, in a general way, such claims reflect major preferences of Americans at certain times in the nation's history, they misrepresent the character of America. Freedom of religion, the basic civil right that allows multiple religions to flourish in America, is a secular value rather than a religious one. So if America indeed does have a religious character, it owes that character to a secular principle.

Recognizing that a secular principle justifies American religious pluralism will help us understand how the First Amendment works. We often suppose that the First Amendment limits only how the government may act, but that view is somewhat misleading. Because it protects the "free exercise" of religious behavior, the First Amendment forbids any religion to use the legal system to restrict another religion. No religion in America can plausibly claim that it is the only one here or that it alone has a mandate to shape, govern, or monitor people's values and behaviors. The legal scholar Stephen L. Carter notes that the "fundamental message of the Establishment Clause . . . is one of religious *equality*. . . ."[6] As its earliest advocates intended, the First Amendment protects and preserves the perspective of religious minorities. It thereby makes religion into an effective vehicle for the expression of dissent.

The First Amendment limits the way religion can manifest power in American life. Although religions may seek to affect the government, they cannot control it. In America, religions can attempt to influence the government by persuading individual voters or elected officials—as they have done on a host of important issues, including slavery, prohibition, civil rights, the war in Vietnam, and abortion—but religions cannot become the government or advance or enforce their doctrines through it. American culture regards religion and government as distinct categories, and the two in principle are not to be confused with one another.

Because they cannot have the backing, confirmation, and power of governmental resources and agencies, religions in America are by necessity voluntary. Many observers think that religions retain their strength among Americans—as they decline in importance in other nations—because, with the separation of church and state, they have to earn their keep. To persist, religions in America must know how to appeal to, and engage the interest of, a broad public audience. Moreover, they must perpetually contend with one another as well as with non-religion and even anti-religion. As they compete to keep their members and attract new ones, religions in America watch one another and adapt—as in the case of Hanukkah and Christmas.

But the adaptation of America's diverse religions to a context of freedom and competition—and the constant option of non-religion—can only go so far. By their nature, religions tend not to compromise on their core beliefs, teachings, and rituals but to affirm that they are right and that they work. As readers of this book doubtless have already learned, different religions really are different, and their values, practices, and worldviews often are irreconcilable. In a word, for all their capacity to adapt to different political and social settings, at a fundamental level religious teachings are non-negotiable. That is another reason religious difference makes people uncomfortable. Often there is no way to overcome the difference. When it comes to religion, people are not "the same underneath," as Joey's teacher claimed.

The American doctrine of religious liberty, as expressed in the First Amendment, holds out the promise that American society can maintain the delicate and exquisite balance of the absoluteness of religious teaching and the relativism of religious pluralism, that it can allow religions to be true to themselves and to the American vision of a diverse society. It can make this promise, and make good on it, because the separation of church and state frees American society from needing to decide among religions, to prefer one over all, or all over none. The world's religions can thrive in the American setting because, although each may judge the others misguided, in error, or just plain wrong, America as a nation cannot, and need not, pass such a judgment on any of them.

To see what is at stake in America's religious pluralism, let us conclude with an instructive historical example. In 1863 a group known as the National Reform Association, composed of eleven Protestant denominations, sought to amend the Constitution of the United States to say that America was a Christian nation. In place of the Constitution's preamble, which reads

> We the People of the United States, in order to form a more perfect Union, establish Justice, insure domestic Tranquility, provide for the common

defense, promote the general Welfare, and secure the Blessings of Liberty for ourselves and our Posterity . . .

they advocated the following words:

> We the people of the United States, humbly acknowledging Almighty God as the source of all authority and power in civil government, and the Lord Jesus Christ as the Ruler among the nations, His revealed will as the supreme law of the land, in order to constitute a Christian government . . .[7]

In light of the First Amendment, the differences between these two texts are stark and require no comment. Needless to say, the proposed amendment was defeated.

Two years later, in 1865, in his Second Inaugural Address, Abraham Lincoln reflected on how both sides in the Civil War had invoked religion in behalf of their cause:

> Both read the same Bible, and pray to the same God; and each invokes his aid against the other. It may seem strange that men should dare ask a just God's assistance in wringing their bread from the sweat of other men's faces; but let us judge not that we not be judged. The prayers of both could not be answered—that of neither has been answered fully.

The American concept of religious liberty holds out the possibility that different religions—despite their often irreconcilable worldviews, value systems, and patterns of behavior—can coexist freely in a single country, and that, in Lincoln's terms, though the prayers of all will be offered, none will be answered fully. Religion is at the core of America's pluralism, and the First Amendment to the Constitution has made the recognition of religious difference in American life both a promise and a reality.

NOTES

1. Leonard W. Levy, *The Establishment Clause: Religion and the First Amendment* (New York: Macmillan, 1986), 123.

2. Ibid., 124.

3. Ibid., 123–124.

4. *Stone v. Graham* (1980).

5. *Wisconsin v. Yoder* (1972).

6. Stephen L. Carter, *The Culture of Disbelief* (New York: Basic Books, 1993), 93.

7. Cited in James E. Woods, Jr., and Derek Davis, eds., *The Role of Religion on the Making of Public Policy* (Waco, Tex.: J. M. Dawson Institute of Church-State Studies, 1991), 8–9.

STUDY QUESTIONS

1. Why, when it comes to religion, does the author believe that America is different? How do the ideas of Christmas and Hanukkah reflect the author's claim? Do you agree that America has a national commitment to religious liberty? Why?
2. Is the First Amendment to the Constitution a religious statement, a political statement, or both? What do you think the First Amendment says about the separation of church and state? Be specific.
3. What are the Establishment Clause and the Free Exercise Clause of the First Amendment? How is each important for religious liberty in America?
4. Why does the author believe that religion is a "natural part" of the way things are in America? Do you agree? What are the implications of such a statement for our understandings of religion? Does it help to explain the world's, as well as America's religious diversity?
5. What is the meaning of religious pluralism? Is America religiously pluralistic?

ESSAY TOPICS

David Koresh and the Branch Davidians: An Abuse of Religious Freedom?
Is America a Religious Nation?
The Christmas Holiday: Is It about Religion?
Prayer in School: Both Sides of the Issue

WORD EXPLORATION

The following words play significant roles in any discussion of religion and society in America and are worth careful reflection and discussion.

Liberty	First Amendment	Pluralism
Disestablishment	Religious Liberty	Civil Rights

INDEX